Quail Country

RECIPES
FROM
THE JUNIOR LEAGUE OF ALBANY, GEORGIA

Smith House Publications
Junior League of Albany, Georgia, Inc.
516 Flint Avenue
Albany, Georgia 31701

© *1983   The Junior League of Albany, Georgia,
Inc.*

Printed in the United States of America
Rose Printing Company
Tallahassee, Florida

First Published in February 1983

*The proceeds from the sale of this book will be returned to the community
through projects sponsored by the Junior League of Albany, Georgia, Inc.*

Quail Country Committee

Editors

Betty Friday Moulton   Rosemary Rhyne Wetherbee

Committee Chairmen

Lynda Medley Campbell   Anne Churchwell Hall
Donna Dudney Davis   Jane Gardner Margeson
Bonnie Henry Warren

Cover Design and Illustrations
by
Rena Lippitt Divine

Committee: Dorothy W. Bishop, Judy B. Gray, Mamie P. Hall, Marilyn C. Hedrick, Anita M. Hudgens, Linda J. Johnson, Nancy H. Martin, Louise H. Mills, Lucille S. Russell, Nealy W. Stapleton. Typist: Brenda Lee Jones.

A special acknowledgement to the Junior League actives, sustainers and friends who gave so generously of their time and efforts to make the publication of this cookbook possible, also to Louise O. Whiting for her special writing.

iii

ABOUT THE ARTIST

Primarily a wildlife watercolorist, Rena Lippitt Divine received her formal training at the Ringling School of Art. Her quail lithograph of "The Governor's Quail Family" has been offered as a limited edition print by the Georgia Cancer Society. A large portion of her work has been donated to the State of Georgia and to charity.

A print of Brown Thrashers, the Georgia state bird, is given to visiting dignitaries and Heads of State by Governor and Mrs. George Busbee. The original painting is in the private collection of H.R.H. The Prince of Wales. Other collections in which the artist's work appears include Governor and Mrs. George Busbee, former President Jimmy Carter, Mr. Robert W. Woodruff, Burt Reynolds, former Vice President Walter Mondale, Duke and Duchess Visconti, former Ambassador to Belgium Ann Cox Chambers and H.R.H. Queen Beatrix of the Netherlands.

The artist's work has been displayed in museums, the Georgia State Capitol, and the Fernbank Science Center in one man shows. The broad appeal of her subjects, her attention to detail and the unusual use of soft colors help to create in us a deeper appreciation of nature.

Contributors

Mrs. Peter Abt
Ms. Mary Lou Addison
Mrs. Robert Allen
Mrs. Phillips Allum
Mrs. L. Carlton Anderson
Mrs. Floyd Edward Armstrong
Mrs. Baby Arnold
Mrs. Zack Aultman
Mrs. James L. Bacon, Jr.
Mrs. Steve Bailey
Mrs. William C. Banks, Jr.
Mrs. Al W. Barrett, Jr.
Mrs. Martha Barrs
Mrs. Richard M. Bartlett
Mrs. Thomas T. Basil
Mrs. J. Daniel Bateman
Mrs. L. H. Bateman
Mrs. James B. Baxter
Mrs. Rembert Bayne, Jr.
Mrs. John B. Beauchamp
Mrs. Cyril Beck
Mrs. John Beck
Mrs. Walter Beck
Mrs. Joseph Berg
Mrs. R. H. Bickerstaff
Mrs. B. W. Bird
Mrs. Eugene C. Black, Jr.
Mrs. Hill Blackett
Mrs. John C. Boesch
Mrs. Jim Bowles
Mrs. Lee Bradbury
Mrs. Thomas J. Brice
Ms. Barbara Brown
Mrs. Jerry Brown
Mrs. Myrtlene Bryan
Mrs. J. C. Burger, Jr.
Mrs. William E. Burgess
Mrs. Harry Burnette
Mrs. Walter H. Burt, Jr.
Mrs. Walter Burt, III
Mrs. George Busbee
Mrs. Mary A. Caines
Mrs. A. Douglas Calhoun
Mrs. Thomas J. Callaway, Jr.
Mrs. Bruce Campbell
Mrs. Virginia W. Campbell
Mrs. L. E. Cannon
Mrs. Thomas Cannon
Mrs. J. Fred Carson
Mrs. Guy C. Carter, Jr.
Mrs. O. B. Carter, Jr.
Mrs. Claud Chambless
Mrs. James P. Champion, Jr.
Mrs. Randolph E. Champion, Jr.
Mrs. Doug Chapman
Mrs. Lyle Charles
Mrs. Ralph Cheatham
Mrs. C. M. Clark
Mrs. Eugene R. Clark, Jr.
Mrs. E. Todd Clay
Mrs. Donald R. Cleesattle
Mrs. Lamar Clifton
Mrs. W. L. Clifton, Jr.

Mrs. Buford Collins
Mrs. Chappell Collins
Mrs. H. C. Colvin
Mrs. Ed Cooling
Mrs. Ed Copelan
Mrs. Randall Cothren
Mrs. Ray Council
Mrs. Sue P. Cowan
Mrs. James Craig
Mrs. Bess Crittenden
Mrs. John D. Cromartie
Mrs. Hugh Cunningham
Mrs. Seaborn Curry
Mrs. S. J. Curry
Mrs. Doug Curtis, Jr.
Mrs. Jody Webb Custer
Mrs. J. I. Davis, Jr.
Mrs. Phillip H. Davis
Mrs. R. H. Dickinson
Mrs. Gordon Dixon
Mrs. George P. Donaldson, III
Mrs. Vince Dooley
Mrs. Roy Dorminy
Miss Susan Dowdell
Mrs. Don Dozier
Mrs. G. Gerry Dozier, Jr.
Mrs. Wesley Dozier
Mrs. A. Donald Dudney
Mrs. Henry C. Duggan, III
Mrs. Harold Durrett
Mrs. Ann O. Duskin
Mrs. John Duval
Mrs. William Eckhardt
Mrs. R. R. Fairburn
Mrs. Leonard Farkas
Mrs. Roger Farrar
Mrs. Richard Fields
Mrs. Stephen Fink
Miss Betty Fleming
Mrs. Garrett Fleming, III
Mrs. G. N. Fowler
Mrs. John A. Fowler
Mrs. Deanna D. Fox
Mrs. Eley C. Frazer, III
Mrs. Ed Freeman
Mrs. A. D. Friday
Mrs. Jimmy Fuller
Mrs. Chick Gatewood
Mrs. A. W. Gay
Mrs. Charles A. Gay
Mrs. Corinne C. Geer
Mrs. Arnold Geeslin, Jr.
Mrs. Vincent Geiger
Mrs. William George
Mrs. Thad Gibson
Mrs. Warren Gill
Mrs. Charles B. Gillespie
Mrs. C. R. Gillespie
Mrs. H. H. Gillespie
Mrs. Hill Gillespie, Jr.
Mrs. Robert D. Gowan, Jr.
Mrs. Russell L. Grace, Jr.
Mrs. Edith Y. Grant

Mrs. John Grant
Mrs. James H. Gray, Jr.
Mrs. Loring Gray
Mrs. Peyton Greaves
Mrs. David L. Green
Ms. Lou Green
Mrs. Robert Green
Mrs. William J. Greggs
Mrs. J. Bruce Gunnels
Mrs. J. H. Hackney
Mrs. Narvella Hadley
Mrs. Herbert Haley
Mrs. W. Banks Haley, Jr.
Mrs. William Thomas Haley
Mrs. Curt O. Hall, Jr.
Mrs. Gina P. Hall
Mrs. James C. Hall
Miss Menard Hall
Mrs. Conway Hamilton
Mrs. J. B. Hanchey
Mrs. Carl Hancock
Mrs. Miriam Flynt Hand
Mrs. Bill Harbert
Mrs. Gordon Harden
Mrs. Joanne J. Harden
Mrs. W. Ferrell Harper
Mrs. Dan B. Harrison
Mrs. Carey Hatcher, Jr.
Mrs. Charles F. Hatcher
Mrs. James Hattaway
Mrs. Frank H. Hedrick
Mrs. Charles Heinemann, Jr.
Mrs. Michael Hendley
Mrs. Wade Hester
Mrs. Edna Lane Higgins
Mrs. Drew D. Hill, Jr.
Mrs. K. B. Hodges
Mrs. K. B. Hodges, Jr.
Mrs. Shelby Hodges, Jr.
Mrs. James B. Holloway
Mrs. John C. Holman
Mrs. Kenneth Holman
Mrs. Michael W. Houston
Mrs. Jack Howard
Mrs. Kenneth L. Howze
Mrs. Claude Hughes
Mrs. Walter Hurtienne
Mrs. Guy Inman
Mrs. Robert Inman
Mrs. Smith Jackson
Mrs. Stewart Jackson
Mrs. Kent Jacobs
Mrs. Emma James
Mrs. Suellen H. James
Mrs. Carl "Bucky" Jenkins
Mrs. John Jenkins
Mrs. Mary Louise Johnson
Mrs. J. B. Johnson
Mrs. Paul Johnson
Mrs. Thomas D. Johnson
Mrs. Michael Johnston
Mrs. Forrest B. Joiner
Mrs. Parks Jones, Jr.

v

Mrs. E. L. Jordan
Mrs. Ladd Jordan
Mrs. Wiley Jordan
Miss Bebe Kilpatrick
Ms. Suzanne King
Mrs. Joanie Kirkpatrick
Mrs. Gilbert S. Klemann
Mrs. Robert Knight
Miss Virginia Lanier
Mrs. Darrell Laird
Mrs. Richard Langley
Mrs. Robert B. Langstaff
Mrs. Chris Lawson
Mrs. J. L. Leach
Mrs. Michael Lee
Mrs. W. Spencer Lee, IV
Mrs. Yates Lee
Ms. Sue Lehr
Mrs. Mark O. Lively
Mrs. Russell Looney
Ms. Wilma Jean Lovett
Mrs. Frank Lowe, Jr.
Mrs. William Lowe
Mrs. Marion W. Luckey, Jr.
Miss Karen L. Lundy
Mrs. W. H. Lundy
Mrs. Len MacDougald
Mrs. William P. McAfee, III
Mrs. Charles McCall
Mrs. James D. McCollum
Mrs. Jerry C. McCroskey
Mrs. Robert H. McGarity, III
Mrs. C. R. McKemie, Jr.
Mrs. H. M. McKemie
Mrs. Ray L. McKinney
Miss Diane McKnight
Mrs. Harry Malcom, Jr.
Mrs. Margaret Mann
Mrs. Felix Marbury, Jr.
Mrs. Robert Margeson, Jr.
Mrs. John S. Martin
Mrs. C. Russell Martin, Jr.
Mrs. Russell E. Martin
Mrs. Jack Mason
Mrs. Robert M. Matre, Jr.
Mrs. James C. Matthews
Mrs. Walter Matthews
Mrs. F. Hill Mauldin
Mrs. William E. Mayher, III
Mrs. Coby Menning
Mrs. Frank F. Middleton, III
Mrs. Jane H. Miller
Mrs. Otis Z. Miller, Sr.
Mrs. Steve Miller
Mrs. David Mills
Mrs. Marvin Mixon
Mrs. Ryan Mock
Mrs. David Moncrief
Mrs. Rusty Moulton
Mrs. Wandell Murphy
Mrs. Marjorie M. Musgrove
Mrs. Tom Myers
Mrs. Logan "Buzzy" Nalley
Mrs. Robert Newcomb
Mrs. Gary Nichols
Mrs. Doug Nipper
Mrs. Steven Norman

Mrs. Doug Oliver
Mrs. Charles T. Oxford
Mrs. Dixon Oxford
Mrs. Lanier H. Oxford
Mrs. Havner Parish
Ms. Claudia Parker
Ms. Grace Parrott
Mrs. David Patten
Mrs. James M. Patterson, Jr.
Mrs. M. Jackson Pennington
Mrs. Del Percilla, Jr.
Mrs. Buddy Persall
Mrs. Jerry Phillips
Mrs. John T. Phillips
Mrs. John T. Phillips, Jr.
Mrs. John Temp Phillips, III
Mrs. Evans J. Plowden, Jr.
Mrs. Joe B. Powell, Jr.
Mrs. J. G. Pritchett
Mrs. Sallie Pritchett
Mrs. Jerry Pulley
Mrs. Ella Puiszis
Ms. Sue Radebaugh
Mrs. R. Kelley Raulerson
Mrs. J. Lamar Reese, Jr.
Ms. Mary Lou Reeves
Mrs. James E. Reynolds, Jr.
Mrs. Robert W. Reynolds
Mrs. Thomas Rhodes
Mrs. W. P. Rhyne
Mrs. A. E. Richardson
Mrs. George Riles
Mrs. Glen P. Robinson, Jr.
Mrs. Jack Rogers
Mrs. Mills P. Rooks
Mrs. Mark Rosenberg
Mrs. Lillian G. Rudolph
Mrs. Erk Russell
Mrs. Paul T. Russell
Mrs. Bill Russell
Mrs. Paul T. Russell, Jr.
Mrs. James R. Salley
Mrs. Joe Salter
Mrs. James E. Sapp
Mrs. Gene Seegmueller
Mrs. Brandon Seely
Mrs. John F. Shackelford
Mrs. Paige Shaver
Mrs. Cecil Shepard
Mrs. Steve Shephard
Mrs. Max A. Sheppard, Jr.
Mrs. John M. Sherman
Mrs. Jeffrey Sikora
Mrs. Bennie Silas
Mrs. Lawton Sims
Mrs. Fred Slaughter
Mrs. Bruce Smith
Mrs. Phil Smith
Mrs. John H. Sperry
Mrs. Scott Sperry
Miss Karen Ward Spooner
Mrs. William T. Stanfill
Mrs. Frank Stimpson
Mrs. J. E. Stimpson
Mrs. Malissa Stokes
Mrs. Don Strickland

Ms. Gladys Strickland
Mrs. Thomas Strickland
Mrs. Mrs. Walter Strom
Mrs. Carlysle Sullivan, Jr.
Mrs. Fred N. Sumter, Jr.
Mrs. Mack Sutton
Mrs. William L. Swan
Mrs. Jack Taylor
Mrs. William Timmerman
Mrs. John Steven Tkac
Mrs. Herb Turner
Mrs. Terry Trojan
Mrs. Robert Truitt
Mrs. William F. Underwood
Mrs. J. C. Varn
Mrs. John Ventulett
Mrs. John P. Ventulett, Jr.
Miss Anne Van Deventer
Mrs. E. F. Wacklin
Mrs. B. L. Waite
Mrs. Donald Wakeford
Mrs. Mack Wakeford
Mrs. Larry Walden
Mrs. Tommy Walden
Mrs. Carole Lowe Walters
Mrs. J. W. Walters
Mrs. Lee H. Walters
Mrs. Harold Watkins
Mrs. J. P. Watkins, Jr.
Mrs. Perry F. Webb
Mrs. James Roland Wetherbee, II
Mrs. Michael Wetherbee
Mrs. W. P. Whelchel, Jr.
Mrs. Bill Whitaker
Mrs. Evelyn White
Mrs. Hugh White
Ms. Marilyn White
Mrs. Albert Whitehead
Mrs. Deming Whiting
Mrs. James D. Whiting
Mrs. W. L. Whittle
Mrs. George S. Whittlesey, Jr.
Mrs. Wendell B. Wight
Ms. Linda Wilder
Mrs. E. B. Wilkin, Jr.
Mrs. Cleone Williams
Mrs. Doug Williams
Mrs. Fannie Lou Williams
Mrs. Hubert Williams
Mrs. Lasse D. Williams
Mrs. Rose Lee Williams
Mrs. T. Glenn Williams
Mrs. Ed Willis
Mrs. Harvey Willis
Mrs. Sherman Willis
Mrs. Dennis Wilson
Mrs. Rick Winston
Mrs. Paul H. Winter
Mrs. James Wray
Mrs. Henry W. Wright
Mrs. William B. Wright, Jr.
Mrs. Don Wylie
Mrs. M. Lynn Wylie
Mrs. R. Sam Yarborough
Mrs. M. C. York
Mrs. Gordon Zeese

Men's Recipes

Mr. Buddy Allen
Mr. Chris Anderson
Mr. Carlton Bullock
Mr. Dick Bullock
Mr. Tommy Chambless
Mr. Charles Fussell
Mr. Ronald Gann
Mr. John Gargano
Mr. Geoff Gray
Mr. Phil Greene
Mr. Curt Hall, Jr.
Mr. J. O. Hall
Mr. David T. Hastie
Mr. William H. Hedrick
Mr. K. B. Hodges, Jr.
Mr. Huddy Hudgens
Mr. Bill Hughey
Mr. Billups Johnson
Mr. Proctor Johnston
The Reverend Howard F. Kempsell, Jr.
Mr. Tom King
Mr. Billy McAfee
Mr. Harry Malcom, Jr.
Judge Hudson Malone
Mr. A. E. Moncrief
Mr. E. R. Moulton
Mr. John L. Moulton
Senator Sam Nunn
Mr. Milton Robinson
Mr. Jack Rogers
Mr. Curt Ross
Mr. Tom Seegmueller
Mr. Brandon Seely
Mr. Cecil Shepard
Mr. Steve Shephard
Mr. Frank Stimpson
Mr. John Tkac
Mr. Ernest Wetherbee, Jr.
Mr. Frank Wetherbee
Mr. Harold B. Wetherbee
Mr. Mike Wetherbee
Mr. Roland Wetherbee
Mr. Hal Wightman

Professional Cooks and Caterers

Miss Katherine Moseley
Mrs. Colette Norris
Mrs. Jean Owens
Mrs. Effie M. Scarborough
Mrs. Dixey Smith

Plantations

BLUE SPRINGS
Mr. and Mrs. Paul Mountcastle
BYRON
Mrs. Clayton Ralph Hodges
Mr. C. Ralph Hudges, Jr.
DUCKER
Mr. and Mrs. Henry M. Goodyear, Jr.
FAIR OAKS
Mr. and Mrs. Brigham Britton
GILLIONVILLE
Mr. Lewis S. Thompson, III
GRAVEL HILL
Family of Francis P. Wetherbee
HOLLY
Family of Charles Allen Thomas
NILO
Mr. and Mrs. John Olin
PEBBLE RIDGE
Family of Kenneth B. Hodges
PINEBLOOM
Mr. and Mrs. John M. Harbert, III
PINELAND
Family of Richard K. Mellon
PINEWOOD
Mr. and Mrs. Harold B. Wetherbee
RIVERVIEW
Mr. and Mrs. Cader Cox
TALLASSEE
Mr. and Mrs. Raymond F. Evans
TOLEE
Dr. and Mrs. Charles Finney
WILDFAIR
Family of John Grant, Jr.
WILLOW OAK
Mr. and Mrs. Edward A. Davis

Introduction

Quail Country *preserves the heritage of Southern hospitality known for more than a century in this southwestern corner of Georgia. Within these pages you will find recipes for native wild game, family favorites that have passed through generations, and unique recipes that have combined the tastes of the Indian, Negro and European settlers. This unique ethnic collection makes up what is known in the deep South as "Southern cookin'."*

"Quail country," rich in Indian and pre-Civil war history, was once a favorite hunting ground for the Creek Indians. Hernando DeSoto and his soldiers in 1540 were the first Europeans to invade this Indian territory. Amid centuries-old live oaks, tall pines and lush swamp foliage, the beautiful Flint River still winds its way to the Gulf of Mexico. The banks and waters of this peaceful river provided the fish and game for those early inhabitants. Called "Thronateeska" (meaning giving of flint) by the Indians, it also provided the native flintrock used to make arrowheads and implements for their everyday life. Young hunters today prize the arrowheads still found deep in those same dense woods.

In 1836 Albany was founded on the banks of the Flint River by Col. Nelson Tift, bringing taste, refinement and culture to the area. With the removal of the Creeks to the Indian territory west of the Mississippi, this same year saw the first log houses and cotton shed constructed. The "Mary Emeline," a steamboat and barge, brought goods upriver from Apalachicola, Florida, to this newly developed settlement which had attracted many new citizens. Albany quickly evolved from a rough frontier settlement to a stable community. Many planters moved into this area from other parts of Georgia, bringing the first Negro families to the area to develop the beautiful plantations throughout "Quail Country." With the abundance of wild game, fruits and vegetables grown in the pleasant climate of South Georgia and the winter riverboats bringing oysters from the Gulf, Albanians truly enjoyed a bountiful table. The area soon became well known for the "sociable" parties, picnics and barbecues hosted by the more prosperous landowners on their plantations.

The plantation houses, many dating back to the pre-Civil war period, were gracefully surrounded by the native wild azaleas, dogwood and occasional magnolias and live oaks. Some spacious old dwellings still stand proudly today with these same plantations in operation as game preserves, for general farming and cattle raising. Today's plantation owners place special attention on raising the population of that regal American game bird, the Bob White Quail, that once made this area the "Quail Capital of the World."

Although Albany is considered one of the fastest growing industrial and agricultural areas of Georgia, today finds Albanians with a strong commitment toward preserving their treasured heritage and the natural beauty of this area. The lakes, ponds and native trees have been enhanced with new varieties of azaleas, camellias, roses and flowering fruit trees. Huge agricultural operations thrive in the surrounding countryside where corn, cotton, peanuts, tobacco, soybeans and watermelons are grown. Vast pecan orchards can be found here and the growth of the pecan industry in the past two decades gives the area its reputation as the "World's Greatest Pecan Center."

It is evident by her history that Albany has enjoyed a heritage of beauty, hospitality and successful growth. This heritage continues today and we graciously offer our Quail Country style to you.

We hope "you all" will find it pleasing.

TABLE OF CONTENTS

Appetizers

Unless the refreshments served at receptions or teas could be considered hors d'oeuvres, appetizers as we know them were not common fare in the early days. There were nuts, of course, from woods and orchards, including walnuts, hickory nuts, chestnuts and the now indispensable pecans. Oysters, we know from early accounts of life in this section, were brought in the winter from the Gulf of Mexico. At receptions or teas, coffee or Russian tea were offered with chicken salad, cheese straws, beaten biscuits, rosettes (made on rosette irons cooked in deep fat) served with sweet sauce and cakes.

Regional

DEEP FRIED PEANUTS

raw peanuts   *salt*
peanut oil

Put peanuts into a frying basket. Submerge in peanut oil preheated to 350° F and fry for 2 minutes. Drain on paper towels. Sprinkle with salt. Serve warm.

BOILED PEANUTS

"Freshly pulled" green   *salt*
*   peanuts, unshelled*

Wash peanuts thoroughly in cool water; then soak in clear cool water for about 30 minutes before cooking. Drain.

Put peanuts in a saucepan and cover completely with water. Add 1 tablespoon salt for each pint of peanuts. Boil the peanuts for about 35 minutes; then taste. If they are not salty enough, add more salt. Taste again in 10 minutes both for salt content and to see if the peanuts are fully cooked. The texture of the peanut when fully cooked should be similar to that of a cooked dry pea or bean. If not ready, continue tasting every 5 minutes until they have a satisfactory texture.

Drain peanuts after cooking or they will continue to absorb salt and become over salted. Cooked peanuts can be frozen. Thaw in boiling water before serving.

DRY ROASTED PEANUTS

green peanuts, shelled   *salt*
butter

Spread raw peanuts in one layer in a shallow baking pan. Heat in a slow oven at 300° F for 30 to 45 minutes until brown. Stir peanuts frequently. For salted peanuts, add 1 teaspoon butter to each cup of peanuts immediately after removing from oven. Stir until peanuts are evenly coated and sprinkle with salt to taste.

ROASTED SALTED PECANS

1 teaspoon salt
1 teaspoon sugar
1 teaspoon milk

1 teaspoon water
1 egg white, stiffly beaten
1 quart pecan halves

Mix salt, sugar, milk, and water with egg white. Add pecans. Cover nuts well. Pour on foil lined cookie sheet. Bake at 250° F - 300° F for 1 hour. Stir every 15 minutes. Yield: 1 quart pecans.

TOASTED PECANS

pecans
butter

salt

Place pecans in shallow pan in 200° F oven. When pecans take on a shiny appearance, add melted butter (2 tablespoons for 8 ounces of pecans, 4 tablespoons for 16 ounces). Stir to coat pecans and salt to taste while stirring. Place pecans back in oven for at least 4 hours.

PECAN CANAPES

pecan halves
cream cheese
Roquefort cheese

mayonnaise
few drops of lemon juice

Use very large pecans for this recipe. Make a filling of cream cheese, Roquefort cheese and mayonnaise. Squeeze a few drops of lemon juice into cheese mixture. Spread a bit of mixture between two pecans. Refrigerate to harden.

VARIATION:

large pecan halves

tube of Anchovy paste

"Glue" 2 halves together with Anchovy paste.

PECAN CHEESE CRACKERS

1 pound sharp Cheddar
    cheese, grated
1 cup butter or margarine

cayenne pepper to taste'
3 cups flour, sifted
1 cup chopped pecans

Combine cheese and butter, cream thoroughly; add cayenne pepper. Add flour and pecans; mix thoroughly (will be very stiff). Shape into rolls and refrigerate overnight. Slice ¼ inch thick and bake in 350° F oven for 12 to 15 minutes. Do not brown. Can be frozen before or after baking. Yield: 100 crackers (approximately).

COCKTAIL PECAN PIE

1 (3 ounce) jar dried beef, chopped
1 (8 ounce) carton sour cream
1 (8 ounce) package cream cheese, softened

½ cup minced green pepper
2 teaspoons minced onion
¼ teaspoon garlic salt
1 cup chopped pecans
2 tablespoons butter

Thoroughly combine dried beef, sour cream, cream cheese, green pepper, onion and garlic salt. Put mixture in ovenproof casserole. Top with chopped pecans which have been sautéed in butter. Bake at 350° F for 20 minutes. Serve with crackers or chips. May be frozen when cooked. Yield: 10-12 servings.

FOOD PROCESSOR BEATEN BISCUIT

2 cups all purpose bread flour
1 teaspoon salt

½ cup butter, cut into pieces
½ cup ice water

Preheat oven to 350° F. Adjust oven rack to center position.

With metal blade in place, add flour and salt to work bowl of food processor. Turn machine off and on twice to aerate mixture. Add butter and process until mixture is consistency of corn meal. With machine running, pour ice water through feed tube in a steady stream. Process until mixture forms a ball; then process for an additional 2 minutes.

Carefully remove dough from blade and work bowl. Roll dough out on a lightly floured surface to a rectangle ⅛ inch thick. Fold dough in half to form 2 layers. Cut through both layers of dough with a 1½ inch cutter with fluted edge.

Place biscuits on ungreased cookie sheet and bake in preheated oven for 25 to 30 minutes or until golden brown. Remove from oven and split biscuits immediately. If centers are soft, return split biscuits to oven for 3 or 4 minutes to assure crisp base for spreads before serving. Yield: 30 biscuits.

SPREADS FOR BEATEN BISCUITS

ROQUEFORT PECAN SPREAD

¼ cup pecans
2 ounces Roquefort cheese
2 tablespoons sour cream

¼ cup pot style cottage
cheese

Add pecans to work bowl of food processor fitted with metal blade. Coarsely chop nuts. Remove from work bowl and set aside. Add Roquefort cheese and sour cream. Process until smooth. Add cottage cheese and process until completely mixed. Spread on split beaten biscuits. Garnish tops of biscuits by dipping them into reserved chopped pecans. Yield: about ¾ cup spread. A sliver of baked ham is sometimes served between beaten biscuits.

CURRIED CHICKEN PATÉ

1 whole chicken breast,
*   poached and cut into 1*
*   inch pieces*
1 shallot
¼ red delicious apple, peeled
*   and cored*

½ cup butter
1 teaspoon lemon juice
¼ teaspoon curry powder
freshly ground pepper

Add chicken, shallot and apple to work bowl of food processor. Process until mixture is finely chopped. Add remaining ingredients. Process until smooth. Taste for seasoning.

Serve on split beaten biscuits. Garnish with chopped parsley, chopped toasted pecans or thinly sliced pitted black olives. Yield: 1½ cups paté.

GRANDMOTHER'S CHEESE STRAWS

6 cups New York extra sharp
*   Cheddar cheese, softened*
1½ cups butter

3½ cups plain or self rising
*   flour*
¼ teaspoon red pepper

Grate cheese. Mix with butter. Add flour and red pepper. Mix well. Press out with a cookie press. Bake at 350° F on ungreased cookie sheet on bottom rack until bottom begins to brown; then move to top rack. Cook approximately 20 minutes. Yield: 100 cookies.

CHEESE STRAWS

1¾ cups self-rising flour
½ cup margarine or butter,
  softened

1 (5 ounce) jar Kraft Old
  English-sharp cheese
cayenne pepper to taste

Place all ingredients in mixer and mix well. Push through cookie press with star disc. Place on ungreased cookie sheet. Cook at 350° F until light brown, approximately 12 to 15 minutes. Yield: 4 dozen.

Appetizers

CRABMEAT REMICK

1 pound lump crabmeat
6 slices crisp bacon
1 scant teaspoon dry
  mustard
½ teaspoon paprika

½ teaspoon celery salt
½ teaspoon Tabasco sauce
½ cup chili sauce
1 teaspoon tarragon vinegar
1½ cups mayonnaise

Divide crabmeat into 6 individual shells or ramekins. Heat in oven and top with strips of crisp bacon. Blend together mustard, paprika, celery salt, and Tabasco sauce. Add chili sauce and vinegar. Mix well; blend with mayonnaise. Spread the warm crabmeat with this sauce and glaze under broiler. Yield: 6 servings.

Pontchartrain Hotel

SHRIMP PATÉ

½ pound fresh shrimp,
  cooked and peeled
3 tablespoons lemon juice

4 tablespoons butter
salt and pepper to taste

Grind shrimp very fine and add lemon juice and butter in small amounts until used, adding salt and pepper to taste. This should be a smooth paste. Pack in a small dish and refrigerate for a few hours. Serve with crisp brown toast or a good crisp cracker. Yield: 10 to 12 servings, 25 to 30 crackers.

SHRIMP IN LEMON SHELLS

12 ounces fresh shrimp
lemon juice
6 lemons

homemade mayonnaise
fresh chives
fresh dill

Cook shrimp in boiling water for 3 minutes. Drain. Pour cold water over shrimp to stop cooking process. Clean, devein, sprinkle with lemon juice and refrigerate until ready to serve. Cut lemons in half lengthwise. Scoop out pulp. Add chives and dill to mayonnaise and add to shrimp. Fill lemon shells and serve with crackers. Tomatoes may be substituted for lemon shells. See recipe for homemade mayonnaise. Yield: 6 servings.

SLANG JANG

1 to 2 tablespoons parched
    cumin seed (do not use
    ground powder)
2 (1 lb. 13 oz.) cans
    tomatoes, chopped, well
    drained

2 green peppers, chopped
2 onions, chopped
1 small can oysters, drained
    and chopped (canned are
    better than fresh)
salt to taste

Brown cumin seed in oven in pie pan about 10 minutes at 350° F. Pound to release flavor. Mix all ingredients and chill for several hours. Drain before serving. Serve cold as appetizer with crackers. Yield: 16 servings.

FRENCH MARINATED EGGPLANT

3 quarts water
6 cups eggplant, cut into
    1-inch cubes
¼ cup wine vinegar
¼ teaspoon minced garlic
½ teaspoon dried basil

½ teaspoon dried oregano
⅛ teaspoon coarse ground
    pepper
½ teaspoon salt
¼ cup olive oil

Bring the water to a boil. Drop in the cubed eggplant; reduce heat and simmer uncovered for 10 minutes. Drain. Rinse with cold water. Mix vinegar, garlic, basil, oregano, pepper and salt in a large bowl. Add the eggplant and toss gently. Marinate in refrigerator for at least 1 hour. Before serving, add olive oil, toss again and serve with crackers. Yield: 20 servings.

LE CRUETTE ST. JOHN

1 pound shrimp, peeled and
    deveined
¼ cup butter
2 tomatoes, peeled and diced
1 garlic clove, minced
½ cup chopped onions
10 large mushrooms, sliced
4 shallots or green onions,
    chopped

½ cup dry white wine
½ teaspoon tarragon leaves
salt to taste
red pepper to taste
¼ teaspoon oregano
½ cup bread crumbs
½ cup grated Parmesan
    cheese

Peel and devein shrimp. Sauté tomatoes, garlic, onions and mushrooms in butter. Remove and reserve mixture. Sauté shrimp. Add shallots, and when they are clear, add white wine, tarragon leaves. Return first mixture to skillet; simmer 5 minutes. Season to taste with salt, red pepper and oregano. Place in four individual baking dishes and top with crumbs and cheese. Broil for 1 to 2 minutes to melt cheese. Yield: 4 servings.

Wash, shake free of water a bunch of parsley. Drop in glass jar, close top and place in refrigerator. It will crisp and keep well.

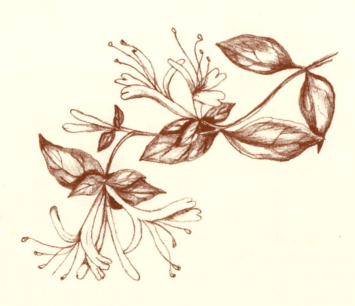

Cocktail Buffet

ARTICHOKE NIBBLES

2 jars marinated artichoke
   hearts
1/3 cup finely chopped onion
1 clove garlic, minced
4 eggs
1/4 cup fine, dry bread
   crumbs
1/4 teaspoon salt
1/8 teaspoon pepper
1/8 teaspoon oregano
1/8 teaspoon Tabasco sauce
1/2 pound sharp Cheddar
   cheese, grated
2 teaspoons minced parsley

Drain marinade from 1 jar of artichokes into a skillet. Sauté the onion and garlic in the marinade for 5 minutes. Set aside.

Drain the other jar of artichokes and discard marinade. Chop the artichokes finely. Beat the eggs; add crumbs and seasonings. Stir in cheese, parsley, artichokes and onion mixture; pour into a buttered 7 × 11 inch baking dish. Bake at 325° F for 30 minutes. Allow to cool 15 minutes before cutting. Cut into 1-inch squares. Serve hot or cold. Yield: approximately 1½ dozen.

TO PREPARE IN ADVANCE: When cool, wrap airtight in aluminum foil. These squares may be stored for up to 4 days in the refrigerator or for up to 3 months in the freezer. If frozen, thaw and heat at 325 ° F for 10 minutes.

CRAB AVIGNON

3 (8 ounce) packages
   cream cheese
2 (6 ounce) cans crab
   meat
1/2 cup mayonnaise
2 tablespoons prepared
   mustard
2 teaspoons onion juice
2/3 cup white wine
dash Lawry's seasoning salt

Soften cream cheese. Combine crab meat, mayonnaise, mustard, onion juice, wine and seasoning salt with cream cheese. Heat in a double boiler. Serve hot in a chafing dish with melba toast or toast points. Yield: 20 servings.

SEAFOOD MOUSSE

2 cups cooked shrimp and
    crab, or lobster meat, cut
    in small pieces
1 cup chopped celery
½ cup finely chopped green
    pepper
2 tablespoons grated onion
1 teaspoon salt
3 tablespoons lemon juice
1 tablespoon Worcestershire
    sauce

15 drops Tabasco
1 can tomato soup
3 (3 ounce) packages
    cream cheese
3 envelopes unflavored
    gelatin
1 cup cold water
1 cup mayonnaise

Combine seafood, celery, green pepper, onion, salt, lemon juice, Worcestershire sauce and Tabasco. Mix well. Let stand to blend flavors. Combine tomato soup and cream cheese in top of double boiler. Stir until cheese is melted. Soften gelatin in cold water for 5 minutes; add it to hot soup and cheese mixture. Stir until dissolved. Remove from heat and cool. When mixture begins to thicken, add mayonnaise. Stir in seafood mixture; pour into lightly greased 1½- quart mold. Chill until set. Yield: 12 to 16 servings.

SHRIMP MELT

1 (8 ounce) package cream
    cheese
¾ cup mayonnaise
3 tablespoons chopped green
    pepper
1 tablespoon fresh lemon
    juice

1 tablespoon Worcestershire
    sauce
1 teaspoon salt
1 teaspoon pepper
1 cup chopped cooked shrimp
2 loaves party rye bread

Mix softened cream cheese with next 6 ingredients. Add shrimp last. Put a teaspoon of mixture on each slice of party rye bread. Place on cookie sheet and bake at 350° F for 15 minutes or until tops begin to brown. Yield: 40 servings.

CHICKEN LIVER PATÉ

1 quart chicken stock
1 stalk celery, diced
2 sprigs parsley, minced
6 whole peppercorns
12 ounces chicken livers, diced
½ cup finely chopped onions
2 cloves garlic
½ teaspoon ground nutmeg
cayenne pepper to taste
2 teaspoons dry mustard
¼ teaspoon ground cloves
1 tablespoon cognac
2 cups sweet butter, softened
lettuce leaves and small sweet gherkins

Heat chicken stock. Add celery, parsley, and peppercorns; simmer 7 minutes. Add livers, onions and garlic; simmer 5 minutes; strain and reserve stock. Blend vegetables and livers in food processor or blender until mixture is like a paste. Add nutmeg, pepper, mustard, cloves and cognac. Mix well and add small amount of stock if needed. Blend butter 1 stick at a time to mixture in blender and blend until smooth. Place in mold and chill. Serve on lettuce and garnish with small gherkins. Serve with crackers. Do not freeze. Yield: 10 to 12 servings.

RED SALMON MOUSSE

2 envelopes unflavored gelatin
½ cup water
6 tablespoons lemon juice
1 tablespoon Worcestershire sauce
1 cup boiling water
1 tablespoon vinegar
dash Tabasco
1 (16 ounce) can red salmon
½ cup grated onion
1 cup mayonnaise
½ cup sour cream
2 cups finely chopped celery

Soften gelatin in water. Add lemon juice, Worcestershire sauce, boiling water, vinegar, and Tabasco to gelatin. Let congeal slightly. Then add salmon which has been drained, boned, skinned and flaked. Stir in onion, mayonnaise, sour cream, and celery. Pour into fish mold. Garnish with parsley and olive slice for fish's eye. May be served with a side dish of sour cream and capers and crackers. Yield: 50 servings.

11

OYSTERS AND ARTICHOKE HEARTS

1 cup butter
1 heaping cup flour
1 quart milk
½ pint light cream
6 dozen oysters, drained
2 teaspoons salt
1 teaspoon black pepper
dash Tabasco

2 teaspoons Worcestershire
  sauce
½ cup dry white wine
8 frozen artichoke hearts,
  cooked and finely
  chopped
¼ cup bread crumbs

Melt butter and blend in flour. Remove from heat. Combine and warm milk and cream; add slowly to butter and flour mixture, stirring constantly. Heat oysters to remove extra liquor; drain, and then add oysters to cream sauce. Simmer until mixture thickens. Add seasonings, Worcestershire sauce, wine and artichoke hearts. Serve in chafing dish. Sprinkle the bread crumbs on top. Serve with toasted bread rounds. Yield: 25 servings for cocktail buffet.

OYSTERS OLIVER

1 pound butter
1 (5 ounce) jar creamed
  horseradish
1 can cream of mushroom
  soup

dash of Worcestershire sauce
salt to taste
1 gallon oysters, drained

Combine butter, horseradish, soup, Worcestershire and salt in a saucepan. Heat until butter melts. Add well-drained oysters but DO NOT COOK. Let stand over low flame in chafing dish and serve with toast points. Yield: 50 servings.

Serve cheese spreads or dips in a hollowed out bell pepper. Decorate tray with seasonal leaves.

Garnish a platter of Brie cheese with a covering of pecans or almonds. Surround with crackers.

SHORE SEAFOOD DIP

1 green pepper, chopped
1 cup chopped onion
2 stalks celery, chopped
2 tablespoons butter
½ can cream of shrimp
　　soup
1 cup mayonnaise

8 ounces Parmesan cheese,
　　grated
1 (6 ounce) can crab meat,
　　drained
1 (6 ounce) can shrimp,
　　drained
½ teaspoon white pepper

Sauté green pepper, onion and celery in butter. Combine shrimp soup, mayonnaise, Parmesan cheese, crab meat, shrimp and pepper. Stir in vegetables. Bake in a shallow casserole at 325° F for 30 minutes. Yield: 12 servings.

PARTY EYE OF THE ROUND

eye of the round roast (2
　　ounces per person)
1 envelope Italian dressing
　　mix

salt
½ cup bourbon
¼ cup vegetable oil
coarse ground pepper

Marinate roast overnight in dressing mix, salt, bourbon and oil. Next day wipe meat dry with paper towel and coat heavily with coarse ground pepper and a little salt. Roast uncovered at 325° F until desired doneness (2 hours for a 5 to 6 pound roast, medium rare). Serve with horseradish sauce (see recipe).

CAVIAR PIE

1 (8 ounce) package cream
   cheese
1/4 cup mayonnaise
2 to 3 teaspoons grated onion
1 to 2 teaspoons
   Worcestershire sauce

1 to 2 teaspoons lemon juice
red caviar
parsley, chopped
1 hard cooked egg, grated
1 onion, finely chopped
melba toast rounds

Soften and blend the cream cheese with mayonnaise. Season cheese with onion, Worcestershire sauce and lemon juice. Spread in center of plate or tray in a circle about 1 inch thick. Cover top with red caviar and parsley. Sprinkle hard cooked egg and onion on top. Chill and serve with melba rounds. Yield: 8 to 12 servings.

CAVIAR MOUSSE

3/4 cup sour cream
1/4 cup chopped onion
3 hard cooked eggs, chopped
3 tablespoons mayonnaise
4 tablespoons lemon juice
1/2 teaspoon salt
1/2 teaspoon Worcestershire
   sauce

1/4 teaspoon Tabasco
1/4 teaspoon white pepper
2 tablespoons unflavored
   gelatin
2 tablespoons hot water or
   vodka
1 (2 ounce) jar red caviar

Mix all ingredients except gelatin, water and caviar in blender. Add gelatin that has been dissolved in 2 tablespoons hot water or vodka. Fold in caviar. Pour into mold and chill. Yield: 20 servings.

14

EGGPLANT CAVIAR

2 pounds firm eggplant
2 cups ground pecans
1/2 teaspoon Tabasco
1/4 teaspoon ground allspice
3/4 teaspoon salt
1/8 teaspoon pepper

1 to 4 cloves garlic, minced
1 teaspoon freshly grated
    ginger root or 1/4 teaspoon
    powdered ginger
5 to 8 tablespoons olive oil

Bake whole eggplant, first cutting off green cap, in preheated 425° F oven. Bake 30 to 35 minutes or until thoroughly soft to touch. Cut in half lengthwise and scoop flesh into mixing bowl. Beat several minutes to purée the eggplant. Beat in pecans and all seasonings. By driblets, beat in olive oil as though making mayonnaise. Beat in only enough to make a creamy mass when lifted by spoon. Taste; correct seasoning. Can be kept in refrigerator several days or may be frozen. Serve with crackers. Yield: 8 to 10 servings.

Cut a wedge from a round cheese, such as Brie or Edam, before serving.

HOT SPINACH DIP

2 (10 ounce) packages frozen
    chopped spinach
1/4 cup butter, melted
2 tablespoons chopped onion
3 tablespoons flour
1/2 cup evaporated milk
1 (6 ounce) roll Jalapeno
    cheese, softened

1/2 teaspoon pepper
3/4 teaspoon celery salt
3/4 teaspoon garlic salt
1 tablespoon Worcestershire
    sauce
dash red pepper

Thaw and drain spinach well, reserving 1/2 cup liquid. Set spinach aside. Combine butter, onion and flour; cook about 1 minute. Gradually add reserved spinach liquid and evaporated milk; cook until slightly thickened, stirring constantly. Add cheese and seasonings to sauce, stirring until cheese is melted. Add spinach. Serve hot in chafing dish with toast rounds. May be frozen. Yield: 1¾ cups.

INDIAN CHICKEN BALLS

½ pound cream cheese
2 tablespoons mayonnaise
1 cup chopped, cooked
chicken (2 or 3 breasts)
1 cup chopped pecans
1 tablespoon chutney

½ teaspoon salt
dash garlic salt
dash onion salt
2 teaspoons curry powder
½ cup grated coconut

Soften cheese; mix with mayonnaise. Add chicken, pecans, chutney, salt, garlic salt, onion salt and curry powder. Refrigerate until firm. Shape into balls and roll in coconut. Cover; chill for 24 hours before serving. If freezing, do not roll in coconut and do not let balls touch. Thaw; then roll in coconut. Yield: 8 servings.

STUFFED MUSHROOMS

1 loaf thinly sliced bread
2 (4 ounce) cans button
mushrooms
1 (8 ounce) package cream
cheese
¼ cup minced onion

2 egg yolks
pinch garlic powder
pinch Jane's Krazy Mixed-up
salt
pepper to taste

Cut bread in small rounds. Place a mushroom cap in the center of each round. Mix cream cheese, onion, egg yolks, garlic powder, salt, and pepper. Cover mushrooms with cheese mixture. Place under broiler until brown and fluffy. Serve while hot. Yield: 16 canapes.

CRAB STUFFED MUSHROOMS

3 dozen large whole fresh
mushrooms
1 (7½ ounce) can crabmeat,
drained and flaked
1 tablespoon chopped
parsley

1 tablespoon chopped
pimento
1 teaspoon capers
¼ teaspoon dry mustard
½ cup mayonnaise or salad
dressing

Wipe mushrooms with damp cloth. Remove stems. Combine crab meat, parsley, pimento and capers. Blend dry mustard into mayonnaise; toss with crab mixture. Fill each mushroom crown with crab mixture. Bake in a moderate oven (375° F) for 8 to 10 minutes. Yield: 36 appetizers.

CROUSTADES AU CHAMPIGNONS

4 tablespoons butter
18 (3 inch) circles of thin
    sliced bread
3 tablespoons finely minced
    green onions
1 pound mushrooms, finely
    minced
1 cup heavy cream

2 tablespoons flour
1/8 teaspoon cayenne pepper
1/2 teaspoon salt
1 tablespoon parsley
3 teaspoons chives
1/2 teaspoon lemon juice
fresh Parmesan, grated

CROUSTADES: Heavily butter tiny muffin tins. Cut 3-inch circles from thin sliced bread. Flatten and roll thin with rolling pin. Press into cups and up against the sides with fingers. Bake at 400° F. for about 12 minutes. Can be frozen for later use.

CHAMPIGNONS: Take finely minced green onion and mushrooms and put in a kitchen towel and twist to remove liquid. Melt remaining butter. Add onions and mushrooms and cook until all liquid has evaporated. Remove from heat. Stir in flour and cream. Return to stove and cook until thick. Stir in remaining ingredients except Parmesan and then set aside to cool. Fill toast cups with mixture. Sprinkle with fresh Parmesan. Bake at 350° F for 20 to 30 minutes. Yield: 18 servings.

VARIATION: Cut crusts from thin slices of fresh bread, butter thickly and spread 1/4 inch thick with creamed mushroom mixture. Roll like a jelly roll and secure with toothpicks. Can be cut in two if too large to serve. Place on cookie sheet and toast in a hot oven, turning to brown on all sides. Serve hot.

PEPPER JELLY TURNOVERS

1 (5 ounce) jar Old English
    cheese
1/2 cup butter

1 cup flour
2 tablespoons water
hot pepper jelly

Cut cheese and butter into flour. Stir in water and shape into a ball. Refrigerate overnight. Roll out dough very thinly and cut into 2-inch circles. Place 1/2 teaspoon of pepper jelly in center of each. Fold over and crimp edges with a fork. Bake for 10 to 15 minutes at 375° F. May be frozen before or after baking. Reheat before serving. May also use orange marmalade for morning coffee. Yield: 2 to 3 dozen.

MUSHROOM TARTS

PIE CRUST:

1 (8 ounce) package cream
   cheese, softened
1 cup butter, softened

2¼ cups flour
1 teaspoon salt
MUSHROOM FILLING

Blend cream cheese and butter. Add flour and salt and work with fingers or pastry blender until smooth. Chill well for 4 hours or overnight.

Roll the dough to ⅛-inch thickness on a lightly floured surface and cut into rounds with a 3-inch biscuit cutter. Place a teaspoon of MUSHROOM FILLING on each and fold the dough over the filling. Press the edges together with a fork. Prick top crusts to allow for the escape of steam. May be frozen on cookie sheet, then placed in plastic bag. Bake at 450° F for 15 minutes.

MUSHROOM FILLING:

3 tablespoons butter
⅔ cup finely chopped onion
½ pound mushrooms, finely
   chopped
¼ teaspoon thyme

½ teaspoon salt
freshly ground black pepper
   to taste
2 tablespoons flour
¼ cup sweet or sour cream

In a skillet, heat the butter, add onion and brown lightly. Add the mushrooms and cook, stirring often, about 3 minutes. Add the thyme, salt and pepper and sprinkle with flour. Stir in the cream and cook gently until thickened. Yield: 2 dozen tarts.

VARIATION:

1 cup chopped chicken, shrimp, crab or lobster may be added to mushroom filling.

CHICKEN LITTLE FINGERS

6 whole chicken breasts
1½ cups buttermilk
2 tablespoons lemon juice
2 teaspoons Worcestershire
    sauce
1 teaspoon soy sauce
1 teaspoon paprika
1 tablespoon Greek
    seasonings

1 teaspoon salt
1 teaspoon pepper
2 cloves garlic, minced
4 cups soft bread crumbs
¼ cup sesame seeds
¼ cup butter, melted
¼ cup shortening, melted

Cut chicken into ½-inch strips. Combine next 9 ingredients; add chicken, mixing until well coated. Cover and refrigerate overnight. Drain chicken thoroughly. Combine bread crumbs and sesame seeds, mixing well. Add chicken and toss to coat. Place chicken in two greased 13 × 9 × 2-inch baking dishes. Combine butter and shortening; brush on chicken. Bake at 350° F for 35 to 40 minutes and serve with PLUM SAUCE. Yield: 12 servings.

PLUM SAUCE:
1½ cups red plum jam
1½ tablespoons prepared
    mustard

1½ tablespoons prepared
    horseradish
1½ teaspoons lemon juice

Combine all ingredients in a small saucepan, mixing well. Place over low heat until warm, stirring constantly. Yield: 1¾ cups.

PINEAPPLE CHEESEBALL

2 (8 ounce) packages cream
    cheese, softened
4 ounces crushed pineapple,
    drained well
¼ cup finely chopped green
    pepper

1 tablespoon seasoned salt
2 tablespoons grated onion
1 cup chopped pecans

Mix ingredients together. Form into two balls. Chill. Roll in pecans. Chill again. Serve with crackers. Yield: 20 servings.

Tea Party, Wine and Cheese

DECORATED CHEESE BALL

6 (8 ounce) packages cream
   cheese
½ pound Roquefort cheese
½ pound sharp Cheddar
   cheese, softened
½ cup chopped chives or
   green onion
1 garlic clove, minced
2 tablespoons red caviar
2 tablespoons black caviar
2 tablespoons chopped green
   olives

2 tablespoons finely chopped
   parsley
2 tablespoons chopped capers
2 tablespoons chopped
   pimento
2 tablespoons crisp diced
   bacon
2 tablespoons chopped black
   olives

Soften cream cheese; divide into three parts. Mix one part
with the Roquefort, one part with the Cheddar, one part with
the chives and garlic. Pile each part on top of one another and
shape into a ball. Mark the ball with a knife into eight
sections. Cover each section with one of the following: red
caviar, black caviar, green olives, parsley, capers, pimento,
bacon, and black olives. Refrigerate. When you cut the cheese,
you taste the different flavors. Yield: 60 servings.

CREAM CHEESE DELIGHT

12 ounces cream cheese
½ cup butter
½ cup sour cream
¼ cup sugar
1 envelope unflavored gelatin
¼ cup cold water

½ cup Major Gray's Chutney
   or Dundee Ginger
   Marmalade
1 cup toasted, chopped,
   salted pecans
rind of 2 lemons, grated

Bring cream cheese, butter and sour cream to room temperature. Cream well. Add sugar. Soften gelatin in cold water.
Add to cream cheese mixture. Add chutney, pecans and lemon
rind. Put in 1-quart mold. Refrigerate. When firm, unmold
and serve with crackers. May be frozen. Yield: 25 servings.

EGG MOLD

1 envelope unflavored gelatin
½ cup water
1 cup mayonnaise
1 teaspoon salt
¼ teaspoon pepper
2 tablespoons lemon juice
¼ teaspoon Worcestershire
  sauce

½ cup finely chopped parsley
¼ cup chopped pimento
½ cup finely chopped green
  onion
dash Tabasco
5 hard cooked eggs

Sprinkle gelatin over water and cook on low for 3 to 4 minutes. Cool; then mix with mayonnaise, salt, pepper, lemon juice, Worcestershire sauce, parsley, pimento, onion and Tabasco. Stir in eggs which have been sliced. Turn into mold which has been greased with mayonnaise. Chill several hours before serving. Yield: 8 servings.

CRABGRASS

1 (8 ounce) package chopped
  spinach
1 (10 ounce) can crabmeat
1 cup mayonnaise
1 cup sour cream
juice of 1 lemon

½ cup thinly sliced green
  onions
1 cup chopped parsley
1 teaspoon dill weed
1 teaspoon salt

Thaw spinach in colander or strainer. Squeeze well. Mix with all other ingredients combining well. Chill several hours. Serve as a dip with carrots, celery, cauliflower, raw squash, cherry tomatoes or with crackers. Yield: 2 cups.

PINK SHRIMP

2 (3 ounce) packages cream
  cheese, softened
⅓ cup mayonnaise or Ranch
  dressing
3 tablespoons chili sauce
2 tablespoons lemon juice

½ teaspoon onion juice
¼ teaspoon Worcestershire
  sauce
1 (5 ounce) can shrimp,
  finely chopped

Blend cream cheese and seasonings well in mixer. Add shrimp. Chill for several hours. Serve with crackers. Keeps several days refrigerated. Yield: 2 cups.

DIP FOR APPLES

½ cup mayonnaise
2 teaspoons horseradish
2 tablespoons guava or
    apple jelly
1 tablespoon tarragon
    vinegar
1 teaspoon prepared mustard

dash salt
dash Tabasco
½ cup whipping cream,
    whipped
1 tablespoon dry sherry
apples, unpeeled
lemon juice

Mix mayonnaise and horseradish. Beat jelly in small bowl to soften, add to mayonnaise mixture. Stir in vinegar, mustard, salt, and Tabasco. Fold into whipped cream. Add sherry just before serving. Each guest dips slice of apple into dip. Five apples yield 100 thin slices. Leave slices in lemon juice for a few minutes. Drain; cover and refrigerate. Yield: 1 cup.

Cheese should be cut in such a way as to retain its original shape. For example, a wedge should be cut from a wheel of cheese and a square slice cut from a block.

CHICKEN CHEESE PARTY LOAF

2 (8 ounce) packages cream
    cheese
4 teaspoons milk
2 cups minced cooked
    chicken
3 tablespoons finely grated
    onion

1 tablespoon salt
dash pepper
large loaf of unsliced white
    bread

Soften 1 package cream cheese with 2 teaspoons of milk. Combine with chicken, onion, salt and pepper; mix well. Chill loaf bread, trim all sides and slice into 4 slices lengthwise. Spread the bread with the filling as one would a cake and stack. Use extra package of cream cheese, softened, with 2 teaspoons of milk to spread over the entire outside of the loaf as icing on a cake. Can be tinted or decorated. Yield: 20 servings.

EGG SALAD PARTY SANDWICHES

1 cup finely chopped pecans
1 hard-cooked egg, finely
  chopped
1 (2 ounce) bottle Spanish
  olives, drained and finely
  chopped

1 tablespoon minced onion
1 cup mayonnaise
16 slices sandwich bread,
  crusts removed

Combine pecans, egg, olives, onion and mayonnaise; mix well.
Chill 3 to 4 hours. Spread filling on 8 slices of bread; top with
remaining slices. Cut each sandwich into thirds. Garnish with
piece of fresh parsley or small piece of pimento. Yield: 24
small sandwiches.

CUCUMBER RIBBON SANDWICHES

FILLING:
6 unpeeled cucumbers,
  grated
2 (8 ounce) packages cream
  cheese, at room
  temperature
1 bunch spring onions, finely
  chopped
2 tablespoons lemon or lime
  juice

1 teaspoon salt
1/4 teaspoon red pepper
1/4 cup mayonnaise
8 drops green food coloring
1/4 teaspoon garlic powder
  (optional)
3 or 4 loaves day old sliced
  white bread

Drain grated cucumbers very well on paper towels. Mix
cucumbers with remainder of filling ingredients. If mixture is
very juicy, place in refrigerator for about an hour before
spreading. Trim crusts from bread—stack sandwiches using 3
slices of bread, alternating with filling mixture. Cut each
stacked sandwich into 8 equal pieces. Pack close together in
an air tight container and keep chilled until ready to serve. A
damp tea towel or paper towel placed around sandwiches,
inside the container, keeps these from drying out. Do not
freeze. Yield: 200-250 sandwiches.

Informal Entertaining and Sandwiches

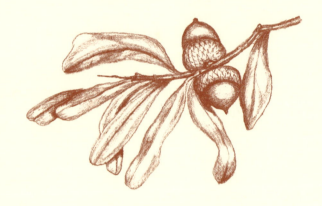

SNOW CAP SPREAD

2 (4½ ounce) cans deviled
  ham
1 tablespoon minced onion
1 (8 ounce) package cream
  cheese

¼ cup sour cream
2½ teaspoons hot mustard

Combine deviled ham and onion. Mound on plate. Frost with blend of cream cheese, sour cream and mustard. Garnish for color. Chill and serve with assorted crackers. Yield: 10-12 servings.

HOMEMADE BOURSIN CHEESE

1 (8 ounce) package cream
  cheese
2 tablespoons mayonnaise
1 teaspoon dill weed

1 teaspoon lemon pepper
½ teaspoon carraway seed
½ teaspoon celery seed
1 clove garlic, minced

Soften cream cheese using a fork. (Do not use a processor). Add remaining ingredients. Refrigerate. Best if made a day ahead to enhance the flavor. Use as a spread on crackers or on French bread. Yield: 1 cup.

CRESCENT SHRIMP SANDWICH

1 pound cooked shrimp,
    finely chopped
1 tablespoon minced onion
1 tablespoon minced celery
1 tablespoon minced green
    pepper

4 to 5 drops Tabasco
1 teaspoon lemon juice
¼ teaspoon salt
dash pepper
1 teaspoon grated lemon rind
¾ cup mayonnaise

Thoroughly combine all ingredients with mayonnaise. Spread on bread which has had crust removed and has been cut into crescent shapes. Pack tightly in an air tight container. Place damp towel or paper towel over sandwiches before closing container. Chill until ready to serve. May be garnished with parsley or olive slice. Yield: 3 cups of spread for party sandwiches.

To keep sandwiches fresh and moist, cover with a damp cloth.

OPEN-FACED SHRIMP SANDWICHES

¼ cup butter, softened
2 tablespoons mayonnaise
1 teaspoon snipped dill
Tabasco to taste
salt to taste
1½ pounds shrimp
1 bay leaf
1-inch piece lemon peel
1 sprig parsley

½ teaspoon thyme
6 slices square Pumpernickel
    bread
24 sprigs watercress
6 hard-boiled eggs, sliced
salt and pepper to taste
red caviar
snipped dill (for garnish)

In small bowl cream butter, mayonnaise, dill, Tabasco and salt. Plunge shrimp into a kettle of boiling, salted water seasoned with bay leaf, lemon peel, parsley and thyme and return the water to a boil. Drain and rinse the shrimp; then peel and devein. Spread bread with butter mixture and on each slice arrange decoratively 4 sprigs of watercress and 1 hard boiled egg, sliced. Divide the shrimp among the sandwiches. Garnish with red caviar and snipped dill. Yield: 3 to 6 servings.

CRAB QUICKEE

1 (8 ounce) package cream
cheese

1 (6 ounce) can crabmeat,
drained

SAUCE:

½ cup chili sauce
1 teaspoon horseradish
1 teaspoon Worcestershire
sauce

2 tablespoons lemon juice
1 teaspoon chopped chives
¼ teaspoon chopped parsley
Tabasco to taste

Slice cream cheese in half horizontally and arrange on a serving dish. Cover with crab meat. Just before serving, top with SAUCE. Serve with crackers. Yield: approximately 10 servings.

HOT CRAB TRIANGLES

8 ounces cream cheese,
softened
½ teaspoon dry mustard
1 tablespoon milk
¼ teaspoon salt
dash cayenne pepper
1 (6 ounce) can white crab
meat, drained and flaked
or shrimp

2 tablespoons chopped chives
2 tablespoons chopped
blanched almonds
12 slices white bread, crusts
trimmed off
paprika

Combine cream cheese with mustard, milk, salt, pepper, crab meat, chives, and almonds. Spread mixture on bread slices. Cut each into 4 triangles. Sprinkle with paprika. Bake at 400° F for 10 to 12 minutes or until browned. Yield: 48 triangles.

CHEESE DREAMS

8 slices bacon
4 slices bread
mayonnaise

4 slices American cheese
8 slices tomatoes

Fry bacon and crumble. Place bread slices on cookie sheet. Spread with mayonnaise; add cheese slices and tomatoes. Top with a tablespoon of mayonnaise. Bake at 350° F for approximately 10 minutes or until cheese is melted and tomatoes heated through. Top with crumbled bacon and serve immediately. Yield: 4 servings.

OYSTERS CHAMPAGNE

6 French rolls
butter
1½ pints oysters, drained
salt

freshly ground pepper
fresh parsley, minced
⅓ cup champagne (or dry
white wine)

Cut tops off French rolls; hollow slightly and spread inside with butter. Butter soft side of tops also. Heat rolls briefly in 400° F oven or toast lightly under broiler. Set aside. Heat ¼ cup butter in heavy skillet. Add oysters and baste with the butter. Season with salt and a few grindings of pepper. Add parsley and champagne. Cover and heat until oysters become plump and edges curl, just a few minutes. (Do not overcook). Pile hot into French rolls. Spoon pan juices on top. Serve at once. Yield: 6 servings.

HOT CRAB SANDWICHES

1 pound fresh crab
6 tablespoons mayonnaise
2 tablespoons chopped onion
1 teaspoon Worcestershire
    sauce
8 drops Tabasco sauce

2 tablespoons lemon juice
11 ounces cream cheese,
    softened
8 pieces Holland Rusk
8 slices tomato
8 slices sharp Cheddar
    cheese

Combine crab, mayonnaise, onion, Worcestershire sauce, Tabasco and lemon juice. Add to cream cheese. Refrigerate overnight. To serve, pile crabmeat mixture at least 1-inch thick on Holland Rusk. Top each with a salted tomato slice and a slice of cheese. Bake at 300° F for 30 to 40 minutes. Yield: 8 servings.

SEAFOOD ROUNDS

1 (15½ ounce) can salmon or
    2 (6½ ounce) cans tuna
4 teaspoons mayonnaise
2 teaspoons grated onion
2 teaspoons finely chopped
    green pepper

dash Tabasco
salt to taste
white pepper to taste
6 Holland Rusks
½ pound sharp Cheddar
    cheese, grated

Mix all ingredients except rusks and cheese. Mound mixture on rusks; top with cheese. Run under broiler until hot. Yield: 6 servings.

ARTICHOKES ALENE

½ cup melted butter
¼ pound bleu cheese,
    crumbled
4 (14 ounce) cans artichoke
    hearts, undrained
2 tablespoons flour

sliced baked country ham
8 to 10 English muffins,
    halved and toasted
4 to 5 hard cooked eggs,
    quartered
pimento strips

Combine butter and cheese in a saucepan; stir until cheese melts. Drain and chop artichoke hearts, reserving liquid. Add artichokes to cheese mixture. Combine flour and ¼ cup artichoke liquid; mix well and add to cheese mixture. Cook over low heat, stirring constantly, until thickened; do not boil. If sauce is too thick, add additional artichoke liquid. Arrange ham slices on English muffins; cover with sauce and top with egg and pimento strips. Yield: 16 to 20 servings.

HOT LUNCHEON SANDWICH

16 slices sandwich bread,
    crusts removed
8 slices boiled ham, chicken
    or turkey
8 slices sharp cheese
6 eggs

3 cups milk
½ teaspoon mustard
½ teaspoon salt
2 cups crushed cornflakes
½ cup melted butter

Butter bread and place 8 slices on bottom of greased 13 × 9½ inch baking pan. Top each slice with meat, cheese and remaining bread. Mix eggs, milk and seasonings. Beat and pour over sandwiches. Refrigerate overnight. Sprinkle sandwiches with cornflakes mixed with melted butter. Bake at 350° F for 45 minutes. Let stand 5 minutes before cutting. Yield: 8 servings.

BACON CRISPS

8 ounces Parmesan cheese
1 pound box Waverly Wafers

2 pounds of bacon, cut in
    half

Put cheese on top of each cracker. Wrap in bacon; no toothpick required. Place on broiler pan rack. No need to turn. Bake at 200° F. for 2 hours. Leave on pan to drain. Serve hot. Yield: 66 canapes.

PUMPERNICKEL STRATA

*1 round loaf pumpernickel
bread*
*½ cup butter or margarine,
softened*

*HORSERADISH-HAM
FILLING*
CHICKEN FILLING
DILLED EGG FILLING

Cut bread horizontally into 5 equal slices. Place bottom slice on serving platter or tray. Spread with butter; cover with half of HORSERADISH-HAM FILLING. Repeat process using CHICKEN FILLING next, the DILLED EGG FILLING, and ending with remaining half of HORSERADISH-HAM FILLING. Top with last slice of bread. Refrigerate the loaf until ready to serve. Cut in wedges.

HORSERADISH-HAM FILLING:

*2 (4½ ounce) cans deviled
ham*
1 stalk celery, minced

*1 tablespoon prepared
horseradish*
2 tablespoons mayonnaise

Combine all ingredients, mixing well. Chill. Yield: about 2 cups.

DILLED EGG FILLING:

4 hard cooked eggs, chopped
2 tablespoons mayonnaise
*2 teaspoons prepared
mustard*

1 teaspoon dill weed
1 teaspoon salt
¼ teaspoon pepper

Combine all ingredients, mixing well. Chill. Yield: about 1¼ cups.

CHICKEN FILLING:

*2 ounces bleu cheese,
crumbled*
*2 tablespoons butter or
margarine, softened*

*1 (7½ ounce) can chicken,
drained and chopped*
1 green onion, chopped
1 whole pimento, chopped

Blend bleu cheese and butter; add chicken, onion and pimento. Mix well. Chill. Yield: about 1¼ cups. NOTE: Tuna or crabmeat may be substituted for chicken.

Yield: 6 to 8 servings.

R. DIVINE ©

Beverages

From mint juleps to sparkling non-alcoholic punch, bever-
ages are important to the hospitable Southerner. "Come for a
drink" can mean a highball, or something similar, and some
nibbles or a heartier repast including sausage biscuits, salted
pecans, cheesestraws and perhaps some small sandwiches. An
early popular drink was blackberry acid, a homemade, refresh-
ing beverage. Blackberry nectar, too, was made during the
blackberry season, bottled and sealed to be served later. Home-
made wines were popular too. Eggnog has long been a Christ-
mas season favorite. No Sunday School picnic would have been
complete without a washtub of lemonade.

Beverages

Here is a checklist of items needed for a complete bar:

1 cocktail shaker with top
1 bottle opener
1 corkscrew
1 set of ice tongs
1 bar strainer
1 large mixing pitcher
1 jigger (1¼ ounces)

1 lemon/lime squeezer
1 stainless steel knife
1 ice bucket
1 serving tray
1 long-handled mixing spoon
stirrers
napkins

Suggested liquor supplies:

Gin	Bourbon	Perrier	Tonic Water
Scotch	White wine	Club Soda	
Vodka	Red wine	Ginger Ale	
Rum	Beer	Cola Drinks	

How much liquor should be bought?

One fifth of liquor makes 17 of most popular drinks, using 1½ ounces per drink.

If you are having	For Pre-Dinner Cocktails, you will average	For a Party, you will average
4 people	8 to 12 drinks (1 fifth required)	12 to 16 drinks (1 fifth required)
6 to 8 people	12 to 24 drinks (2 fifths required)	18 to 32 drinks (2 fifths required)
12 people	24 to 36 drinks (3 fifths required)	36 to 48 drinks (3 fifths required)
20 people	40 to 60 drinks (4 fifths required)	60 to 80 drinks (5 fifths required)

For a party of 25, you will need 1½ dozen highball glasses, 1½ dozen old-fashioneds, and 1½ dozen wine glasses.

To insure the comfort of non-smoking guests, place several lighted candles around the room. The lighted candles help to clear the air of smoke.

MINT JULEP

4 mint leaves

1 tablespoon sugar

1½ ounces bourbon whiskey

1 sprig mint

Use a mortar and pestle to crush the mint leaves with the sugar into a paste. Put the mint paste and the bourbon in a highball glass and fill with crushed ice. Stir until the glass frosts on the outside. Serve garnished with a sprig of mint. Yield: 1 serving.

SCARLET O'HARA

1½ ounces bourbon

1 ounce lime juice

3 ounces cranberry juice

ice

Shake with ice; then strain into a champagne glass. Yield: 1 serving.

PEACH DAIQUIRI

1 medium-size fresh peach, peeled and pitted

1 ounce lime juice

1 or 2 teaspoons sugar

3 ounces Bacardi Rum

1 cup cracked ice

Mix in blender until smooth and serve unstrained in cocktail glasses. Yield: 2 servings.

DEEP FREEZE DAIQUIRI

2 (6 ounce) cans pink lemonade, thawed

1 (6 ounce) can frozen limeade, thawed

1 fifth light rum

6 lemonade cans of water

Juice of 2 lemons

Mix all ingredients. Store in glass jar in deep freeze overnight. About 30 minutes before serving remove from freezer. Mixture should be icy. Will not freeze solidly. Yield: 2 quarts.

HOT BUTTERED RUM

1 pound butter, softened
1 pound light brown sugar
1 pound confectioners' sugar
 2 teaspoons ground
   cinnamon

2 teaspoons ground nutmeg
1 quart vanilla ice cream,
  softened
light rum

Combine butter, sugars and spices; beat until light and fluffy. Fold in ice cream, stirring until well blended. Freeze mixture. To serve, place 2 heaping tablespoons butter mixture and 1 jigger rum in large mug. Fill with boiling water; stir well. Refreeze any unused mixture. Yield: 25 cups.

HOT SPICED APPLE CIDER

1½ cups sugar
2 cups water
2 tablespoons whole allspice
½ gallon sweet apple cider

1 (18 ounce) can pineapple
  juice
1 (18 ounce) can orange juice
1 (6 ounce) can frozen
   lemonade concentrate

Make a syrup of sugar and water. Tie allspice in a cloth and let stand in syrup until it is flavored and then remove. Mix all ingredients. This can be served cold but is better served hot. Yield: 15 to 20 servings.

HOT CRANBERRY PUNCH

1¾ cups water
½ cup brown sugar
1 tablespoon whole allspice
½ tablespoon whole cloves
⅛ teaspoon salt
3 sticks cinnamon

2 lemons, sliced
1 (46 ounce) can pineapple
  juice
1 (32 ounce) bottle cranberry
   juice cocktail

Bring water, sugar and spices to a boil. Remove from heat and add lemons and fruit juices. Remove cloves, allspice and cinnamon. Serve hot. Yield: 15 to 18 servings.

KAHLUA MILKSHAKE

6 ounces Kahlua   ½ cup milk
1 quart good quality vanilla
    ice cream

Add Kahlua, ice cream and milk in blender. Blend until it has a smooth texture. Pour into small glasses. Yield: 4 servings.

VELVET HAMMER

1½ ounces brandy   3 ounces vanilla ice cream
1 ounce Creme de Cacao   ice
    white (or dark)

Put in a blender with cracked ice to thicken to a slush. Pour into wide champagne glass (conventional) and serve. Yield: 2 servings.

QUICK CHOCOLATE FIZZ

2 cups milk   4 scoops vanilla ice cream
½ cup chocolate syrup   2 cups chilled sparkling
⅛ teaspoon orange extract or   water
    2 tablespoons Cointreau

Combine milk, chocolate syrup and orange extract; divide evenly into 4 (12-ounces) glasses. Place a scoop of vanilla ice cream in each of the 4 glasses. Fill glass with sparkling water. Stir to blend. Serve immediately. Yield: 4 servings.

FRENCH CHOCOLATE

2½ squares unsweetened   ¾ cup sugar
    chocolate, finely cut   pinch of salt
½ cup cold water   ½ pint whipped cream

Cut chocolate in small bits, place in cold water and heat over low fire until melted; stir constantly. Add sugar and salt and stir until dissolved. Cool. Add whipped cream. To serve, place one tablespoon of this mixture in cup and fill with hot milk. Yield: 15 servings.

CAFÉ BRÛLOT

Peel of 1 orange, cut in 1 x
  ⅛ inch strips
Peel of 1 lemon, cut in 1 x ⅛
  inch strips
3 sugar lumps
6 whole cloves
1 (2 inch) cinnamon stick

1 cup Cognac
½ cup curacao, Grand
  Marnier or other orange
  liqueur
2 cups fresh strong black
  coffee (preferably from
  dark roast Creole-style
  ground coffee)

Assemble ingredients at dinner table. Light a burner with a stand under a brûlot bowl or chafing dish and adjust heat to low. Drop the orange and lemon peel, sugar, cloves and cinnamon stick into bowl. Pour in Cognac and curacao and stir to dissolve sugar. When mixture is warm, ignite it with a match. Stirring gently, pour in the coffee in a slow, thin stream and continue to stir until the flames die. Ladle café brûlot into brûlot or demitasse cups and serve at once. Yield: 6 servings.

BRANDY CAFÉ

1 jigger brandy
1 cup hot black coffee

Twist of lemon peel

Pour brandy into hot coffee. Add a twist of lemon peel. Yield: 1 serving.

COFFEE FRAPPÉ PUNCH

2 cups water
2 ounces instant coffee
2 cups sugar
1 tablespoon vanilla extract

1 gallon milk
½ gallon vanilla ice cream
½ gallon fudge ripple ice
  cream

Bring to boil 2 cups water. Remove from heat and add the instant coffee and sugar. Stir well and dissolve as much as possible. Allow to cool. When cool, add vanilla. Pour this mixture into 5 gallon container. Add milk. Set ice cream out to soften slightly and add both flavors. Keep stirring from the bottom. Yield: 32 cups (punch size).

CAFÉ AU LAIT COOLER

3 cups milk
2 tablespoons sugar
red food color

1 tablespoon sugar (optional)
2 cups milk
2 cups cold double-strength
    coffee

Prepare ice cubes by combining 1½ cups milk and 1 table-spoon sugar; pour into freezing tray. Combine remaining 1½ cups milk, 1 tablespoon sugar and a few drops red food color for pink cubes; pour into second freezing tray. Freeze both trays. Serve by alternating white and pink cubes in each of 4 large glasses or mugs. Add 1 tablespoon sugar to 2 cups milk. Pour milk and coffee simultaneously into a pitcher so the milk and coffee blend as they are poured; fill glasses. Yield: 4 servings.

SANGRÍA

2 fifths Burgundy wine
1 (6 ounce) can frozen
    orange juice concentrate,
    thawed

1 (6 ounce) can frozen
    lemonade concentrate,
    thawed
2 quarts club soda
2 tablespoons sugar

Mix wine with fruit juices. Add club soda and sugar. Pour over ice and serve in punch bowl or serve in individual wine glasses. Garnish with slices of lemon or orange. Yield: 32 servings.

PEACH FLOAT

1 (10 ounce) package frozen
    sliced peaches, thawed,
    undrained
1 cup peach ice cream,
    softened

2 cups milk
⅛ teaspoon almond extract
4 scoops peach ice cream

In a small mixing bowl, beat peaches until fairly smooth; add softened ice cream. Gradually stir in milk and almond extract. Pour into 4 (10 ounce) glasses. Top each with scoop of ice cream. NOTE: Vanilla may be substituted for peach ice cream. Yield: 4 servings.

MIMOSAS

1 bottle champagne, chilled   4 cups orange juice, chilled

In a pitcher, combine champagne and orange juice. Stir once. Serve in chilled champagne glasses. Yield: 8 servings.

CAMARGO

1 bottle claret   *1 (32 ounce) bottle soda*
1 bottle port   *water*
juice of 6 oranges   *block of ice*
1 cup sugar

Stir all ingredients except soda water until sugar is well dissolved. Pour over block of ice and serve in large punch bowl; add soda water. Yield: 20 to 25 cups.

ICE RING FOR PUNCH

Fill a mold with 1 to 2 inches of water and freeze. Then add another 1 to 2 inches and freeze. Continue this until the mold is almost to the top. Cover the entire top with fruits of your choice: grapes, lemon and lime slices, orange slices, strawberries. Kumquats are very nice used whole with grapes in small bunches. Add water to the top of the mold and return to freezer.

NOTE: The method of freezing a small amount of liquid at a time avoids the unevenness created when a large amount of liquid is frozen and expands on freezing to make a hump in the ice ring.

SUMMER FRUIT PUNCH

1 cup sugar
1 cup hot water
2 (48 ounce) cans pineapple
 juice
1 (12 ounce) can frozen
 orange juice
1 (12 ounce) can frozen
 lemonade
1 package whole strawberries
mint leaves
2 quarts ginger ale

Dissolve sugar in hot water. Mix all ingredients. Make sure to add the ginger ale last. Pour over a block of ice in a large punch bowl. Yield: 40 to 50 servings.

WHITE GRAPE JUICE PUNCH

2 (24 ounce) bottles white
 grape juice, chilled
2 (32 ounce) bottles ginger
 ale, chilled
white grape juice
fruit

Pour white grape juice and ginger ale into cold punch bowl. Make ice ring with grape juice and fruit. Serve in wine glasses. Can pour half grape juice and half ginger ale into chilled pitcher. Pour into chilled glasses when ready to serve. Yield: 28 cups (punch size).

ORANGE JULIUS

1 (6 ounce) can frozen
  orange juice
2 cups milk

¼ cup sugar
2 or 3 ice cubes

Combine all ingredients in blender at high speed for 30 seconds. Yield: 4 servings.

EGGNOG

1 quart whipping cream
12 eggs
1 cup sugar
pinch of salt

1 cup bourbon
1 cup rum
1 cup brandy (optional)
1 pint milk

Whip cream. Set aside. Beat eggs until lemon colored, about 20 minutes at high speed of mixer. Add sugar and salt. Slowly add bourbon, rum and brandy. Add milk. Fold in whipped cream and place in refrigerator for 2 days to mellow. Yield: 24 cups.

"For a gift, deliver in a pitcher with a bow on handle. Tie on recipe and instructions."

MILK PUNCH

⅘ quart bottle bourbon
3 quarts half and half
4 tablespoons vanilla extract

SIMPLE SYRUP
ground nutmeg

Combine bourbon, half and half and vanilla in a gallon container; add SIMPLE SYRUP to desired sweetness. Chill thoroughly. Sprinkle with nutmeg before serving. Serve in chilled julep cups. Yield: 1 gallon.

SIMPLE SYRUP:

1 cup sugar

1 cup water

Combine sugar and water in a small sauce pan; boil 5 minutes. Cool completely before using. Yield: 1¼ cups.

PARTY ICED TEA

4 sprigs fresh mint
8 to 12 whole cloves
3 quarts water
12 tea bags
juice of 8 lemons (about 1¼ cups)

juice of 6 oranges (about 2¼ cups)
1 (46 ounce) can pineapple juice
2 cups sugar

Add mint and cloves to water and bring to a boil. Simmer 10 to 15 minutes. Remove from heat; add tea bags and steep about 10 minutes. Strain. While still hot, add juices and sugar. Stir to dissolve sugar. Yield: 4½ quarts.

TO MAKE GOOD ICED TEA, pour 1 quart of boiling water over 2 ounces of tea. Steep 6 minutes; stir and remove bags. Pour tea mixture into 3 quarts of cold tap water. (Do not pour water into the hot concentrate). Do not refrigerate or ice the tea prior to service. If tea clouds, reduce brewing time, but not less than 4 minutes. If clouding continues, add a small amount of boiling water. Make fresh iced tea for each meal. Finished iced tea can be held for 4 hours at room temperature without loss of flavor.

TO BREW GOOD HOT TEA, water must be boiling. Merely hot water from the urn isn't hot enough for proper extraction from the tea leaves. Only a bitter taste is released. The water must be poured over the tea bag in a cup or pot. Never serve hot water in a cup with a dry tea bag on the side.

RUSSIAN TEA MIX

2 cups Tang
2 (6½ ounce) packages instant lemonade mix
¾ cup instant tea

1¼ cups sugar
1 teaspoon cinnamon
1 teaspoon cloves
1 teaspoon allspice

Mix all ingredients. Store in airtight containers. To serve, put one heaping tablespoon into each cup and add boiling water. Yield: 4 cups.

THINK AHEAD WHEN GIVING HOMEMADE LIQUEURS, as most cordials need three to eight weeks to age. Make liqueurs when the fruits needed are in season. May through August is the time to make Blackberry Brandy and Plum Cordial. Fall is best for Apple Cordial.

PEACH CORDIAL

*3 pounds fresh peaches,
   pitted and quartered
4 cups bourbon
2½ cups sugar*

*4 strips lemon peel, each 2
   inches long
4 inches stick cinnamon,
   broken
6 whole cloves*

In gallon screw-top jar, mix all ingredients. Cover tightly. Invert jar; let stand 24 hours. Turn jar upright; let stand 24 hours. Repeat turning until sugar dissolves. Store in cool dark place at least 2 months. Strain through cheesecloth into decanters. Cover. Yield: 6 cups.

BLACKBERRY CORDIAL

*4 cups fresh blackberries
2 cups brandy
¾ cup sugar*

*¾ teaspoon whole allspice
12 whole cloves*

Wash fruit; drain. In gallon screw-top jar, mix fruit and remaining ingredients. Cover tightly. Invert jar; let stand 24 hours. Turn jar upright; let stand 24 hours. Repeat turning process until sugar is dissolved. Store in cool, dark place at least 2 months. Strain through cheesecloth into a decanter. Cover. Yield: 3½ cups.

PLUM CORDIAL

3 pounds (7 cups) fresh
    purple plums, halved and
    pitted

4 cups sugar
4 cups gin

In gallon screw-top jar, mix all ingredients. Cover tightly. Invert jar; let stand 24 hours. Turn jar upright; let stand 24 hours. Repeat turning process until sugar dissolves. Store in cool, dark place 2 months. Strain through cheesecloth into decanters. Cover. Yield: 8 cups.

APPLE CORDIAL

4 cups coarsely chopped
    apple
2 cups brandy

1 cup sugar
4 inches stick cinnamon,
    broken

In large screw-top jar, combine all ingredients. Cover tightly. Invert jar; let stand 24 hours. Turn jar upright; let stand 24 hours. Repeat turning process until sugar dissolves. Store in cool, dark place 4 to 6 weeks. Strain through cheesecloth into decanter. Cover. Yield: 2½ cups.

ORANGE LIQUEUR

4 medium oranges
water

2 cups sugar
2 cups vodka or rum

Squeeze juice from oranges; reserve peel from one orange. Scrape white membrane from reserved peel; cut into strips. Add water to juice to make 2 cups. Bring orange juice mixture, peel and sugar to boiling. Reduce heat; simmer over low heat 5 minutes. Cool. Pour into large screw top jar. Stir in vodka. Cover. Let stand at room temperature for 3 to 4 weeks. Strain into decanters. Cover. Yield: 5 cups.

APRICOT LIQUEUR

1 pound dried apricots
1 quart vodka

1 cup sugar

Combine all ingredients in large glass or stainless steel container. Cover and let stand 4 to 7 weeks. Stir once every 2 weeks. Yield: 1½ quarts.

"Nice gift to fill a pretty bottle or decanter."

Soups

"Soup, soup, beautiful soup" can be the beginning of a meal or a meal in itself with bread and salad. It can help the busy cook or it can rescue about-to-be discarded leftovers. There is no hurrying the thick hearty kind, it must simmer for a long time to develop full flavor. But there are commercial aids now which would amaze our grandmothers. For instance an old cookbook tells how to make "gumbo fillet powder" which we now purchase already bottled as gumbo filé. This is how it was made in an earlier day: Take very young, tender leaves of sassafras, spread on white paper and dry in a cool, airy place. When dry, pound in a mortar, press through a sieve and keep in a well corked bottle. In a gumbo, one heaping teaspoonful could be used in place of okra.

Soups

BASIC BROWN STOCK

2½ quarts cold water
6 pounds beef soup bones
1 stalk celery with leaves
1 onion, quartered

4 sprigs parsley
1 bay leaf
8 peppercorns
2 teaspoons salt

Place water and meat bones in a large kettle. Simmer uncovered 3 hours. Remove bones; cut off meat and chop. Return meat to stock, add remaining ingredients and simmer uncovered 2 hours longer. Strain. Chill and lift off fat. Yield: 2 quarts.

CHICKEN STOCK

1 chicken
1 onion, quartered
1 stalk celery, quartered
4 sprigs parsley
2 cloves garlic
1 carrot, quartered

1 bay leaf
¼ teaspoon thyme
salt
2 whole cloves
5 whole peppercorns

Wash chicken. Place it in a large kettle and add remaining ingredients. Cover with water and bring to a boil. Reduce heat and simmer gently for 2 hours. Remove chicken from stock and cut the meat from the bone. Return the bones, only, and simmer another 30 minutes. Chill and lift off fat.

SOUP GARNISHES:

Egg yolks sieved on hot cream soups.
Watercress on cream of asparagus and mushroom soup.
Popcorn on green pea and tomato soup.
Chopped apple for curried soups.

Sour cream alone or with horseradish, watercress or chives.
¼ cup whipped cream with ½ teaspoon horseradish on split pea soup.

Crisp bacon on black bean and cheddar chowder.
Lemon slices on fish soups, clear soups, black bean soup.

CLEAR MUSHROOM SOUP

4 tablespoons butter or
    margarine
4 cups sliced mushrooms
1 cup sliced onion
2 tablespoons chopped fresh
    parsley

2 tablespoons flour
1/4 teaspoon pepper
5 cups chicken broth, fresh
    or canned

Melt butter in large saucepan. Sauté mushrooms, onion and parsley until tender. Stir in flour and pepper. Remove from heat. Gradually stir in chicken broth. Bring to a boil, stirring constantly. Reduce heat; simmer 5 minutes. Yield: 6 to 8 servings.

GREEK LEMON-EGG SOUP

8 cups homemade chicken
    broth
2/3 cup white rice
4 eggs, separated

4 to 5 tablespoons lemon
    juice
salt and pepper to taste

Cook rice in broth for 30 minutes. Beat the whites until frothy. Beat egg yolks. Add the lemon juice to the yolks. Blend yolks into egg whites. Add 2 cups of broth to egg mixture. Beating all the while, add mixture to soup; continue beating. Simmer 15 more minutes. DO NOT BOIL. Garnish each bowl with a lemon slice. Yield: 8 servings.

POTATO SOUP WITH SOUR CREAM

2 cups potatoes, diced
1 cup boiling water
1 teaspoon salt
1 small onion, sliced

1/2 teaspoon pepper
2 cups sour cream
minced parsley

Combine potatoes, water, salt, onion and pepper and cook together for 15 minutes. Add sour cream and cook until potatoes are tender. Serve hot. Garnish with parsley. Yield: 6 servings.

47

SOUR CREAM GARNISH FOR SOUP

sour cream
horseradish

watercress
chives

Mix sour cream with horseradish, watercress or chives; or just use sour cream. Put teaspoon or tablespoon of mixture on soup just before serving.

QUICK SENEGALESE
(COLD CURRIED CHICKEN SOUP)

1 can cream of chicken soup
1 teaspoon curry powder
½ cup milk

½ cup light cream
1 cup crushed ice
chopped chives for garnish

Place soup, curry powder and milk into blender. Cover and blend for about 15 seconds. Add cream and crushed ice. Cover and blend about 10 more seconds or until mixture is well blended. Chill for at least 1 hour and garnish with chopped chives. Yield: 4 servings.

CORN CHOWDER

½ cup butter
1 onion, chopped
1 green pepper, chopped
2 tablespoons flour
1 can beef broth
1 (16 ounce) can cream-style
   corn
1 (28 ounce) can tomatoes

1½ teaspoons salt
1 tablespoon soy sauce
2 beef bouillon cubes
1 (16 ounce) can whole
   kernel corn
1 cup milk
1 green onion, chopped

Sauté onion and peppers in butter until transparent. Add flour and cook for 1 minute. Add next 7 ingredients. Bring to a boil and purée. Add corn, milk and green onion. Heat and serve with croutons. Yield: 16 to 20 servings.

48

HOT TOMATO SIP

2 cans beef bouillon
2½ cups tomato juice
2 lemon slices
6 cloves
⅛ teaspoon basil
½ teaspoon salt

½ teaspoon sugar
¼ teaspoon monosodium
  glutamate
1 tablespoon sherry
grated cheese

Simmer bouillon, tomato juice, lemon, cloves and basil for 30 minutes; strain. Add seasonings. Simmer until ready to serve. Serve with grated cheese sprinkled on top of soup. Yield: 6 servings.

VEGETABLE SOUP

1 beef soup bone
½ pound stew beef
1 quart water
2 bay leaves
1 tablespoon sugar
2 large onions, sliced
4 carrots, thinly sliced
6 stalks celery, sliced

3 cups okra, cut
3 cups fresh corn
3 (12 ounce) cans tomato
  juice
2 (16 ounce) cans tomatoes
  OR 3 pounds fresh
  tomatoes
salt to taste

Put soup bone, stew beef, water, bay leaves and sugar in soup kettle. Bring to a boil and allow to simmer for 3 hours. Remove bone and cut off meat. Return meat to kettle. Skim off fat. Add all other vegetables. Salt to taste. Simmer until vegetables are done. Yield: 12 servings.

VEGETABLE BEEF SOUP

1 pound ground beef
1 onion, chopped
1 cup chopped celery
3 small potatoes, cubed
2 zucchini, sliced

1 (8 ounce) can corn
1 (14½ ounce) can stewed
  tomatoes
3 (12 ounce) cans tomato juice
salt and pepper to taste

Cook beef and onion; drain fat. Add all other ingredients and simmer about 2 hours. Add enough water for desired thickness. Best if made a day ahead. Yield: 8 to 10 servings.

"A hearty one dish meal for a cold winter evening."

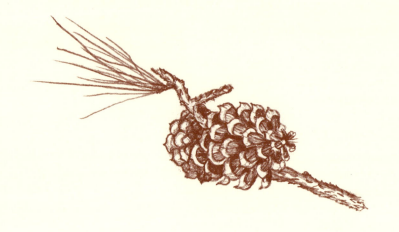

CHINESE CHICKEN SOUP

3 or 4 pieces of chicken
1 (1 inch) piece fresh ginger
   root
1 tablespoon soy sauce
1 teaspoon salt
½ teaspoon pepper
2 to 3 garlic buds

6 to 8 green onions
1½ tablespoons oil
very fine noodles or Misua
   (in Chinese grocery store)
4 tablespoons chopped celery
   leaves, for garnish

Put chicken in about 1½ quarts of water and boil for 15 minutes. Add chopped ginger, soy sauce, salt and pepper and cook for ½ hour. Remove chicken pieces and discard bones and skin. Skim off fat. Put chicken back into pot. In another pan, lightly fry garlic and onions using oil, above. Then add this to soup. Add about 2 handfuls of very fine noodles. Serve in bowls garnished with celery leaves. Yield: 4 servings.

Make your own croutons and season with:
1. *Basil or oregano to serve on tomato or minestrone soup.*
2. *Parmesan cheese for vegetable or green pea soup.*
3. *Garlic for vegetable or beef noodle soup.*

CREAM OF ARTICHOKE SOUP

½ cup chopped shallots or
    green onion
1 stalk celery, chopped
1 medium sized carrot,
    chopped
1 bay leaf
⅛ teaspoon thyme

4 tablespoons butter
1 quart chicken consommé
1 cup cooked and sliced
    artichoke hearts
2 egg yolks, beaten
1 cup heavy cream
salt and pepper to taste

Sauté shallots, celery, carrot, bay leaf and thyme in butter. Add consommé and simmer 10 to 15 minutes. Add artichoke hearts and simmer 5 to 10 minutes. Remove from heat and add beaten egg yolks mixed with cream. Salt and pepper to taste. Yield: 1½ to 1¾ quarts.

CREAM OF ASPARAGUS SOUP

1 pound fresh asparagus
    spears
¼ large onion, thinly sliced
4 tablespoons chicken stock
6 tablespoons butter
3 tablespoons flour

2 cups chicken stock
salt and pepper
2 cups heavy cream
1 tablespoon chopped parsley
grated rind of ½ lemon

Break off tough ends of asparagus. Wash and slice into one-inch segments. Combine with onion and four tablespoons of chicken stock and butter. Cook until tender. Remove asparagus, stir in flour until blended. Add chicken stock, stir and bring to boil. Season with salt and pepper. Add asparagus and purée in blender until smooth. Add heavy cream to blender, mix and then strain if desired. To keep warm, place in double boiler. Garnish with parsley and lemon. Yield: 6 servings.

OYSTER STEW

1 pint half and half
¼ cup butter
1 pint oysters

salt
fresh ground pepper

Heat half and half to scalding in saucepan. Melt butter in another pan (10 or 12 inch skillet). Add oysters and liquor to butter and simmer until edges curl. Add butter and oysters to half and half. Salt and pepper to taste. Serve immediately. May use milk and part heavy cream, if desired. Yield: 2 generous servings.

CREAM OF TOMATO SOUP

2 pounds tomatoes, peeled
  and chopped
½ cup sliced onion
1¼ teaspoons salt
1 teaspoon sugar

½ teaspoon white pepper
1 tablespoon butter, melted
1 tablespoon flour
1 cup cream

Cook tomatoes with onion, salt, sugar and pepper over low heat for 30 minutes, stirring frequently. Melt butter, whisk in flour as you cook 1 minute over medium heat; add butter-flour mixture to tomato mixture, stirring well until smooth. Add cream. Before serving, heat almost to boiling. Yield: 6 servings.

CREAM OF MUSHROOM SOUP

½ pound mushrooms,
  chopped
1 onion, chopped
1 cup chopped parsley
¼ cup butter

1 tablespoon flour
2 cups chicken broth
salt and pepper to taste
1 cup sour cream

Sauté mushrooms, onions and parsley in butter. Stir in the flour and add the chicken broth, salt and pepper. Simmer for 10 minutes. Put in food processor and blend until smooth. Add sour cream a little at a time, stirring constantly. Reheat and serve. Yield: 6 servings.

CAULIFLOWER SOUP

4 cups cooked cauliflower
10 tablespoons unsalted
  butter
2 cups new potatoes, peeled
  and quartered

1 quart milk
1¼ cups chicken stock
1 tablespoon salt
milk or water to thin
buttered croutons

Clean and parboil cauliflower; rinse and drain. Place in saucepan with 7 tablespoons melted butter. Simmer for 20 minutes. Add potatoes, milk, stock and salt. Cook slowly for 20 minutes. Remove from heat. Put in blender and purée. Add hot milk or water to thin to desired consistency. Add remaining butter to soup just before serving. Add croutons and serve. Yield: 6 to 8 servings.

SEAFOOD CHOWDER

6 slices bacon, chopped
1 cup chopped onion
1 cup chopped celery
½ lemon, thinly sliced
1 quart water
2 (16 ounce) cans tomatoes
1 clove garlic
¼ cup catsup
½ teaspoon curry powder
2 teaspoons salt

½ teaspoon Tabasco sauce
1 tablespoon Worcestershire
   sauce
1 pound scallops, cleaned,
   drained
1 pound shrimp, cleaned
1 pound filet of fish, cut in
   pieces
⅔ cup sherry
4 tablespoons butter

Cook bacon until brown. Add onions and celery. Cook covered for 5 minutes. Add next 9 ingredients. Reduce heat; cook slowly for 30 minutes. Add scallops and shrimp. Cook slowly 20 minutes. Add fish, sherry and butter. Cook 10 minutes longer. Yield: 8 to 10 servings.

Best made the day before and reheated.

CRAB-SHRIMP SOUP

1 pound crabmeat
1½ pounds shrimp, peeled
   and deveined
1 (6 ounce) can mushrooms
2 cans celery soup
3 cups milk

½ cup butter
½ pint heavy cream
2 lemons, sliced
salt and pepper to taste
minced parsley for garnish

Mix all ingredients except parsley; simmer. DO NOT BOIL. Garnish with parsley. Yield: 6 servings.

CRAB SOUP

½ cup butter (do not
   substitute)
2½ tablespoons flour
1 quart milk
1 tablespoon McCormicks
   Good Seasoning Chicken
   Stock Base

1 slice pimiento, finely
   chopped
1 dash parsley flakes
1 pound crab meat

Blend butter and flour; slowly add milk, stirring to combine. Cook until smooth. Add chicken stock base, pimiento and parsley flakes. Before serving, add crab meat. Yield: 6 servings.

OYSTER AND ARTICHOKE SOUP

3 tablespoons butter
1 bunch green onions,
   chopped
2 stalks celery, chopped
2 small cloves garlic, pressed
1 (14 ounce) can artichoke
   hearts, washed, drained
   and quartered
1½ tablespoons flour

1 to 1½ pints chicken stock
½ teaspoon cayenne pepper
½ teaspoon salt
1½ teaspoons Worcestershire
   sauce
1 pint oysters, drained and
   chopped (liquor reserved)
½ cup evaporated milk
½ cup milk

Melt butter in a heavy four-quart pot. Sauté onions, celery and garlic until soft. Add artichokes. Sprinkle with flour and stir to coat well, but do not brown. Add stock and seasonings. Cover and simmer 1 hour. Add oysters and liquor. Simmer for 10 minutes, but do not boil. Stir in milk and refrigerate at least 8 hours or up to 3 days. Reheat gently and serve. Yield: 4 to 6 servings.

CHILLED TOMATO SOUP WITH DILL

2 tablespoons butter
1 cup minced onions
2 garlic cloves, minced
2 pounds ripe tomatoes,
   peeled, seeded and
   chopped
1 cup chicken broth
2 cups chicken broth

2 tablespoons tomato paste
2 tablespoons cornstarch,
   dissolved in ¼ cup cold
   chicken broth
½ cup heavy cream
¼ cup snipped dill weed
1/16 teaspoon salt
1/16 teaspoon white pepper

In a 1½ quart boiler, sauté onions and garlic cloves in butter until onion is soft. Add tomatoes and 1 cup chicken broth. Simmer 20 minutes until tomatoes are very soft. Add 1¾ cups chicken broth, tomato paste and cornstarch mixture. Bring to a boil over high heat. Reduce heat and simmer for 10 minutes, stirring occasionally until mixture thickens. Let the mixture cool; force it through a sieve into a soup tureen. Chill mixture, covered, overnight. Just before serving, stir in heavy cream, dill weed, salt and white pepper. Yield: 5 to 6 servings.

CUCUMBER SOUP

1 medium cucumber, peeled
   and sliced
1 (10¾ ounce) can condensed
   cream of chicken soup
1 cup sour cream

¾ cup milk
salt and pepper to taste
dash of curry powder
dash of dill weed

Place cucumber, soup, sour cream, milk and seasonings in blender. Blend until smooth. Chill. To serve, stir and pour into cups. Garnish with dill weed. Yield: 6 servings.

CHILLED CREAM OF BROCCOLI SOUP

1 small onion, sliced
1 garlic clove, sliced
2 tablespoons butter
1 tablespoon flour
3 cups chicken broth
¼ cup dry white wine

1 bunch fresh broccoli, cut in
   pieces
1 dash mace
1 cup half and half
salt and pepper

Sauté the onion and garlic in butter over low heat. Blend in flour, add chicken broth and wine and bring to boil. Add broccoli. Simmer, covered, until broccoli is tender. Add mace and cool. Whirl in blender and chill several hours. Before serving, mix in half and half, salt and pepper to taste. Yield: 4 servings.

TOMATO COB SOUP

8 large tomatoes, peeled and
   finely chopped
1 cup diced celery
1 red onion, diced

salt and pepper
1 teaspoon curry powder
2 cups Hellman's
   mayonnaise

Put tomatoes through blender or food processor. Combine with celery and onion. Salt and pepper to taste. Mix well and chill overnight. Before serving, combine curry and mayonnaise. Put a generous tablespoon or more on each serving. Have soup cups or mugs chilled and serve icy cold. Yield: 8 cups.

CLASSIC VICHYSSOISE

4 leeks, sliced (white part)
1 onion, sliced
¼ cup butter
5 potatoes, thinly sliced
1 quart water or chicken broth

1 tablespoon salt
3 cups milk
2 cups heavy cream
chives, finely chopped

Brown leeks and onion in butter; add potatoes, water or chicken broth, and salt. Boil 35 to 40 minutes. Add milk and cream. Blend, season and sprinkle with chopped chives. Serve well chilled. Yield: 12 servings.

BLENDER VICHYSSOISE

½ small onion, chopped
½ teaspoon salt
¼ teaspoon white pepper
2 cups rich chicken broth (or canned)

1½ cups diced potatoes, cooked
½ cup half and half
1 cup crushed ice
chopped chives

Into container of blender put onion, salt, pepper, chicken broth and potatoes. Cover and blend about 8 seconds. Add half and half, crushed ice, and blend for another 10 seconds. Thin to desired consistency with milk. Serve quite cold, garnished with chopped chives. Yield: 6 servings.

WHITE GAZPACHO

4 cups chicken broth
2 cups Chablis or dry white wine
½ cup lemon juice
3 cucumbers, thinly sliced
3 tomatoes, peeled, seeded and chopped

¾ cup thinly sliced scallions
½ cup fresh minced parsley
¼ teaspoon Tabasco, or to taste
salt and pepper to taste

Bring first three ingredients to a boil, cool. Chill, covered, for 4 hours or overnight. Add the remaining ingredients. Ladle the soup into chilled bowls. Yield: 6 servings.

GAZPACHO

1 medium onion, chopped
1½ cucumbers, chopped
1 medium bell pepper,
   chopped
1 jar chopped pimentos
5 unpeeled tomatoes, chopped
1 quart tomato juice
1 can beef consommé

¼ cup olive oil or vegetable
   oil
1 tablespoon Worcestershire
   sauce
2 tablespoons wine vinegar
3 tablespoons lemon juice
dash of Tabasco
salt and pepper to taste
¼ teaspoon garlic powder

Combine chopped vegetables in a large bowl. Add remaining ingredients. Stir well. Let stand at room temperature to blend flavors (about 2 hours). Chill 6 to 24 hours. Garnish with lemon slices or a dollop of sour cream at serving time. Yield: 8 servings.

SOUP TOASTS

loaf of stale white bread
softened or melted butter

salt
cayenne pepper

Cut nine ⅓ inch thick slices from a loaf of stale white bread and remove the crusts. With a 1½ inch cutter, cut out rounds from 4 of the slices. With a smaller cutter, cut out the center of each round, leaving a ⅓ inch ring. Cut the remaining slices into ⅓ inch strips. Spread the rings and strips with softened butter or dip them in melted butter and sprinkle them with salt and cayenne pepper. Arrange the rings and strips on a buttered baking sheet and toast them in a preheated very slow oven (200° F) for 20 minutes or until they are lightly browned. Slip 2 of the toast strips into each ring. Yield: 16 toasts.

Serve cool soups well chilled in bed of crushed ice.

Top jellied Madrilene with dollop of sour cream.

Serve beef broth "on the rocks" with dash of Tabasco sauce.

Salads

Salads are a healthful part of today's diet and also had a prominent place in old cookbooks. Chicken salad was probably the most popular of the meat category for it played an important role in home entertaining. Potato salad was one of the mainstays of the picnic menu along with fried chicken and ham. Beautiful red ripe tomatoes, so abundant in this area, were served sliced, unaccompanied, or mixed with other raw vegetables such as the famous Vidalia onions.

Once the variety of commercial salad dressings now offered was not available on the grocery shelves and neither were the premeasured mixing bottles and packaged seasonings. Then as now a good rule of the thumb is the old-time advice "have a spendthrift for oil, a miser for vinegar, a wise man for salt and a madcap to stir the ingredients up and mix them together." Cooks of yesteryear advised using mayonnaise dressing for fish, meats and some vegetables, such as cauliflower, tomatoes and celery, but the simple French dressing for lettuce. In preparing these dressings, it was advised, to use a silver spoon or wooden fork and a large soup plate, very cold. Never beat, but stir one way continually. Now, the blender is pressed into service for a quick tasty mayonnaise.

Salads

SIMPLY SPLENDID FRUIT SALADS

Fresh peach halves filled with cottage cheese on lettuce, garnish with watercress.

Romaine, alternating sliced red delicious apples and avocado, topped with chopped pecans with mayonnaise dressing.

Lettuce, sliced oranges, red delicious apples and pears with mayonnaise dressing.

Grapefruit, orange and avocado slices, garnished with green pepper with French dressing.

Alternating slices of fresh pineapple, grapefruit on Bibb lettuce leaves, garnish with pecans with French dressing.

Lettuce, sliced avocado, seedless green grapes.

Fresh pineapple sprinkled with sugar, sprigs of fresh peppermint tucked through the bowl.

Wedges of melon (cantaloupe or honeydew) wrapped with thinly sliced ham.

PINEAPPLE-OLIVE SALAD

2 cups pineapple juice and water
2 (3 ounce) packages lemon Jello
1 (2 ounce) jar Spanish Olives, sliced
1 (17 ounce) can pineapple chunks
½ bell pepper, chopped
2 teaspoons Worcestershire sauce
3 tablespoons lemon juice
1 tablespoon grated onion

Add enough water to pineapple juice to make 2 cups of liquid. Add Jello and bring to a boil. Chill. When partially set, stir in remaining ingredients. Chill until congealed. Yield: 4 to 6 servings.

AMBROSIA CREAM CHEESE MOLD

1 envelope unflavored gelatin
½ cup cold water
1 (15½ ounce) can
   unsweetened pineapple
   chunks, undrained
⅓ cup sugar
juice of 1 lemon
2 (3 ounce) packages cream
   cheese, softened

1 orange, peeled, sectioned
   and diced (chill several
   hours until firm)
½ cup chopped pecans
½ cup flaked coconut
lettuce (optional)
lemon slices (optional)

Soften gelatin in water. Drain pineapple and reserve juice; add enough water to juice to make 1 cup. Place juice in a 2 quart saucepan. Heat to boiling. Add gelatin mixture and stir until dissolved. Remove from heat; stir in sugar, lemon juice and cream cheese, using a wire whisk to blend. Chill until gelatin partially sets; fold in pineapple chunks, orange, pecans and coconut. Spoon mixture into a lightly greased 1 quart mold. Chill until firm. Unmold on lettuce leaves and garnish with lemon slices. This recipe must be done ahead. Yield: 6 servings.

APRICOT CONGEALED SALAD

1 (16 ounce) can apricots,
   halved, drained (reserve
   juice)
1 small can seedless white
   grapes, drained (reserve
   juice)
1 (6 ounce) package apricot
   Jello

1 package unflavored gelatin
2 tablespoons lemon juice
½ teaspoon salt
1 cup mayonnaise or plain
   yogurt
1 (3½ ounces) package
   slivered almonds

Add enough water to the fruit juices to make 4 cups; heat to boiling. Stir the hot juice into the Jello and gelatin (which have been mixed together.) Add lemon juice and salt. Whip in the mayonnaise with a hand mixer; stir in fruit and nuts; let congeal. Yield: 8 servings.

TO UNMOLD GELATIN, first rinse platter with cold water. To loosen mold, run top of knife between gelatin and pan. Dip mold, just to rim, in warm water for a few seconds. Place wet platter on top of mold; hold tightly and invert quickly. Lift off pan.

SPICED PEACH SALAD

1 cup juice from peaches
1 (3 ounce) package lemon
    Jello
1 envelope unflavored
    gelatin, dissolved in 2
    tablespoons water
½ cup orange juice

1 (29 ounce) jar spiced
    peaches
1 (8¼ ounce) can crushed
    pineapple, drained
¼ (10 ounce) jar orange
    marmalade

Heat peach juice and dissolve Jello and gelatin in hot juice. Add orange juice. Cool slightly. Slice peaches; add to gelatin with pineapple and marmalade. Pour into mold and set. Yield: 8 servings.

STUFFED SPICED PEACH RING

3 tablespoons mayonnaise
juice from peaches
2 (3 ounce) packages orange
    Jello
1 (8 ounce) package cream
    cheese

¼ cup chopped pecans
2 tablespoons mayonnaise
2 (29 ounce) jars spiced
    peaches with juice OR 12
    home-canned peaches
    with juice

Grease ring mold or bundt pan with 1 tablespoon mayonnaise. Bring peach juice to boil and add Jello until dissolved. Cool. Mix cream cheese, nuts and mayonnaise. Remove seeds from peaches (carefully) and stuff with about 1 tablespoon of cheese mixture. Press peach halves back together. Place stuffed peaches in mold and pour Jello mix over them. Chill until congealed. Yield: 12 servings.

GRAPEFRUIT MOLD

3 large grapefruit
1½ tablespoons gelatin
1 cup grapefruit juice, cold
1 cup grapefruit juice,
    boiling

3 tablespoons lemon juice
¾ cup sugar
¾ cup chopped celery
½ cup slivered almonds

Peel grapefruit and remove membranes. Let gelatin soften in cold grapefruit juice; add boiling grapefruit juice, lemon juice and sugar. Allow gelatin to partially set before adding grapefruit, celery and almonds. Put in a 1-quart ring mold, and chill overnight. Serve on bed of lettuce. Yield: 8 servings.

"Especially good with ham or turkey."

BLUEBERRY SALAD

2 (3 ounce) packages
    blackberry Jello
2 cups boiling water
1 (15 ounce) can blueberries
1 (8 ounce) can crushed
    pineapple

1 (8 ounce) package cream
    cheese
½ cup sugar
½ pint sour cream
½ teaspoon vanilla extract
½ cup chopped pecans

Dissolve gelatin in boiling water. Drain blueberries and pine-apple and measure liquid. Add enough water to make 1 cup and add to gelatin mixture. Stir in drained blueberries and pineapple. Pour into a 2-quart rectangular dish; cover and refrigerate until firm. Combine cream cheese, sugar, sour cream and vanilla and spread over congealed salad. Sprinkle with chopped pecans. Yield: 10 to 12 servings.

FRESH CRANBERRY SALAD MOLD

1 quart cranberries
1½ cups sugar
2 envelopes unflavored
    gelatin

½ cup orange juice
1 (6½ ounce) can crushed
    pineapple
1 cup pecans, chopped

Grind cranberries; add sugar and let set a few minutes. Dissolve gelatin in orange juice and bring to a boil. Add to ground cranberry mixture. Stir in pineapple and pecans. Pour into greased 2-quart mold. Chill until congealed. Serve on bed of lettuce. Yield: 10 to 12 servings.

FROZEN CHERRY SALAD

1 (16 ounce) can pitted, dark
    sweet cherries
1 (8¾ ounce) can crushed
    pineapple
1 (8 ounce) package cream
    cheese

1 cup sour cream
½ cup sugar
¼ teaspoon salt
2 cups miniature
    marshmallows
½ cup chopped nuts

Strain all fruits. Soften cream cheese and whip until fluffy. Blend in sour cream, sugar and salt. Fold in fruit, marsh-mallows and nuts. Freeze in loaf pan or paper-lined muffin tins for at least 6 hours. Set out 10 minutes before serving. Yield: 6 to 8 servings.

SOUTHERN POTATO SALAD

4-6 baking potatoes
3 eggs, boiled
3 tablespoons mayonnaise
2 tablespoons Durkee sauce
½ cup sour cream

2 teaspoons oil and vinegar
*   dressing*
½ teaspoon Dijon mustard
½ cup minced onion
salt and pepper to taste
fresh parsley

Cook unpeeled potatoes in salted water until tender. While potatoes are cooking, mash hard boiled eggs in a bowl. Combine mayonnaise, Durkee sauce, sour cream, dressing, mustard and onion. Add salt and pepper. When potatoes are done, peel and cube. While warm, mix with eggs and dressing. Adjust salt and pepper. When serving, decorate with parsley. Yield: 12 servings.

SOUR CREAM POTATO SALAD

1½ cups mayonnaise
1 (8 ounce) carton sour
*   cream*
1½ teaspoons prepared
*   horseradish*
1 teaspoon celery seed

8 medium potatoes, cooked,
*   peeled and sliced*
1 cup fresh minced parsley,
*   divided*
¾ cup chopped green onion,
*   divided*

Combine first 4 ingredients and set aside. Place ½ of sliced potatoes in medium bowl; sprinkle with ⅓ cup parsley and ¼ cup onion. Top with ½ of mayonnaise mixture. Repeat layers. Use remaining parsley and onion to garnish top. Cover and chill. Yield: 8-10 servings.

SALAD NIÇOISE

SALAD DRESSING:

1 cup wine vinegar
1 cup oil
½ teaspoon garlic powder

⅓ cup sugar
dash Worcestershire sauce
dash soy sauce

Combine all ingredients and mix well.

POTATO SALAD:

2 Idaho potatoes, cooked and
    thinly sliced

SALAD DRESSING

Prepare potatoes and marinate for several hours in ½ cup SALAD DRESSING.

SALAD:

3 cups lettuce (salad bowl,
    leaf or red leaf)
2 (7 ounce) cans solid-pack
    white tuna, drained
1 cup cooked, chilled green
    beans
potato salad
½ cup thinly sliced celery
1 green pepper, cut in thin
    rings
1 small red onion, thinly
    sliced

1 cup cherry tomatoes
4 canned artichoke hearts,
    halved
1 small cucumber, thinly
    sliced
2 hard-boiled eggs, quartered
1 (2 ounce) can anchovy
    fillet, drained and cut in
    half
4 green onions, thinly sliced
½ cup ripe olives
salad dressing

To serve: Line the container you have chosen with leaves of salad bowl, leaf or red leaf lettuce. Place a mound of tuna in the center if the container is round or at one end if it is oval or rectangular. Arrange around it or radiating out from it separate mounds of green beans, potato salad, celery, green pepper, onion, cherry tomatoes, artichokes and cucumbers. Arrange quarters of egg topped with anchovy fillet, among the mounds. Sprinkle them with green onions, including some of the tops. Scatter olives over the composition. In a separate bowl or cruet serve the remaining SALAD DRESSING.

Yield: 4 servings.

"Making this salad will satisfy the artist that lurks in the soul of every cook."

POTATO SALAD

1½ teaspoons mustard seed
1 teaspoon celery seed
3 tablespoons white vinegar
½ cup chopped green onions
  with tops

5 cups diced, cooked potatoes
¾ cup mayonnaise
2 boiled eggs, diced
salt and pepper

Soak seeds in vinegar overnight. Combine onions, potatoes, mayonnaise and eggs with vinegar and seeds. Mix well. Salt and pepper to taste. Chill thoroughly. Yield: 8 servings.

GERMAN POTATO SALAD

4 potatoes
4 slices bacon
2 tablespoons bacon fat
2 tablespoons flour

½ cup vinegar
½ cup water
1 cup sugar
2 onions, chopped

Peel, slice and parboil potatoes approximately 10 minutes. Fry bacon; drain and crumble. Mix flour and bacon fat. Add vinegar, water, sugar and onions. Add potatoes and bacon; stir; simmer for 10 minutes. Yield: 8 servings.

"A different dish for outdoor barbecues. Good with hot dogs."

SHRIMP AND RICE SALAD

¾ pound fresh mushrooms,
  coarsely chopped
2 tablespoons salad oil
2 tablespoons lemon juice
1 teaspoon salt
3¼ cups cooked rice (half
  white, half wild)

1 green pepper, coarsely
  chopped
1½ pounds shrimp, cleaned
  and cooked
2 hard-cooked eggs

Sauté mushrooms in oil. Add lemon juice and salt and cook until tender (about 10 minutes). Mix rice, green pepper, mushrooms and shrimp together. Refrigerate overnight. Toss with GARLIC MAYONNAISE before serving. Garnish with sliced eggs.

GARLIC MAYONNAISE:

1 clove garlic
¼ teaspoon paprika
½ teaspoon dry mustard

⅛ teaspoon pepper
1 teaspoon warm water
¾ cup mayonnaise

Blend well all ingredients. Yield: 10 servings.

NAIROBI AVOCADO NEPTUNE

WHITE SAUCE:

2 tablespoons butter	½ teaspoon salt
2 tablespoons flour	¼ teaspoon white pepper
1 cup half and half	1½ teaspoons curry powder

Heat butter in skillet until bubbly; add flour and cook at least 1 minute. Gradually add half and half; stir until thickened and add seasonings.

SALAD:

1 large avocado	1 cup WHITE SAUCE
8 ounces fresh or canned crabmeat	¼ cup medium Cheddar cheese, grated

Halve avocado; take out inside and leave shells intact. Chop up avocado; set aside. Mix crab meat with WHITE SAUCE; heat until bubbly. Put chopped avodaco into shells; pour crab mixture over. Sprinkle with cheese; run under the broiler to melt the cheese. Yield: 2 servings.

"Recipe from Chef of the Old Norfolk Hotel in Nairobi, Kenya, Africa. It was served with white wine, small bran muffins, and tomato aspic for luncheon."

CLAMATO-SHRIMP MOLD

3 packages unflavored gelatin	¼ cup vinegar
½ cup cold water	½ cup mayonnaise
3 cups Clamato juice	1½ cups chopped shrimp
1 teaspoon salt	½ cup chopped celery
1 teaspoon onion juice	¼ cup chopped green pepper

Dissolve gelatin in water and 1 cup Clamato juice and bring to a boil. Add remaining Clamato juice, salt, onion juice and vinegar. Chill ¼ of the liquid in the mold. Chill rest of the liquid in a bowl. When contents of bowl are chilled and beginning to congeal, beat in mayonnaise. Fold in shrimp, celery and green pepper. Pour this into the mold on top of the completely set ¼ liquid which was placed in the mold earlier. Yield: 6 to 8 servings.

Center a ring mold with an open head of Bibb lettuce.

SHRIMP MOUSSE

6 cups cooked shrimp, peeled and deveined
1 pound cream cheese, softened
1 cup mayonnaise
2 cups sour cream
½ cup finely minced bell pepper
½ cup finely minced green onion
¼ cup finely minced pimento
½ cup chili sauce
2 tablespoons unflavored gelatin
6 tablespoons lemon juice
¼ cup cold water
⅛ teaspoons Tabasco sauce
1 teaspoon salt
1 tablespoon Worcestershire

Finely chop shrimp. Cream cheese, mayonnaise and sour cream. Add bell pepper, onion, pimento, and chili sauce. Dissolve gelatin in the lemon juice and water mixture. Heat in a double boiler for five or ten minutes. Gradually stir this into the cheese and seasoning mixture. Add shrimp and blend well. Pour into a chilled ring mold and refrigerate overnight. Unmold and garnish with watercress or parsley. Serve as hors d'oeuvre or as a main course with a salad. Yield: 6 to 8 servings.

SALMON OR TUNA MOLD

16 ounces salmon or tuna
2 envelopes gelatin
½ cup cold water
1 can tomato soup
8 ounces cream cheese
3 tablespoons A-1 sauce
1 cup mayonnaise
1 cup finely chopped celery
2 tablespoons finely chopped onion
¼ teaspoon salt
dash of red pepper

Dissolve gelatin in water. Heat soup and cheese in double boiler until smooth. Add gelatin, let cool, then add fish which has been drained, boned and flaked. Add remaining ingredients, pour into mold, and refrigerate. Serve with additional mayonnaise and giant white asparagus. Yield: 8 servings.

To make celery crisp and crackly, place it in cold water with several slices of lemon for one hour.

Garden Salads

TOMATO
Leaf lettuce topped with fresh cooked green beans, bordered by tomato wedges with French dressing.

ASPARAGUS
Romaine lettuce, cooked asparagus tips, sliced beets, with wedges of bleu cheese with oil and vinegar dressing.

AVOCADO
Lettuce, slices of avocado, pimento and ripe olives dressed with French dressing.

PEPPER AND AVOCADO
Bibb lettuce, alternate strips of red and green peppers with avocado slices with French dressing.

SPINACH
Shredded spinach topped by alternate slices of Provolone cheese and tomatoes, sprinkled with fresh basil and parsley dressed with oil and vinegar dressing.

STRING BEANS
Fresh cooked young string beans and mushrooms, cut in julienne strips, topped with tomato wedges and finely chopped onion with vinaigrette.

DUTCH SLAW

1 head cabbage	¾ cup oil
2 large yellow onions	1 teaspoon celery seed
1 cup sugar	1 tablespoon salt
2 teaspoons sugar	1 cup vinegar
1 teaspoon dry mustard	

Grate or thinly slice cabbage. Slice onions. Make a layer of cabbage in bowl, top with layer of onions. Pour 1 cup sugar over this. Bring to a boil 2 teaspoons sugar, the dry mustard, oil, celery seed, salt and vinegar. Immediately pour over cabbage and onions and refrigerate for 6 hours. Toss and drain well to serve. Yield: 6 servings.

Hollow out center of a head of cabbage. Turn outer leaves out to curl like a flower. Fill with slaw, dip or other salad.

69

TOMATO ASPIC with SHRIMP DRESSING

3 cups tomato juice
2 envelopes unflavored
   gelatin
¼ cup cold water
1 teaspoon salt
1 teaspoon sugar
½ teaspoon dried green
   onion
½ teaspoon dried parsley

2 teaspoons Worcestershire
   sauce
1 tablespoon onion juice
4 drops Tabasco
2 teaspoons lemon juice
1 tablespoon horseradish
½ cup chopped celery
½ cup sliced stuffed olives
1 can artichoke hearts OR
   avocado cut into chunks

Heat tomato juice. Dissolve gelatin in cold water and add to tomato juice with salt, sugar, onion and parsley. Allow mixture to cool and add Worcestershire sauce, onion juice, Tabasco, lemon juice and horseradish. Taste for salt. Add celery, olives and artichoke hearts or avocado. Pour into mold and chill. Yield: 8 to 10 servings.

SHRIMP DRESSING:

½ pound boiled shrimp
1 clove garlic
1 pint sour cream
½ cup catsup
2 tablespoons Worcestershire
   sauce

1½ tablespoons grated onion
1 teaspoon salt
2 tablespoons horseradish
1 tablespoon lemon juice
1 teaspoon paprika
¼ teaspoon dry mustard

Cut up shrimp. Rub bowl with garlic and discard clove. Add remaining ingredients except shrimp. Stir and blend well but do not beat. Add shrimp. Chill and serve with tomato aspic. Yield: 3½ cups.

A TOMATO WELL STUFFED

2 cups canned, artichoke
   hearts, chopped
½ cup chopped celery
½ cup chopped green onions
   and tops

1 cup Hellman's mayonnaise
8 tomatoes
1½ cups cooked shrimp,
   shelled and deveined
12 slices of bacon, cooked

Combine artichoke hearts with celery, green onions and mayonnaise. Peel and scoop out 8 tomatoes; stuff with mixture. Just before serving, add shrimp to stuffing. Place on lettuce. Sprinkle with crumbled bacon on top. Filling is better if made ahead. Yield: 8 servings.

TOMATO ASPIC

4 packages unflavored
   gelatin
½ cup water
4 cups tomato juice
3 tablespoons lemon juice
2 teaspoons salt

pinch red pepper
1 teaspoon onion juice
   (optional)
small bottle stuffed olives,
   sliced
4 stalks celery, chopped

Let gelatin stand in ½ cup of water for 10 minutes. Put tomato juice, gelatin and seasonings in double boiler and bring to boil. Add olives and celery. Mold. Refrigerate until congealed. Yield: 6 to 8 servings.

COLD ARTICHOKE RICE SALAD

1 package chicken flavored
   Rice-A-Roni
4 thinly sliced green onions
½ green pepper, chopped
12 pimento olives, sliced

2 (6 ounce) jars marinated
   artichoke hearts
¾ teaspoon curry powder
⅓ cup mayonnaise

Cook entire box of rice according to directions, omitting the first step using butter. Cool rice in a large bowl. Add rice to onions, green peppers and olives. Drain artichokes and reserve the marinade. Slice artichokes and add to rice. Combine marinade with curry powder and mayonnaise. Pour over rice mixture and toss thoroughly. Chill until served. This may be made a day ahead. Yield: 4 to 6 servings.

71

PERSIAN SALAD

MARINADE:
½ cup salad oil
¼ cup lemon juice
1 teaspoon salt
2 teaspoons sugar
¼ teaspoon pepper

¼ teaspoon cumin
1 clove garlic (split and put
    toothpicks through each
    piece)

Combine all ingredients and let stand for 2 or more hours before pouring on vegetables. Remove garlic before serving.

SALAD:
6 large tomatoes, cut in 1
    inch squares
1 green bell pepper, chopped
2 cucumbers, cut in quarters
    and sliced

1 can whole pitted olives,
    drained
½ purple onion, chopped

Combine all vegetables. Pour marinade over vegetables. Cover and let set (not refrigerated) for 1 to 2 hours. Yield: 6 to 8 servings.

MARINATED ASPARAGUS

¼ cup lemon juice
⅓ cup olive oil
½ cup salad oil
½ teaspoon salt
dash of pepper
½ teaspoon dry mustard
1 hard-cooked egg, chopped
1 tablespoon chopped
    pimento

1 tablespoon capers
1 tablespoon chopped green
    onion
1 tablespoon chopped parsley
1 pound fresh asparagus,
    cooked
salad greens

Combine lemon juice, oils, salt, pepper and mustard, stirring until well blended; add egg, pimento, capers, green onion and parsley. Place cooked asparagus in a shallow 1½-quart casserole and pour marinade over all; cover and chill 2 hours. Serve mixture over salad greens. Yield: 4 servings.

VARIATION:
Hearts of palm, broccoli, or artichoke hearts may be used instead of fresh asparagus.

CREAMY ASPARAGUS MOLD

1 (10 ounce) can cream of
  asparagus soup
1 (3 ounce) package lemon
  jello
1 (8 ounce) package cream
  cheese, softened

½ cup cold water
½ cup mayonnaise
¾ cup minced celery
½ cup minced bell pepper
½ cup chopped pecans
1 tablespoon grated onion

Heat soup to boiling. Remove from heat and stir in jello. Add cream cheese and stir until melted; mix well. Stir in rest of ingredients. Turn into mold and chill. Yield: 6 to 8 servings.

ASPARAGUS PECAN MOLD

¾ cup sugar
1 cup water
½ cup white vinegar
½ teaspoon salt
2 envelopes unflavored
  gelatin
½ cup cold water

1 cup chopped celery
½ cup chopped pecans
1 small jar pimento
1 (16 ounce) can cut green
  asparagus
8 green olives, sliced

Mix sugar, water, vinegar, and salt; bring to boil. Add gelatin which has been soaked in ½ cup cold water. Cool in refrigerator. When slightly thickened, add other ingredients. Place in mold and refrigerate until completely congealed. Yield: 8 servings.

"Looks like confetti. A nice Christmas salad."

PERFECTION SALAD

1½ tablespoons unflavored
  gelatin
4 tablespoons vinegar
1 pint hot water
3 carrots, grated
½ cup chopped pimento
1 cup shredded cabbage

1 cup chopped pecans
1 cup chopped celery
1 onion, finely chopped
1 bell pepper, chopped
4 tablespoons sugar
1½ cups mayonnaise

Soften gelatin in vinegar and then dissolve in hot water. Mix in other ingredients. Pour into individual molds (sprayed with vegetable oil) and congeal. Yield: 12 to 14 servings.

LAYERED SPINACH SALAD

2 large bunches fresh
    spinach
1 bunch green onions,
    chopped
4 hard-cooked eggs, sliced
1 to 2 pounds fresh
    mushrooms, sliced

1 cup sour cream
1½ cups mayonnaise
6 ounces Parmesan cheese
4 tablespoons sugar
10 slices bacon, fried crisply

In a large bowl, layer spinach, green onions, eggs and mushrooms. Mix sour cream and mayonnaise. Spread on top of salad. Combine Parmesan cheese and sugar; sprinkle on top of mayonnaise mixture. Crumble bacon on top. Cover and refrigerate overnight. Optional: toss before serving. Yield: 10-12 servings.

WEST INDIES SALAD

1 medium onion, sliced
1 pound fresh lump
    crabmeat
salt and pepper

4 ounces salad oil
3 ounces cider vinegar
4 ounces ice water
shredded lettuce

Spread half of onion over bottom of large bowl. Cover with crabmeat and remaining onion. Salt and pepper. Pour oil, vinegar and ice water over all. Cover and marinate for 2 to 12 hours. Toss lightly and drain before serving with the shredded lettuce. Yield: 4 servings.

RICE SALAD ITALIAN STYLE

1 box long grain and wild
    rice
½ cup black olives, sliced
2 tablespoons capers
2 stalks celery, finely
    chopped
3 green onions, chopped
1 small jar chopped pimentos
1 (6½ ounce) can white tuna

⅓ to ½ cup olive oil
juice of two lemons
salt and ground pepper to
    taste
2 hard-boiled eggs for
    garnish
marinated artichoke hearts,
    drained (optional)

Cook rice according to directions on box. Add olives, capers, celery, onions, pimento and tuna to cooled rice. Add olive oil, lemon juice, salt and pepper. Add artichoke hearts, if desired. Chill before serving. Garnish with eggs. Yield: 6 to 8 servings.

ORIENTAL SPINACH SALAD

DRESSING:

1 cup vegetable oil
¼ cup wine vinegar
⅓ cup ketchup

⅔ cup sugar
1 medium onion, grated
sprinkle of salt

Prepare dressing by mixing oil, vinegar, ketchup, sugar, salt and onion together. Refrigerate while preparing other ingredients.

SALAD:

2 pounds spinach
2 eggs, hard-boiled, grated
8 slices bacon, cooked,
   crumbled

1 (8½ ounce) can water
   chestnuts, diced
½ (16 ounce) can bean
   sprouts

Wash, dry and shred spinach. Grate eggs. Combine spinach, eggs, bacon, water chestnuts and bean sprouts. Add as much dressing as desired. Yield: 8 servings.

SPINACH SALAD MOLD

3 packages frozen chopped
   spinach
3 packages unflavored
   gelatin
½ cup lemon juice
½ cup chopped pimento
1 cup sour cream
1 tablespoon Worcestershire
   sauce
1 large onion, grated

2 stalks celery, finely
   chopped
1 cup mayonnaise
1 tablespoon grated lemon
   rind
2 cups whipping cream,
   whipped
1 teaspoon white pepper
salt to taste
leaf lettuce

Cook spinach until tender; drain. Dissolve gelatin in lemon juice. Stir into hot spinach; add next 7 ingredients. Blend, then cool. Fold in whipping cream, add pepper and salt. Pour into 6-cup mold, chill. Unmold onto serving platter, garnished with leaf lettuce. Yield: 15 servings.

After washing lettuce, roll gently in a towel and refrigerate. It will become crisp.

CHICKEN SALAD VERONIQUE

3 cups cooked chicken, cubed
1 cup seedless green grapes,
   halved
½ cup toasted, chopped
   pecans
½ cup chopped celery
3 tablespoons chopped onion

½ teaspoon celery salt
⅓ cup mayonnaise
⅓ cup lemon yogurt
1 tablespoon dry white wine
½ teaspoon prepared
   mustard
leaf lettuce

In a medium bowl, mix chicken, halved grapes, pecans, celery, onion and celery salt. In a small bowl, mix mayonnaise, yogurt, wine and mustard. Fold mayonnaise mixture into chicken mixture. Refrigerate until serving time. Spoon chicken salad onto lettuce leaves. Garnish with FROSTED GRAPE CLUSTERS. Yield: 6 servings.

Prepare FROSTED GRAPE CLUSTERS as follows: Brush 6 clusters with one slightly beaten egg white or dip into egg white. Sprinkle with lime flavored gelatin. Dry on a wire rack.

CHICKEN AND FRUIT SALAD

2½ to 3 cups cooked chicken,
   diced
1 cup chopped celery
2 tablespoons chopped green
   onion
2 tablespoons capers
1 teaspoon salt
2 tablespoons lemon juice
1 (11 ounce) can mandarin
   oranges, drained

1 (8 ounce) can pineapple
   chunks, drained
½ cup slivered almonds,
   toasted
½ cup Hellman's
   mayonnaise
½ teaspoon grated lemon
   peel
salad greens

Combine chicken with celery, green onions and capers. Mix in salt and lemon juice; cover and chill for several hours. Just before serving, add the oranges (reserve a few for garnish), pineapple, and almonds. Combine the mayonnaise and lemon peel; mix carefully so as not to break the fruit pieces. Spoon into a bowl lined with salad greens. Garnish with reserved oranges. Yield: 6 servings.

CHICKEN-CRANBERRY LAYERS

LAYER 1:

1 tablespoon unflavored
   gelatin
¼ cup cold water
2 cups whole cranberry sauce

1 (9 ounce) can crushed
   pineapple, drained
½ cup chopped pecans
1 tablespoon lemon juice

Soften gelatin in cold water. Dissolve over hot water. Add cranberry sauce, pineapple, pecans and lemon juice. Pour into a 10 × 6 × 1½-inch baking dish; chill until firm.

LAYER 2:

1 tablespoon unflavored
   gelatin
¼ cup cold water
1 cup mayonnaise
½ cup cold water
3 tablespoons lemon juice
¾ teaspoon salt
2 cups cooked or canned
   chicken, diced

½ cup diced celery
2 tablespoons chopped
   parsley
lettuce
mayonnaise
pecan halves

Soften gelatin in ¼ cup water. Dissolve over hot water. Blend in mayonnaise, ½ cup water, lemon juice, salt, chicken, celery and parsley. After first layer is firm, pour second layer over first. Chill until firm. Cut into squares; invert each on lettuce. Top with mayonnaise and pecan halves. Yield: 6 to 8 servings.

CUCUMBERS IN CREAM

2 cucumbers
1 teaspoon salt
½ cup sweet or sour cream

1 tablespoon sugar
1 tablespoon vinegar

Pare and slice cucumbers very thin. Place cucumbers in bowl and add salt. Place in refrigerator for several hours; then rinse and squeeze out as much juice as possible. Make dressing by combining cream, sugar, and vinegar. Pour over cucumbers. Yield: 6 to 8 servings.

Salad Dressings

CLASSIC FRENCH DRESSING

1½ teaspoons salt
1 teaspoon pepper
½ cup wine vinegar
1 tablespoon lemon juice
1 tablespoon Grey Poupon
    Mustard

1⅓ cups olive or salad oil
1 tablespoon egg white,
    slightly beaten
1 clove garlic

Mix salt, pepper, vinegar, lemon juice and mustard using wire whisk. Add oil; mix well, and then stir in egg white. Place in jar with garlic clove. Store in refrigerator. Shake well before each use. Yield: 1 pint.

VINAIGRETTE

¼ teaspoon sugar
¼ teaspoon salt
¼ teaspoon white pepper
1 teaspoon Dijon mustard
2 tablespoons wine vinegar

1 tablespoon lemon juice
3 tablespoons olive oil
3 tablespoons vegetable oil
1 clove garlic (optional)

Beat the first 6 ingredients well with a wire whisk or a fork until they are smooth. Add oil and beat again. Add the clove of garlic whole and remove before serving. Yield: ½ cup.

FRENCH DRESSING AUX FINE HERBES

1 teaspoon salt
¼ teaspoon cracked black
*   pepper*
¼ cup red wine vinegar
¼ cup garlic wine vinegar
1 cup olive or salad oil

1 teaspoon paprika
¼ teaspoon crushed oregano
¼ teaspoon crushed sweet
*   basil*
1 bay leaf

Mix salt, pepper and vinegars. Whisk together. Add oil and herbs, whisking together thoroughly. Store in refrigerator and shake well before using. Yield: 1½ cups.

LE NORMANDIE SALAD DRESSING

4 egg yolks
1 tablespoon Dijon mustard
1 tablespoon coarse black
*   pepper*

1½ teaspoons salt
⅓ cup vinegar
2 cups salad oil

Place yolks, mustard, pepper and salt in a bowl. Whisk together. Add vinegar; whisk until well mixed. Add oil, whisking as you pour, until all ingredients are well blended. Refrigerate. Yield: 2½ cups.

Le Normandie Restaurant
Americus, Georgia

Put a clove of garlic into store-bought French dressing to add zip.

BLENDER MAYONNAISE

1 egg
½ teaspoon salt
¼ teaspoon dry mustard

1 tablespoon lemon juice or
  vinegar
1 cup oil

Break whole egg into blender and, at high speed, blend 30 seconds. Add salt, mustard, lemon juice or vinegar and blend for a few more seconds. With the blender running, add oil in a very thin stream. Yield: 1 cup.

VARIATION:

BASIL MAYONNAISE:

2 cups fresh basil leaves
1 garlic clove, crushed

2 tablespoons lemon juice

Whisk ingredients into Blender Mayonnaise. Yield: about 1½ cups.

Add 1 tablespoon boiling water to homemade mayonnaise; this will prevent it from separating in the refrigerator.

AVOCADO DRESSING

¾ cup avocado pulp
3 tablespoons lemon
   juice
2 tablespoons heavy
   cream

½ teaspoon Worcestershire
   sauce
¾ teaspoon salt
1 teaspoon Dijon mustard

Sieve enough soft ripe avocado to make ¾ cup. Add lemon juice and mix well. Add heavy cream, Worcestershire sauce, salt and mustard. Chill. Yield: 1 cup.

"Especially recommended for fruit salads."

Lemon juice prevents discoloration on cut surfaces of avocados, apples, pears, and mushrooms.

GREEN GODDESS

1 cup mayonnaise
½ cup sour cream
⅓ cup chopped parsley
3 tablespoons chives

3 tablespoons anchovy paste
3 tablespoons vinegar
1 tablespoon lemon juice
dash freshly ground pepper

Combine all ingredients and chill thoroughly. Yield: 2 cups.

POPPY SEED DRESSING

1¼ cups sugar
2 tablespoons dry mustard
2 teaspoons salt
⅔ cup white vinegar

1 tablespoon grated onion
2 cups salad oil
¼ cup poppy seed

In a blender, mix sugar, mustard and salt. Add vinegar and onion; mix well. Very gradually add oil. Mix in poppy seed. Chill. Keeps indefinitely. Yield: 4½ cups.

TO MAKE APPLE SWANS, slice off ⅓ of apple to use later for the neck and head. By removing this portion, you have a flat base for the swan to rest on. Cut a small wedge from apple. Start cutting slices around wedge. The slices are taco shaped and will become larger as more slices are cut. When all slices are cut, fit them back together the way they began by lapping them to form wings and tail. Cut head from reserved apple piece and make eyes with cloves. Attach the head with a toothpick. Rub swan with Fruit Fresh or lemon juice to prevent discoloration.

TO MAKE RADISH MUSHROOMS, remove root end, cutting as little red skin as possible. Make a deep cut around equator of radish. Working from stem end to the cut, carve away part of the radish to form stem. Crisp in salty water. Use in clusters with parsley.

WHEN FREEZING STRAWBERRIES, don't pull the stem off. The juice runs out even more if you do. When you are ready to use them, wash them in ice water and then pull the hull off.

RANCH DRESSING

1 cup mayonnaise
1 cup buttermilk
1½ teaspoons dried onion
    flakes

1 tablespoon dried parsley
1 teaspoon Accent
scant teaspoon onion salt
¼ teaspoon garlic salt

Mix all ingredients. Store in refrigerator. Substitute sour cream for buttermilk to make vegetable dip. Yield: 2 cups.

BLEU CHEESE DRESSING

½ pound bleu cheese,
    crumbled
1 quart Hellman's
    mayonnaise
1 cup milk

1 small onion, minced
2 teaspoons black pepper
½ teaspoon garlic salt
2 teaspoons Worcestershire
    sauce

Mix all ingredients well. Keep refrigerated. If you like a thicker dressing, use less milk. Yield: 1½ quarts.

ROQUEFORT CHEESE DRESSING

2 spring onions (including
    green tops)
2 tablespoons parsley
1 (4 ounce) package
    Roquefort cheese, OR
    bleu cheese

2 cups mayonnaise
1 cup sour cream
¼ cup lemon juice

Finely chop spring onions and parsley. Crumble cheese. Put all of the listed ingredients into a blender. Blend at medium speed until well mixed. Some may prefer a short blending time so that cheese remains in large pieces. Chill for 2 to 3 hours before serving. Yield: 1 quart.

Add flavor to store-bought mayonnaise by adding chopped herbs such as parsley, dill or basil.

FRENCH ROQUEFORT DRESSING

1 can tomato soup
½ cup sugar
1 teaspoon salt
1 teaspoon paprika
1 teaspoon dry
    mustard
½ teaspoon pepper
1 cup salad oil

1 cup vinegar
1 teaspoon Worcestershire
    sauce
1 small onion, grated
½ pound Roquefort OR bleu
    cheese
½ teaspoon garlic minced

Mix all ingredients except cheese and garlic in a blender until creamy. Add crumbled cheese. Put in quart bottle with garlic clove. Chill several hours before using. Yield: 1 quart.

CLOISTER DRESSING

4 eggs
¼ cup chopped onion
½ clove garlic, minced
½ small can anchovies (⅓
    ounce)
1 cup cottonseed oil
½ teaspoon white pepper

½ teaspoon dry mustard
salt to taste
½ cup cider vinegar
juice of ½ lemon
1 teaspoon Worcestershire
    sauce

Place the eggs in a mixing bowl and set them to warm in a sink filled with hot water. Coarsely chop the anchovies. When the eggs are warm, beat with an electric mixer at low speed for 5 to 6 minutes. Gradually add half the oil, onion and garlic, anchovies and dry seasonings. Blend well; then gradually add the remaining oil. Add vinegar, lemon juice and Worcestershire sauce and blend, a little at a time, with the oil and eggs. Continue to mix at low speed for 10 minutes. Keeps for weeks, sealed, in the refrigerator. Stir well before using. Yield: 1¾ cups.

The Cloister
Sea Island, Georgia

Dip boiled egg quarters into chopped parsley for a garnish.

R.D.

Breads

It is often quoted "Truly, bread is the staff of life" and to that can be added, it is an art as well. Corn raised on the plantations was taken to the miller by some family member on horseback. The corn was transported in large white cotton sacks. Some plantations had their own mills and neighbors probably used them also. Wheat for flour was grown on the farms. Milk cows and goats supplied milk. Butter was made in a crockery churn with wooden dasher. Also the cook had at her disposal sweet milk, buttermilk, cottage cheese, cream and clabber. Quick yeast was made at home as were yeast cakes. To test the temperature of the oven when baking bread, an old cookbook says, "if one can hold the hand in the oven to count to 20 it is right, or throw a little flour on the floor of the oven, if it browns quickly, it is right."

Breads

BUTTERMILK CORNBREAD

1 cup yellow cornmeal
   (coarse grind)
1/4 teaspoon baking powder
1/2 teaspoon baking soda
1/2 teaspoon salt

3 tablespoons vegetable
   shortening
1 cup buttermilk
1 egg, slightly beaten

Sift dry ingredients into large bowl. Place shortening in 8-inch iron skillet and heat. Add buttermilk and egg to dry ingredients and mix well. Pour hot shortening into cornbread and stir well. Pour into hot skillet. Bake at 425° F for 25 minutes. May be frozen at completion. This is good when used for making cornbread dressing. Yield: 6 servings.

"Nothing takes the place of iron skillets in real Southern cooking."

CORNBREAD DRESSING

1 recipe (6 servings) of
   BUTTERMILK
   CORNBREAD, crumbled
   (see recipe)
1/2 bell pepper, chopped
3 celery stalks, chopped
3 onions, chopped
3 tablespoons butter
5 chicken bouillon cubes
1 cup boiling water
1 1/2 cups chicken broth

1 1/2 cups butter
1 teaspoon Lawry's seasoning
   salt
1/8 teaspoon cayenne pepper
1/4 teaspoon pepper
1/2 teaspoon poultry
   seasoning
6 eggs, beaten
6 slices of white bread,
   crumbled

Ahead of time, make BUTTERMILK CORNBREAD. Sauté bell pepper, celery and onion in 3 tablespoons butter. Melt bouillon cubes in water. Add chicken broth and butter. Add seasoning salt, cayenne pepper, pepper and poultry seasoning. Stir in beaten eggs. Add crumbled breads. Mix well. Pour into 9 × 11 roasting pan. Bake in 450° F oven, about 1 to 1 1/2 hours, until crust is brown on top. Yield: 14 servings.

SOUTHERN CORNBREAD DRESSING

5 stalks celery, chopped
1 cup finely chopped onion
2 tablespoons salad oil
2 tablespoons butter
broth from a large hen (may
    substitute 2-4 cans chicken
    broth)
BUTTERMILK CORN-
    BREAD baked in large
    iron skillet, crumbled

6 slices stale bread (or
    equivalent of homemade
    biscuits)
10-12 eggs (depending on
    size of eggs)
2 tablespoons drippings from
    turkey
salt and pepper to taste

Sauté celery and onion in combination of oil and butter. Pour broth over CORNBREAD in large mixing bowl. Add stale bread and sautéed celery and onions. Add eggs and mix thoroughly. Add turkey drippings and salt and pepper. Mixture should be very loose. The best way to mix completely and thoroughly is to use your hands. Bake at 400°F until firm in 2 large greased cast iron skillets which have been preheated in the oven. Test for doneness with a knife blade as you would for a custard pie. This dressing is very rich and will be light and quite moist. Spoon onto heated serving platter. Yield: 20 to 25 servings.

"Southerners do not always stuff the Thanksgiving turkey. They like left-over dressing with gravy."

HOECAKE

1 cup cornmeal
1¼ cups water
1 teaspoon salt

bacon drippings (enough to
    cover bottom of skillet)

Combine cornmeal, water and salt. In iron skillet heat bacon drippings, greasing pan very well, on medium heat. Pour half the batter into skillet. Cook until bottom is brown (lift and check with spatula). Flip cooked side of hoecake onto a dinner plate. Regrease skillet, then slide cake into skillet with uncooked side face down. Cook until brown. Repeat steps for second hoecake. Yield: 2 hoecakes.

"An old Southern recipe."

CHARLIE BREAD

3 eggs
½ cup oil
1 cup sour cream

1 cup cream style corn
1 cup cornmeal mix

Preheat oven to 375° F. Beat eggs. Add remaining ingredients and stir until well-blended. Pour into greased baking dish (either 11½ × 7½ × 1½ or brownie pan). Bake at 375° F for about 45 minutes or until top is lightly golden. This cornbread is very moist and can be kept several days in the refrigerator. Charlie Bread is also good as muffins. May be frozen after baking. Yield: 12 servings.

CRACKLIN' CORNBREAD

1¾ cups flour
1 teaspoon salt
4 teaspoons baking powder
1 teaspoon baking soda
¾ cup cornmeal
4 tablespoons cane syrup

1 egg
1 cup cracklings
1¼ cups buttermilk
4 tablespoons melted
  shortening OR bacon
  drippings

Combine flour, salt, baking powder, baking soda and cornmeal. Add syrup and egg to dry ingredients. Stir in cracklings. Add milk and melted shortening. Beat thoroughly and bake at 350° F in greased pan for 40 minutes. Yield: 6 servings.

SPOON BREAD

2 cups meal
2 cups boiling water
3 tablespoons butter
2 teaspoons salt

2 tablespoons baking powder
1½ cups milk
2 large eggs, separated

Preheat oven to 350° F. Sift meal and dissolve in boiling water. Add butter, salt and baking powder. Add milk. Separate eggs. Add yolks to meal mixture. Beat whites until stiff. Fold whites into meal mixture. Pour into buttered baking dish. Bake at 350° F for 30 to 35 minutes until done. Serve hot with butter. Yield: 8 servings.

NATURE'S LOAF

1½ cups hot tap water (100° F -
   115° F)
½ cup non-fat dry milk
2 tablespoons sugar
2 teaspoons salt
2 packages dry yeast
2 cups whole wheat flour

3 teaspoons wheat germ
3½ to 4 cups bread flour or
   flour
2 tablespoons butter, room
   temperature
2 eggs, room temperature

Pour water in mixing bowl and stir in milk, sugar, salt, yeast, whole wheat flour, wheat germ, and 1 cup white flour. Add butter and eggs. Beat with a spoon until batter is smooth and sheets off spoon, or at medium speed of electric mixer for 2 minutes. Scrape bowl occasionally. Stir in remaining white flour, ½ cup at a time, first with spoon, and then by hand. The dough will be a rough, shaggy mass. Scrape down the sides of the bowl with fingertips or spatula. Turn onto lightly floured work surface and knead with rhythmic 1-2-3 motion of push-turn-fold. The dough will become smooth and elastic, and bubbles will form under the surface of the dough. Sprinkle more flour on the ball of dough if it is moist and sticks to hand or work surface. Break the kneading rhythm occasionally by throwing the dough down hard against countertop. Place dough in greased bowl and cover tightly with plastic wrap. Place in draft-free place until dough has risen to about twice its original size (about 1½ hours). Turn back plastic wrap and punch down dough. Fold over, recover, let rise until almost doubled (about 30 minutes). Punch down. Knead for 30 seconds to press out bubbles. Divide into 2 pieces, shape into balls. Let rest under a towel for 3 to 4 minutes. Shape into loaves and place in pans. Cover pan with wax paper and leave in warm place until center of dough has risen to 1 inch above the edge of the pan (about 50 minutes). Bake in preheated 400° F oven about 30 to 40 minutes until loaves are golden brown and test done. Turn one loaf out of pan and tap bottom crust with forefinger. A hard hollow sound means the bread is done. If not, return to oven for an additional 10 minutes. If loaves seem to brown too quickly, cover loosely with foil. Turn from pans and cool on metal racks. For a soft crust, brush with butter and cover with a towel. Yield: 2 loaves.

"The best all around loaf. Toasts beautifully; great sandwich bread; freezes well."

ALL WHOLE-WHEAT BREAD

7¾ to 8¾ cups unsifted
   stoneground whole-wheat
   flour
4 teaspoons salt
2 packages active dry yeast

1½ cups milk
1½ cups water
¼ cup honey
6 tablespoons butter

In a large mixing bowl thoroughly stir together 3 cups of the whole-wheat flour, salt and undissolved yeast.

Into a small saucepan turn the milk, water, honey and butter. Over low heat, heat until liquids are very warm (120° to 130°); butter does not need to melt. Gradually stir into flour mixture and beat 2 minutes at medium speed of electric mixer, scraping bowl occasionally. Add 1 cup flour. Beat at high speed 2 minutes, scraping bowl occasionally. Stir in enough additional flour to make a stiff dough.

Turn out onto lightly floured smooth surface; cover and let rest 10 minutes. Then knead dough until smooth and elastic—about 10 minutes. Place in greased bowl, turning to grease top. Cover; let rise in warm draft-free place until doubled in bulk—about 50 minutes.

Punch down dough. Divide in half; shape each half into loaf. Place each loaf in a greased 8½ × 4½ × 2½-inch loaf pan. Cover; let rise again until doubled in bulk—about 50 minutes.

Bake in a preheated 375° F oven until loaves sound hollow when tapped with knuckles—about 35 minutes. Turn out of pans onto wire rack; turn right side up; cool. Yield: 2 loaves.

To Knead:

Turn dough on a lightly floured work surface. Knead with a rhythmic 1-2-3 motion. Push with heel of your hand - turn - fold. Sprinkle more flour on surface if dough is so moist that it sticks to surface or your hands. Break kneading rhythm by occasionally throwing dough down hard on countertop. Dough will be smooth, elastic and have air bubbles under the surface when sufficiently kneaded. This takes about 5 minutes.

RICH WHITE BREAD

1 package dry yeast
¼ cup sugar
½ cup non-fat dry milk
1½ cups hot water
    (100°-115°)
2 teaspoons salt
¼ cup butter

2 eggs
5 to 5½ cups flour,
    unbleached
1 egg white, beaten with 1
    tablespoon water
sesame seeds

In a large mixing bowl, combine yeast, sugar, dry milk and water. Let the yeast proof for 3 to 5 minutes. Add salt and butter which has been cut into small pieces. Add eggs; mix thoroughly. Gradually add flour while beating with an electric mixer. Scrape bowl occasionally. A stiff dough will be formed. Turn out on a floured board and knead the dough until it is smooth and elastic (about 5 minutes). Work dough into a ball. Put in a buttered bowl. Cover and let rise until double in bulk.

Punch the dough down. Knead a few times. Now you are ready to shape. (1) Divide dough into two equal portions. Roll into a rectangle with the short side as long as the bread pan you are using (for this recipe use a 9 × 5 loaf pan). Roll tightly in jelly roll style. Fold ends under. Place loaf seam side down in greased pan. Repeat for second loaf. (2) For braided loaf, divide dough into three equal portions. Roll each into a thin cylinder about 10 to 12 inches long. Braid together. Place braid on greased baking sheet. (3) Double braided loaf: Make a braid of three larger strips then make a braid of three small strips and put one on top of another. After shaping, cover and allow to rise until double in bulk (about 1½ hours). Brush with egg white-water mixture, sprinkle lavishly with sesame seeds. Bake in a preheated 350° F oven for 40 minutes.

FESTIVE VARIATIONS OF RICH WHITE BREAD

CINNAMON AND SUGAR LOAF

Rich White Bread recipe
1 cup sugar cubes, broken

1 tablespoon cinnamon
butter

Follow basic white bread recipe. Combine sugar cubes and cinnamon. During kneading process flatten dough and sprinkle with ¼ cup sugar cube mixture. Knead; add another portion of sugar cube mixture. Repeat until all is used. Proceed as in basic recipe. Bake in loaf pans. Do not brush with egg white before baking. Rub butter over freshly baked surface for glazed appearance and rich taste.

CURRANT-PECAN BREAD

Rich White Bread recipe
½ cup brown sugar
½ cup butter, softened

1 cup chopped pecans
1 cup currants
butter

Follow basic recipe. Let rise until double in bulk. Punch down. Turn out on lightly floured broad. Knead in sugar, butter, pecans and currants. (Excessive kneading of fruit-filled breads causes the dough to discolor.) Form into loaves. Rub loaves with butter when done. This bread is good served with the following spread.

SPREAD:

8 ounces cream cheese
¼ cup finely chopped pecans

¼ cup sugar
¼ teaspoon almond extract

Mix all ingredients. Strawberry preserves are served with cream cheese spread.

"A prize winner at the National Pecan Festival."

For tender, soft crust, brush bread with shortening after taking it from oven.

CHEESE BREAD

Rich White Bread recipe
*1 cup sharp Cheddar cheese
  grated OR ¾ cup Swiss
  cheese, grated and ¼ cup
  fresh grated Parmesan
  cheese*

1 teaspoon Tabasco sauce
1 egg yolk
1 tablespoon milk

Follow basic white bread recipe. Knead a mixture of cheese and Tabasco into dough. Proceed as in basic recipe. Glaze with egg yolk mixed with milk before baking.

CHRISTMAS HOLIDAY LOAF

Rich White Bread recipe
⅛ teaspoon mace
*½ cup raisins, which have
  been soaked in rum
  overnight, drained
  (reserve rum)*

1 teaspoon orange rind
½ cup chopped pecans
*½ cup candied cherries,
  halved*
½ cup brown sugar
½ cup butter

Follow basic white bread recipe. Let rise until doubled in bulk. Punch down. Knead in the remaining ingredients. Remember that excessive kneading of fruits causes dough to discolor. Braid loaf. Proceed as in basic recipe. Do not glaze before baking. Remove bread from oven; let cool on wire rack. Ice and decorate with the following.

ICING AND DECORATIONS:

1 cup confectioners' sugar
1 tablespoon milk
¼ teaspoon almond extract

¼ cup pecan halves
*red and green candied
  cherries, halved*

Mix sugar, milk and almond extract. Ice bread. Decorate with pecan halves and cherries.

"This makes a beautiful and tasty Christmas gift."

Gift idea: Make homemade bread; wrap in breadcloth and put in a bread basket. A jar of homemade jam would be good, too!

PULL-APART LOAVES

5½ to 6½ cups flour,
  unsifted
3 tablespoons sugar
2 teaspoons salt
1 package dry yeast

1½ cups water
½ cup milk
3 tablespoons margarine
margarine, melted

In large bowl, thoroughly mix 2 cups flour, sugar, salt and undissolved dry yeast. Combine water, milk and 3 tablespoons margarine in a saucepan. Heat over low heat until liquids are very warm. Margarine does not need to melt. Gradually add liquid to dry ingredients and beat for 2 minutes on medium speed of electric mixer, scraping bowl occasionally. Add ¾ cup flour. Beat at high speed for 2 minutes. Stir in enough additional flour to make a stiff dough. Turn out onto lightly floured board. Knead until smooth and elastic, about 8 to 10 minutes. Place in a greased bowl, turning to grease the top. Cover. Let rise in warm place, free from draft, until doubled in bulk, about 1 hour. Punch dough down; divide in half. Cover. Let rise on board 15 minutes. Roll one half to a 12 × 8 inch rectangle. Brush with melted margarine. Cut into 4 equal strips, 8 inches long. Stack strips. Cut into 4 equal pieces, 2 inches wide. Place on edge in greased 8½ × 4½ × 2½ inch loaf pan so that layers form one long row down length of pan. Repeat with remaining dough. Cover. Let rise in warm place, free from draft, until doubled in bulk, about 1 hour. Bake at 400° F. about 30 minutes or until done. Can do ahead and freeze. Yield: 2 loaves.

FOR USE OF FOOD PROCESSOR:
Proof yeast in processor then add other ingredients. Process for 30 seconds to 1 minute. Dough will begin to form a ball and pull away from the sides of the container. NOTE: 3¾ to 4 cups flour is all the average food processor can manage. The motor will stop if overloaded. Dough may rise in the processor bowl. Now proceed as in the above recipe.

For glazed crust, brush top with egg yolk, beaten in 1 tablespoon water, before baking.

REFRIGERATOR ROLLS
(For the Novice Bread-Maker)

½ cup Crisco shortening
¼ cup sugar
scant teaspoon salt
½ cup boiling water
½ cup cold water

1 egg, beaten
1 (¼ ounce) package yeast
3 cups flour, unsifted
1 egg white, beaten

In electric mixer, pour boiling water over Crisco, sugar and salt. Stir until shortening has melted. Add cold water, mix well and add beaten egg. In a separate bowl, sift dry yeast with the first cup of flour. Sift the remaining 2 cups of flour and add to the yeast/flour mixture. Mix. Add flour mixture to the ingredients in mixer. Mix well and place in a large covered, greased bowl. Refrigerate overnight. Shape into rolls. Place on a greased cookie sheet and brush with beaten egg white. Let rise 1 hour or longer before cooking. Bake at 400° F about 10 minutes or until brown. Yield: 2 dozen rolls.

To thaw frozen bread or rolls, wrap them tightly in aluminum foil and heat at 325° F for 5 minutes.

IDIOT ROLLS

1 cup margarine
¾ cup Crisco shortening
1 cup water
2 packages dry yeast
½ cup water
2 eggs

1 cup water
¾ cup sugar
7 cups self rising flour OR 7
    cups flour and 2
    tablespoons salt

Heat in pan until melted, margarine, shortening, and 1 cup water. Cool. Dissolve yeast in ½ cup lukewarm water. In large bowl mix eggs, slightly beaten, 1 cup cold water and sugar. Combine all ingredients in bowl. Stir in sifted flour. Cover and place in refrigerator. Take out amount you need about 3 hours before baking. Roll into balls and put in greased pans and let rise for 3 hours. Bake 7 to 12 minutes in 450° F oven. Yield: 4 dozen rolls.

"This recipe is for cooks who have been afraid to try rolls. More experienced bakers have been known to adopt this recipe."

HOMEMADE ROLLS

¼ cup sugar
⅔ cup Crisco shortening
1 cup buttermilk
½ cup water

3½ cups self-rising flour
1 teaspoon salt
1 package yeast
¼ cup melted butter

All ingredients should be at room temperature. Blend sugar and Crisco with a spoon. Add buttermilk and water and stir. In another bowl, sift flour and salt and then add yeast. Gradually stir dry ingredients into Crisco-milk mixture. Cover and refrigerate overnight. Place dough on well-floured counter and work in more flour until easy to handle. Roll out dough to ½ inch thickness and cut with biscuit cutter. Dip each round piece into melted butter. Roll over Parkerhouse style. Let rise 2½ to 3 hours. Bake in preheated oven at 350° F for 15 minutes or until brown. Yield: 1 dozen.

"Delicate and light."

BUTTERMILK BISCUITS

2 cups flour
2 teaspoons baking powder
1 teaspoon salt
½ teaspoon soda

2 teaspoons sugar
⅓ cup shortening
⅔ cup buttermilk

Preheat oven to 450° F. Sift dry ingredients together. Cut in shortening. Add buttermilk and mix until dough is pliable. Knead dough on a lightly floured board for 30 seconds. Roll ½ inch thick. Cut with biscuit cutter and place close together on an ungreased cookie sheet. Bake 10 to 12 minutes. Excellent for dinner sized biscuits or for small party sized. Butter substituted for shortening makes flavor better. Yield: 1 dozen.

CHEESE BISCUITS

4 teaspoons baking powder
1 teaspoon salt
2 cups flour
4 tablespoons shortening

1 cup grated sharp Cheddar
   cheese
¼ cup Parmesan cheese
¼ teaspoon red pepper
1 cup milk

Sift baking powder and salt with flour. Cut in shortening. Mix in cheeses and red pepper. Add milk and make into a dough. Knead slightly. Roll, cut into biscuits. Bake 10 to 12 minutes at 400° F. Do not crowd in pan. Yield: 18 medium biscuits or 36 small biscuits.

"Great filled with thin slices of ham."

SOUR CREAM MUFFINS

1 cup self-rising flour
½ cup sour cream

½ cup butter, melted

Quickly stir flour and sour cream into melted butter. Drop by heaping tablespoons into slightly greased muffin tins. Bake at 400° F until brown, about 10 to 15 minutes. Serve hot. Yield: 12 medium muffins.

BRAN MUFFINS

4 cups All Bran (Kelloggs)
2 cups 100% Bran (Nabsico)
1 teaspoon salt
2 cups boiling water
1 quart buttermilk

3 cups sugar
1 cup shortening
4 eggs
5 cups flour
5 teaspoons soda

Combine brans and salt. Add water and mix. Add buttermilk and allow mixture to cool. Cream sugar and shortening. Add eggs, one at a time. Add cooled bran mixture. Stir in flour and soda. Bake at 375° F for 20 to 25 minutes in greased muffin tins. Yield: 5 dozen muffins.

NOTE: Uncooked muffin mixture may be stored in the refrigerator for up to one month. Do not stir.

DATENUT MUFFINS

1 egg
½ cup sugar
⅓ cup Crisco, melted
¾ cup flour

¼ teaspoon baking powder
1 cup finely chopped pecans
½ cup chopped dates
½ teaspoon vanilla extract

Preheat oven to 350° F. Cream egg, sugar and Crisco. Blend flour and baking powder. Stir in pecans, dates and vanilla. Grease and heat miniature muffin tins and then flour before filling with one heaping teaspoon in each ring. Bake at 350° F for 8 to 10 minutes. Muffins should not brown and dry out. Yield: 3 dozen.

CINNAMON PECAN MUFFINS

½ cup Crisco
1 cup sugar
2 eggs
2 cups flour
¼ teaspoon salt

2 teaspoons baking powder
3 teaspoons cinnamon
1 cup milk
1 cup chopped pecans

Preheat oven to 450° F. Cream Crisco and sugar. Add eggs one at the time, beating thoroughly after each addition. Combine flour, salt, baking powder and cinnamon. Alternately add dry ingredients and milk to sugar mixture. Stir in pecans. Pour into well greased muffin tins, half filling the cups. Bake for 15 minutes for miniature muffins, 20 minutes for regular sized tins. Yield: 5 dozen miniature muffins.

If muffin batter is lumpy, it is perfect.

"Muffin method": to make muffins, add all liquid ingredients to all dry ingredients.

Muffins freeze well and may be reheated.

DILL BREAD

1/4 cup lukewarm water
1 package dry yeast
1 tablespoon butter, softened
1 cup cottage cheese
1 tablespoon sugar
2 teaspoons dill seed

1 tablespoon dehydrated
    onion flakes
1/4 teaspoon soda
1 teaspoon salt
1 egg, unbeaten
2 1/4 cups flour

Warm large bowl by allowing hot water to stand in it a few minutes. Empty it; now pour in 1/4 cup warm water; add yeast and stir until dissolved. Blend in butter. Warm cheese slightly in top of double boiler over warm (not hot) water. Add to yeast mixture. Beat in sugar, dill seed, onion flakes, soda and salt. Add egg and beat again. Add flour and stir until all flour is moistened. Keeping the sticky dough in the bowl, knead until it appears slightly smooth, adding as little flour as possible. Grease top of dough with a bit of oil. Cover with cloth. Let rise until almost double in bulk, about 1 hour. Punch down; divide into 6 portions; pat each into a well-greased loaf pan or put dough into 1 large loaf pan. Allow to rise about 40 minutes or until dough has risen at least to top of pan. Bake at 350° F for 35 to 40 minutes. When baked, brush with melted butter and sprinkle immediately with coarse (kosher) salt. (This step is optional.) Yield: 1 regular loaf or 6 miniature loaves.

YORKSHIRE PUDDING

1 cup flour
1 teaspoon salt
2 eggs

1 cup milk
2 to 3 tablespoons pan
    drippings or grease

Put flour and salt in bowl. Make a well in middle and add eggs and milk. Beat well. (This can be made in the morning and let stand). Heat oven to 450° F. Melt grease in 9 × 12 pan. Add the above mixture. Bake for 35 to 40 minutes in 450° F oven. Cut into squares and serve immediately with roast beef and gravy. Yield: 4 servings.

POPOVERS

2 eggs
1 cup milk
1 cup flour

½ teaspoon salt
pinch nutmeg
½ cup butter

Preheat oven to 425° F 10 minutes before popover is ready to bake. Liberally grease 8 or 10 custard cups using 6 tablespoons of butter. Heat the custard cups until sizzling hot. Beat eggs for 1 minute with an electric beater. Add milk and gradually beat in flour. Add seasonings and 2 tablespoons of the butter and beat for 1 minute. Let stand at room temperature for 30 minutes. Pour batter into prepared heated custard cups, filling not more than ⅓ full. Bake at 425° F for 30 minutes, then turn oven off. Allow popover to remain in oven 5 to 10 minutes longer. Serve immediately. Yield: 8 to 10 servings.

Bread tricks for a busy life:

In place of scalded milk, use ⅓ cup non-fat dry milk per 1 cup lukewarm water.

Use a food processor. Follow basic recipe but instead of hand kneading, let processor do the job. Process for about 25 to 30 seconds. Continue basic recipe.

CASSEROLE RYE BREAD

1 cup scalded milk
¼ cup brown sugar
¼ cup butter
2 teaspoons salt
2 packages yeast

1 cup warm water
2 tablespoons carraway seed
3 cups white flour
2 cups rye flour

In mixing bowl, pour milk over sugar, butter and salt. Cool. Soften yeast in the warm water. Add to milk mixture. Add carraway seed and half of each of the flours. Mix at medium speed for 2 minutes. Add remaining flours and beat 1½ minutes. Cool and let rise 45 minutes. Stir vigorously. Turn into well greased 2-quart casserole. Brush top with milk. Sprinkle with carraway seed. Bake at 350° F for 45 to 50 minutes. Yield: 1 loaf.

"Marvelous when eaten with sliced corned beef."

SALLY LUNN

1 package dry yeast
¼ cup warm water
1¾ cups milk
2 tablespoons sugar

4 tablespoons butter
2 teaspoons salt
2 eggs, beaten
5 cups flour, approximately

Dissolve yeast in warm water. Heat the milk and pour over sugar, butter and salt in mixing bowl. Cool. Beat the eggs slightly and sift the flour. When mixture has cooled, stir in the yeast, eggs and 3 cups of flour. Add enough additional flour to make a soft dough. Place dough in a buttered angel cake pan or buttered loaf pans. Let rise until double in bulk, about 1 hour. Bake at 400° F for 15 minutes, then reduce heat to 350° F for another 15 to 18 minutes. Serve warm or use toasted. Yield: 10 to 12 servings.

On very humid or rainy days, use 2 to 3 tablespoons less liquid.

CREAM CHEESE CRESCENTS

1 cup butter or margarine
8 ounces cream cheese,
    softened
2 cups flour
¼ teaspoon salt

¾ cup finely chopped pecans
⅓ cup sugar
1½ teaspoons cinnamon
confectioners' sugar

Combine butter and cream cheese, creaming until well blended. Combine flour and salt. Add to creamed mixture, mixing well. Shape dough into 8 balls. Wrap each in plastic wrap. Chill at least 2 hours. Roll each ball of dough into an 8 inch circle on a lightly floured surface. Cut into 8 wedges. Combine pecans, sugar and cinnamon. Sprinkle ¼ teaspoon mixture over each wedge of dough. Starting at wide edge of dough, roll up each wedge; shape into a crescent. Place point side down on ungreased cookie sheet. Bake at 350° F for 12 minutes or until lightly browned. Cool and dust with confectioners' sugar. Yield: 64 crescents.

"Continental breakfasts should adopt!"

CARROT BREAD

4 eggs
2 cups sugar
1¼ cups oil
3 cups flour, sifted

2 teaspoons baking powder
1½ teaspoons salt
2 teaspoons cinnamon
2 cups carrots, shredded

Preheat oven to 350° F. Beat eggs. Gradually add sugar, beating until thick. Add oil slowly and continue beating until thoroughly combined. Sift dry ingredients together. Stir into egg mixture. Add carrots and stir until blended. Divide batter into three greased one pound coffee cans. Bake at 350° F for 45 minutes to 1 hour. Yield: 18 servings.

"Non-carrot lovers dote on this bread. It can be a dessert or served with ham."

STRAWBERRY NUT BREAD

1 cup butter
1½ cups sugar
1 teaspoon vanilla extract
¼ teaspoon lemon extract
4 large eggs
3 cups flour, sifted

1 teaspoon salt
1 teaspoon cream of tartar
½ teaspoon baking soda
1 cup strawberry jam
½ cup sour cream
1 cup pecans, chopped

Preheat oven to 350° F. Cream together butter, sugar, vanilla extract and lemon extract until fluffy. Add eggs one at a time, beating well after each addition. Sift together the dry ingredients. Combine jam and sour cream. Add jam mixture alternately with dry ingredients to creamed mixture, beating until well combined. Stir in pecans. Pour into greased and floured loaf pan. Bake at 350° F for 50 minutes. Yield: 12 servings.

SOUR CREAM TWISTS

3¼ cups flour
1½ teaspoons salt
1 cup butter
2 eggs, beaten
½ cup sour cream

3 teaspoons vanilla extract
1 package yeast, softened in
    ¼ cup lukewarm water
1½ cups sugar

Sift flour and salt together in mixing bowl; cut in butter until particles are small. Blend in eggs, sour cream, 1 teaspoon vanilla extract and the softened yeast. Cover and chill at least 2 hours. Combine sugar and 2 teaspoons vanilla extract. Roll out half the dough on a board which has been sprinkled with vanilla sugar. Fold one end of dough over the center; fold other end to make three layers. Turn ¼ way around and repeat, rolling and folding twice. Sprinkle board and dough with vanilla sugar as needed. Roll out the dough about ¼ inch thick; cut into strips. Twist each strip 2 or 3 times. Place on ungreased baking sheet. Repeat process with remaining dough. Bake at 350° F for 15 minutes. Remove immediately from pan. Yield: 6 dozen.

DANISH BREAKFAST TREAT

½ cup butter
1 cup sugar
2 egg yolks
2 cups plain flour

1 (18 ounce) jar orange
    marmalade or apricot
    preserves
¾ cup chopped pecans

Cream together the butter and sugar. Add egg yolks. Add flour and mix with fork until pastry consistency. Set aside ¼ cup of this mixture. Press the remainder of this mixture into bottom and sides (½″) of 10 × 15 cookie sheet. Spread marmalade or preserves over this. Sprinkle with chopped nuts. Sprinkle the ¼ cup pastry mix over nuts. Bake in 325° F oven 30 minutes, until pastry is *slightly* brown. Let cool 5-10 minutes and cut into squares. Cut into squares when cool but not cold. May be frozen. Yield: 5 dozen.

"Good for brunch, morning coffee or afternoon tea."

APRICOT-CHEESE PASTRIES

1 cup margarine, softened
8 ounces cream cheese,
    softened
2 cups flour

1 teaspoon salt
apricot preserves
1 egg, well beaten
granulated sugar

Mix margarine and cream cheese well. Add flour and salt, mix well and chill. Roll out chilled dough. Cut in circles. Place small amount of preserves in center. Brush edges with beaten egg. Make crescents and seal with fork. Brush top with egg and sprinkle with sugar. Bake at 400° F until lightly brown. Yield: 6 dozen.

"Freezes well."

CHEESE KUCHEN

DOUGH:

1 package yeast
1/4 cup lukewarm water
1/4 cup milk
1/4 cup sugar

1/2 teaspoon salt
1 egg
1/4 cup shortening
2 1/4 cups flour

CHEESE FILLING:

2 (8 ounce) packages cream
    cheese

2 eggs
1/2 cup sugar

TOPPING:

1 tablespoon cinnamon

1/2 cup sugar

Dissolve yeast in warm water. Scald milk. Add sugar and salt to milk and cool to lukewarm. Stir in yeast mixture. Blend in egg and shortening. Mix in flour in 2 additions. Turn dough out onto a lightly floured board. Knead dough until smooth and elastic and does not stick to board. Place in lightly greased bowl. Cover and let rise until double in bulk. Punch down and let rise again until almost double in bulk. Divide dough in half. Heat oven to 350° F. Press each piece into a 9 inch round cake pan, bringing dough up the sides of pan to form an edge. Mix together cream cheese, eggs and 1/2 cup sugar. Divide the mixture and spread onto dough. Sprinkle with mixture of sugar and cinnamon. Bake for 20 to 25 minutes or until crust is brown and filling set. May be frozen. Yield: 6 to 8 servings.

BREAD OF BARBADOS

⅓ cup chopped blanched
   almonds
1 cup flour
¾ cup fine graham cracker
   crumbs
2 tablespoons ground baking
   chocolate

2 teaspoons baking powder
1 teaspoon baking soda
½ teaspoon salt
⅓ cup butter
⅔ cup sugar
2 eggs
1 cup mashed ripe bananas

Combine almonds with flour, graham cracker crumbs, chocolate, baking powder, soda and salt. Mix well. Cream butter with sugar until fluffy. Beat in the eggs, one at a time and then beat in the mashed bananas. Beat until smooth. Stir in the almond mixture. Spoon into well greased 9 × 5-inch loaf pan. Bake at 350° F for 1 hour or until well done. Turn out onto wire rack to cool. Cool before slicing. To serve, cut thin slices. Spread, if you wish, with soft butter or cream cheese. Yield: 12 to 14 servings.

"Never before has banana bread tasted so good!"

BANANA NUT BREAD

2 cups sugar
½ cup shortening
2 eggs
3 cups flour
1½ teaspoons soda
8 to 10 tablespoons
   buttermilk

3 ripe bananas, well mashed
½ cup chopped nuts
pinch of salt
1 teaspoon vanilla extract

Preheat oven to 300° F. Cream sugar and shortening. Add eggs, then beat until fluffy. Gradually add flour. Add soda to buttermilk. Add buttermilk to sugar-flour mixture. Mash bananas thoroughly before adding to the batter. Stir in nuts, salt and vanilla. Bake at 300° F for approximately 1 hour in greased and floured loaf pans. Yield: 2 loaves.

SPICED FRENCH BREAD

½ cup butter
2 tablespoons oil
½ teaspoon powdered
  mustard
½ teaspoon paprika
½ teaspoon Italian herb
  seasoning
½ teaspoon Worcestershire
  sauce

½ teaspoon onion juice
½ teaspoon garlic juice
2 to 3 drops Tabasco sauce
2 tablespoons butter
1 loaf French bread
Parmesan cheese

Preheat oven to 375° F. Melt butter. Turn off heat. Combine spices with melted butter. Do not brown. Butter cookie sheet with 2 tablespoons butter. Cut French bread into 2″ slices. Dip one side in spice mixture. Lay undipped side of each slice on the buttered cookie sheet. Sprinkle Parmesan cheese on top. Bake at 375° F for 8 to 15 minutes, until golden brown. Yield: 1 large loaf.

"An easy accompaniment to quick supper."

OLD FASHIONED PANCAKES

2 cups flour
2 tablespoons sugar
6 teaspoons baking powder
1 teaspoon salt

2 tablespoons margarine,
  melted
2 eggs, well beaten
2 cups milk

Mix dry ingredients. Blend in melted margarine, eggs, then add milk. Have griddle slightly greased and very hot. Spoon mixture to make medium sized pancakes. (Let brown nicely on one side before turning.) Yield: 12 medium size pancakes.

COTTAGE CHEESE PANCAKES

3 eggs
1 cup cottage cheese

2 heaping tablespoons flour
2 tablespoons oil

Mix all ingredients. Cook on a griddle until lightly browned on each side. NOTE: Make pancakes smaller than usual as they will tear when turned if too large. These are good with apricot or strawberry preserves. Yield: 12 small pancakes.

A little sugar in pancakes or waffle batter helps make them brown more quickly.

FLUFFY WAFFLES

2 eggs, separated
¾ cup plus 2 tablespoons
   milk
2 teaspoons cooking oil

2 teaspoons sugar
1 cup flour
½ teaspoon salt
2 tablespoons baking powder

Combine egg yolks, milk and oil. Beat egg whites and fold in milk mixture. Add dry ingredients and beat until smooth. Cook on ungreased griddle (or seasoned waffle iron). Yield: 2 servings.

FLAT BREAD WAFERS

2 cups flour
½ cup yellow cornmeal
½ teaspoon salt

¼ cup butter, softened
⅔ cup warm water

Combine flour, cornmeal, and salt. Cut in butter until mixture is crumbly. Add water, mixing until dry ingredients are moistened. Shape dough into ¾ inch balls. Place 4 inches apart on ungreased cookie sheets. Cover with wax paper and roll with a rolling pin into paper thin rounds. Remove wax paper. Bake at 375° F for 5 to 7 minutes or until lightly browned. Cool and store in tightly covered container. Yield: 85 wafers.

"Serve with cheeses, dips and soup."

PITA TOASTS

¾ cup butter
2 tablespoons minced parsley
1 tablespoon snipped chives
1 tablespoon lemon juice

1 large clove garlic, minced
salt and pepper to taste
6 pita loaves, horizontally
   halved

In a bowl, cream together first 6 ingredients. Halve pita loaves horizontally, separating each half into 2 pieces. Spread the inside of each piece with some of the butter mixture. Arrange the pita on a baking sheet in one layer and bake it in a 250° F oven for 40 to 45 minutes. You may divide them again if you want smaller pieces. Great with most cold and hot soups. Yield: 12 toast pieces

Cheese and Eggs

Cottage cheese was made by the thrifty housewife of yester-year and other cheese was available, though judging by the recipes it was limited to yellow cheese. Cheese straws were popular then as now and so was macaroni and cheese. A turn of the century housewife would look with amazement at the row after row of cheeses, domestic and imported, offered now in supermarkets and specialty shops. Deviled eggs have for many years been popular picnic fare and also find their place on the cocktail buffet table. An egg offers a lot of nutrition in a small package and helps stretch the food dollar. Eggs can be served in many ways and are a mainstay of the brunch, an informal entertainment growing in popularity. A dairy product seldom seen now is clabber, which in a way can be compared to yogurt, but when made fresh on the farm was often served with cream, sugar and nutmeg as a supper dish.

Cheese and Eggs

TOMATO CHEESE PUFFS

6 large tomatoes
½ teaspoon salt
1 cup milk
1 cup soft bread crumbs

1 cup shredded Cheddar
  cheese
1 tablespoon butter
3 eggs, separated

Cut off top of each tomato. Scoop out pulp, leaving shells intact. Pulp may be saved for another recipe. Sprinkle cavity with salt and drain by inverting tomato on paper towel. Combine milk, bread crumbs, cheese and butter in heavy saucepan. Cook over medium heat and stir constantly. Let cheese melt and have mixture thoroughly heated. Beat egg yolks until thick and lemon colored. Gradually stir about ¼ of the hot mixture into yolk; add to remaining hot mixture. Stir constantly. Beat egg whites until stiff peaks form; fold into yolk mixture. Spoon into tomato shells. Place in greased baking dish, bake at 350° F for 35 to 40 minutes until puffed and lightly browned. Serve immediately. Yield: 6 servings.

QUICK CHEESE LAYER BAKE

12 slices bread
1½ cups shredded Cheddar
  cheese
4 eggs, beaten
2½ cups milk

½ teaspoon dry or prepared
  mustard
1 tablespoon minced onion
⅛ teaspoon pepper
1 teaspoon salt

Remove crusts from bread. Arrange 6 bread slices in a greased 12 × 8 × 2 baking dish. Cover bread with sliced cheese, then cover with remaining bread. Beat eggs and add milk and remaining ingredients. Blend. Pour over bread and let stand one hour. Bake in 325° F oven for about 50 minutes. Serve at once. Yield: 6 to 8 servings.

Keep a cloth moistened with vinegar around cheese to keep it fresh.

110

UNSINKABLE CHEESE SOUFFLÉ

2 tablespoons butter
3 tablespoons flour
1 cup scalded milk
1 teaspoon salt
1/8 teaspoon cayenne pepper

1/2 cup sharp Cheddar cheese,
  grated
3 egg yolks, beaten
3 egg whites

Melt butter in 2-quart saucepan; add flour and mix well. Add scalded milk, salt and cayenne pepper; cook until thick over medium heat, stirring constantly. Add cheese gradually and stir until melted. Add egg yolks; mix well. Remove cheese mixture from heat and fold into egg whites, which have been beaten stiff, in a 2-quart casserole. Set the casserole in a shallow pan of water and place in middle of oven. Bake at 375° F for about 35 minutes, until golden on top, but not brown. Yield: 4 servings.

CHEESE FONDUE

1 clove garlic
1/2 pound Swiss cheese
1/2 pound Gruyère cheese
3 tablespoons flour
2 cups dry white wine
1 tablespoon lemon juice

dash pepper
dash nutmeg
1/8 teaspoon salt
2 loaves French or Italian
  bread

Rub inside surface of fondue pot with garlic. Discard clove. Toss grated cheese with flour. Pour wine into fondue pot. Set over low flame. When it begins to bubble, stir in lemon juice and handfuls of cheese, stirring constantly. Stir in spices and serve at once with bread torn or cut into cubes. Yield: 10 servings.

CHEESE AND HAM PIE

1/2 cup mayonnaise
1/2 cup milk
2 eggs
1 tablespoon cornstarch or 2
  tablespoons flour
1 1/2 cups cubed ham

3/4 cup grated Cheddar
  cheese
3/4 cup grated Swiss cheese
1 (9 inch) deep dish pastry
  shell

Preheat oven to 350° F. Mix all ingredients and pour into pastry shell. Bake for 35 to 40 minutes. Yield: 6 to 8 servings.

SPINACH CHEESE PIE

CRUST:

1 cup Bisquick Baking mix
1/4 cup milk

2 eggs
1/4 cup finely chopped onion

Combine baking mix, milk, eggs and onion. Beat 20 strokes. Spread in greased 10-inch pie pan.

FILLING:

1 (10 ounce) package frozen
  chopped spinach, thawed
  and drained
1/2 cup grated Parmesan
  cheese
4 ounces Monterey Jack
  cheese, cut into 1/2 inch
  cubes

1 (12 ounce) carton creamed
  cottage cheese
1/2 teaspoon salt
2 cloves garlic, crushed
2 eggs

Mix all ingredients; spoon evenly over crust. Bake at 375° F for 30 minutes. Let stand for 5 minutes before cutting. Yield: 6 servings.

Brush your grater with a small amount of oil before grating cheese for a faster clean up.

HAM AND BROCCOLI STRATA

12 slices white bread, crusts
  removed
1 (10 ounce) package frozen
  chopped broccoli, cooked
  and drained
2 cups diced cooked ham
6 eggs, slightly beaten

3 1/2 cups milk
1 tablespoon grated onion
1/4 teaspoon dry mustard
3 cups grated Cheddar
  cheese
parsley sprigs
2 hard-boiled eggs, sliced

Cut bread into small cubes. Layer bread cubes, broccoli and ham in 2-quart casserole. Combine eggs, milk, onion, mustard and cheese. Stir well, pour over casserole. Cover and refrigerate 24 hours. Bake uncovered at 325° F for 55 to 60 minutes. Garnish with parsley and hard-boiled eggs. Yield: 6 to 8 servings.

BAKED NOODLES

1 large package thin noodles
2 cups creamy cottage cheese
2 garlic cloves, finely cut
1 medium onion, finely cut
2 tablespoons Worcestershire
   sauce

dash of Tabasco
salt to taste
sour cream, optional
Parmesan cheese, grated
   (optional)

Cook noodles in salted water about 10 minutes; drain. Mix other ingredients and add to noodles. Put in greased baking dish; bake 45 minutes or until brown and crusty on top at 350° F. Serve piping hot. May top with sour cream and/or grated Parmesan.

To avoid the green ring around the center of the hard boiled egg, when cooked, pour off the hot water and put them in cold water to stop the eggs from continuing to cook.

"THE" BRUNCH CASSEROLE

6 hard-cooked eggs, sliced
salt and pepper to taste
1 pound hot sausage, bulk
   type

1½ cups sour cream
1½ cups grated Cheddar
   cheese

Place eggs in a buttered casserole. Season with salt and pepper. Brown sausage in skillet. Drain and sprinkle over eggs. Season. Pour sour cream over sausage; sprinkle cheese over casserole. Cook at 350° F for 25 minutes. Yield: 6 servings.

To shred cheese easier, freeze the cheese for 15 minutes.

When peeling hard boiled eggs, start at the large end. They peel much easier. Pour the hot water off the eggs immediately, shake the pan vigorously, until all are well cracked, and then pour cold water on them. The eggs just sort of scoot out of the shells when the pan is filled with cold water.

BLINTZ CASSEROLE

FILLING:

2 pounds Ricotta cheese
2 eggs
¼ cup sugar
⅛ teaspoon salt

1 lemon, juiced or ¼ cup
    lemon juice
8 ounces cream cheese,
    softened

Place all ingredients for filling in mixer and blend well. Set aside.

BATTER:

½ pound butter, melted
½ cup sugar
2 eggs
1 cup sifted flour

3 teaspoons baking powder
⅛ teaspoon salt
¼ cup milk
1 teaspoon vanilla extract

Mix batter ingredients by hand and spoon ½ batter into two greased 9-inch pie pans. Top this with filling, spreading, not mixing with batter. Spread remaining batter over filling. Bake at 300° F for 1½ hours. Cut in wedges and serve with fresh fruit and grilled Canadian bacon. Yield: 12 servings.

BAKED EGGS

6 teaspoons butter
6 eggs
6 teaspoons grated Cheddar
    cheese
6 teaspoons cooked and
    crumbled bacon
6 teaspoons fresh minced
    parsley

salt
pepper
Worcestershire sauce
paprika
Tabasco

Using a 6-cup muffin tin, place 1 teaspoon butter in each muffin cup. Gently break egg into each cup and sprinkle with 1 teaspoon cheese, 1 teaspoon bacon and 1 teaspoon parsley. Add salt, pepper, Worcestershire sauce, paprika and Tabasco to taste. Bake at 350° F for 15 to 20 minutes or until eggs are done to desired consistency. Yield: 4 to 6 servings.

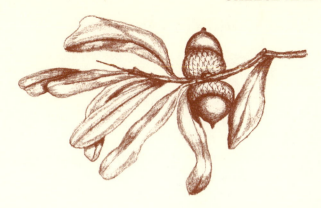

When boiling eggs, put some of the outer skin from onions in the water. The skins will color the shells and you will know which eggs have been cooked when put in the refrigerator.

SCRAMBLED EGG CASSEROLE

*1 cup cubed ham or
    Canadian bacon
¼ cup chopped green onion
3 tablespoons butter
1 dozen eggs, beaten*

*1 (4 ounce) can sliced
    mushrooms, drained
¼ cup melted butter
2¼ cups soft bread crumbs
⅛ teaspoon paprika*

Sauté ham and green onion in 3 tablespoons butter in large skillet until onion is tender. Add eggs and cook over medium-high heat, stirring to form large, soft curds. When eggs are set, stir in mushrooms and CHEESE SAUCE. Spoon eggs into greased 13 × 9 × 2 baking pan. Combine melted butter and crumbs, mixing well; spread evenly over egg mixture. Sprinkle with paprika. Cover and chill overnight. Uncover and bake at 350° F for 30 minutes.

CHEESE SAUCE:

*2 tablespoons butter
2½ tablespoons flour
2 cups milk
½ teaspoon salt*

*⅛ teaspoon pepper
1 cup shredded American
    cheese*

Melt butter in heavy saucepan over low heat; blend in flour and cook 1 minute. Gradually add milk; cook over medium heat until thickened, stirring constantly. Add salt, pepper and cheese and continue stirring until cheese melts and mixture is smooth. Yield: 8 to 10 servings.

SOUTHERN EGG CASSEROLE

8 eggs, hard-cooked
1/4 cup melted butter
1/2 teaspoon Worcestershire
   sauce
1/4 teaspoon prepared
   mustard
1 teaspoon chopped parsley
1 teaspoon chopped chives
1/3 cup chopped ham

3 tablespoons butter
3 tablespoons plain flour
1 cup chicken broth
3/4 cup milk
salt
pepper
1 cup grated American
   cheese

Cut eggs lengthwise and mash yolks. Mix yolks with melted butter, Worcestershire sauce, mustard, parsley, chives and ham. Fill whites with this mixture. Arrange in a greased 1½ to 2-quart baking dish. Make cream sauce with butter, flour, chicken broth, milk, salt and pepper. Pour sauce over eggs. Sprinkle with cheese. Bake for 20 minutes at 350° F. Yield: 6 to 8 servings.

VARIATIONS:

Line casserole with asparagus or ham. Add mushrooms to cream sauce.

CREAMY EGG CASSEROLE

6 slices bacon
2 large onions, thinly sliced
2 tablespoons butter or
   margarine
6 hard cooked eggs, sliced
3/4 cup mayonnaise

1/4 cup milk
3 tablespoons Parmesan
   cheese, grated
1 teaspoon prepared mustard
1/4 teaspoon salt
1/2 teaspoon cayenne pepper

Fry bacon; drain and crumble. Sauté onions in butter. Layer onions and eggs in baking dish. Stir together last 6 ingredients; spread on top. Broil 3 minutes or until brown and bubbly. Top with crumbled bacon and serve. Yield: 3 to 4 servings.

"A great brunch dish. Broiled tomatoes go well with this."

QUICHE LORRAINE

1 deep dish pastry shell
10 slices bacon
6 ounces Gruyere cheese
4 eggs
1½ tablespoons flour
⅛ teaspoon celery salt

½ teaspoon salt
1 teaspoon nutmeg
dash cayenne pepper
½ teaspoon minced onion
2 cups half and half
1½ tablespoons melted butter

Line 9 inch glass pie plate with crust, well built up around edges. Partially bake crust 10 minutes to avoid sogginess. Fry bacon; drain and crumble. Shred cheese and sprinkle, with ¾ of the bacon, over crust. Beat eggs with flour, salts, nutmeg and cayenne. Add onion, cream and butter. Blend. Pour into pastry shell and top with remaining bacon. Bake in 350° F. oven for 50 to 60 minutes until custard is set and browned. Let quiche set for 5 to 10 minutes before serving. Serve in pie-shaped wedges.

Freezes well. Reduce baking time 10 minutes, cool, wrap and freeze. To bake, unwrap and cook frozen in 325° F oven for 40 to 50 minutes. Yield: 6 to 8 servings.

RIPE OLIVE QUICHE

12 slices bacon
1 (9 inch) pastry shell
4 ounces Swiss cheese
3 ounces Gruyère cheese
½ package dry onion soup
    mix

½ cup ripe olives, chopped
2 cups milk
4 eggs
½ cup chopped parsley

Fry bacon; drain and crumble. Put into pastry shell. Grate cheeses and put on top of bacon. Sprinkle onion soup mix over bacon and cheeses and add chopped olives. Beat together the milk and eggs; pour over all. Cover top with parsley. Bake for 10 minutes at 450° F and continue baking for 30 minutes at 350° F. Cool 5 to 10 minutes. Yield: 6 servings.

AVOCADO AND ARTICHOKE QUICHE

1 pastry shell
1 ripe avocado
2-3 tablespoons lemon juice
6-8 canned artichoke hearts
3 eggs
1 cup heavy cream

1/4 teaspoon salt
1/4 teaspoon pepper
1/2 cup grated Gruyère or
   Swiss cheese
fresh parsley, chopped

Preheat oven to 375° F. Bake shell 8 minutes. Peel avocado, cut into slices, discard the pit. Sprinkle with lemon juice. Cut artichoke hearts into quarters. Lightly beat eggs with cream, salt and pepper. Add the avocado and artichoke hearts. Pour the mixture into the pastry shell and sprinkle with cheese. Bake for 25 to 30 minutes until quiche is set, puffed and browned. Garnish with sliced avocado and chopped parsley. Yield: 6 to 8 servings.

CRUSTLESS CARROT QUICHE

2 cups finely shredded
   carrots
6 eggs
1 1/4 cups milk
1 tablespoon instant minced
   onion

1/2 teaspoon salt
1/4 teaspoon ground ginger
1/8 teaspoon pepper
1 cup shredded Cheddar
   cheese

In medium saucepan heat 1 inch water to boiling. Add carrots. Cover and cook until tender, about 5 minutes. Drain well in strainer or colander, pressing out water. Meanwhile, beat together eggs, milk, onion, salt, ginger and pepper until blended. Stir in carrots and cheese. Pour into buttered 10-inch quiche dish or pie plate. Set dish or plate in large baking pan on oven rack. Pour very hot water into baking pan to within 1/2 inch of top of custard. Bake in preheated 350° F oven until knife inserted near center comes out clean, 30 to 35 minutes. Let stand 5 minutes before serving. Yield: 6 servings.

To prevent spills when baking quiche, pour 1/2 of the liquid mixture into pie shell, let bake for 10 minutes. Then pour in the remaining mixture and continue baking until firm.

FRESH APPLE QUICHE

½ pound bulk sausage
½ cup chopped onion
¼ teaspoon thyme
2 Red Delicious apples,
    pared, cored and cut into
    ½-inch cubes
1 tablespoon fresh lemon
    juice

1 tablespoon sugar
½ cup shredded Cheddar
    cheese
4 eggs, beaten
2 cups light cream or milk
pastry for 1 single crust deep
    dish pie

In large skillet cook sausage, onion and thyme until sausage is browned and onion is tender, about 10 minutes. Remove from heat. Drain off excess fat. In a bowl, toss apples with lemon juice and sugar. Add prepared sausage mixture, Cheddar cheese, eggs and cream or milk; mix well. Pour into pie shell. Bake at 350° F for 40 to 45 minutes or until custard is set. Let stand 10 minutes. May be frozen before cooking. Yield: 6 servings.

FLORENTINE CRÊPE FILLING

1 cup grated Swiss cheese
3 cups Medium White Sauce
    (see recipe)
1 tablespoon minced green
    onion

2 tablespoons butter
1½ cups chopped spinach
¼ teaspoon salt
8 ounces cream cheese
1 egg

Add Swiss cheese to white sauce. Set aside. Cook onion in butter for 1 minute. Stir in spinach and salt. Combine cream cheese and egg. Stir 2 cups Swiss cheese sauce and cream cheese mixture into spinach. Fill crepes with spinach mixture. Place crepes in buttered baking dish. Cover with remaining Swiss cheese sauce. Place in the upper third of oven. Bake at 350° F until heated through and lightly browned on top. 4 to 6 servings.

VARIATION:

Add 1 cup minced, sautéed mushrooms to spinach mixture.

119

BASIC CRÊPE RECIPE

4 eggs
1 cup flour
½ cup milk

½ cup chicken stock
½ teaspoon salt
2 tablespoons melted butter

Measure all ingredients, except flour, into a large mixing bowl; beat with electric mixer on medium speed, gradually adding flour until all ingredients are combined. Make crepes on crepe maker or in frying pan. May be made ahead and frozen. (Freezes beautifully for 1 month or more). Yield: 4 to 6 servings.

CRÊPES CAMPAGNE

BASIC CRÊPE RECIPE

FILLING:

4 tablespoons butter or
   margarine
4 tablespoons flour
½ teaspoon salt
dash of white pepper
1 teaspoon dry mustard
1 tablespoon Worcestershire
   sauce
2 cups milk

½ cup chopped green pepper
½ cup chopped onion
½ cup sliced fresh
   mushrooms
1 tablespoon butter
2 cups chopped thinly sliced
   ham
4 hard-cooked eggs, chopped
1 cup grated Swiss cheese

Melt butter in saucepan over low heat. Blend in flour, salt, white pepper, dry mustard and Worcestershire sauce. Add milk and cook, stirring constantly until mixture thickens and bubbles. In a small skillet, sauté the green pepper, onion and mushrooms in 1 tablespoon of butter. Stir sautéed vegetables, ham, chopped eggs and Swiss cheese into the white sauce. Set aside. Fill each crepe with about ¼ cup of filling, roll it and place it, seam down, in a greased baking dish. Stack crepes in about three layers. Thin the remaining sauce with some milk and pour over the entire dish. Cover with foil and bake 20 minutes; uncover and brown for 10 minutes. Yield: 4 to 6 servings.

CHICKEN CRÊPE FILLING

1½ tablespoons minced green
  onion
2 tablespoons butter
1¼ cups diced, cooked
  chicken
⅓ cup dry white wine

salt and pepper to taste
2 cups Medium White Sauce
  (see recipe)
½ cup grated Swiss cheese
1 egg yolk
¼ cup whipping cream

Cook onion in butter for 1 minute. Stir in chicken. Add wine. Simmer for 2 minutes, covered. Uncover, boil until liquid has evaporated. Salt and pepper to taste. Stir 1 cup white sauce, ¼ cup cheese, egg yolk and whipping cream into chicken mixture. Fill crepe with chicken filling; cover with remaining white sauce, sprinkle with remaining cheese. Yield: about 2 cups.

SHRIMP AND CRABMEAT CRÊPE

BASIC CRÊPE RECIPE

FILLING:

3 tablespoons butter
3 tablespoons flour
1 cup chicken bouillon
½ cup half and half
1 egg yolk
1 tablespoon sherry

1 cup fresh raw shrimp,
  cleaned and deveined
1 cup fresh crabmeat
1 cup fresh mushrooms,
  sliced and lightly sautéed
  in butter
paprika

After preparing basic crepe recipe, prepare filling by melting butter over low heat in a 1-quart saucepan. Add flour and stir until smooth and bubbly. Remove from heat. Add bouillon and half and half. Return to heat. Heat mixture, stirring constantly. Add small amount of heated mixture to egg yolk and combine. Pour into bouillon mixture, continuing to stir until thickened. Transfer to double boiler and add sherry. Add shrimp and heat until shrimp is almost cooked. Add crabmeat and mushrooms. Spoon onto crepes and fold. Top with additional mixture and sprinkle with paprika. Yield: 4 large servings.

R.D.

Poultry

While fried chicken was the earlier piece de resistance of picnics and Sunday dinners, the turkey reigned supreme on Thanksgiving and Christmas. The table was covered with a linen damask cloth and set with linen damask napkins. A crystal bowl centered the table and held roses, or at Christmas, white narcissi. China, crystal and silver made the table sparkle with beauty. The turkey was served with dressing, rice, vegetables in season, sweet potato soufflé, peach pickle, cranberry sauce, biscuits or rolls, ambrosia and cake. Now of course, turkey is available the year round and is no longer just a holiday bird. It can be bought whole or the breast alone. Chicken is one of the most versatile meats and can be served in a variety of ways. Some outstanding recipes have been contributed for this section.

Poultry

SOUTHERN FRIED CHICKEN

1 chicken, cut up
salt
black pepper, freshly ground

1 egg, beaten
1 cup flour
3 cups vegetable shortening

The trick to true Southern fried chicken is to fry it quickly over medium high heat in a deep, heavy skillet, turning the pieces only once.

Wash the chicken pieces well, and pat dry with paper towels. Sprinkle individual pieces with salt and add pepper to taste. Beat egg and thin with a little water. Dip the chicken in the egg mixture then dredge in flour. Set aside. Melt vegetable shortening in a deep, heavy cast-iron skillet. There should be enough oil to almost cover the chicken. The oil is ready when it just begins to smoke. Drop the chicken pieces into the oil and cook uncovered at medium heat for about 10 minutes on each side. Turn only once. Drain on paper towels. Serve with cream gravy.

CREAM GRAVY

2 tablespoons pan drippings
  (from frying chicken)
2 tablespoons flour

1 cup milk or cream
salt and pepper to taste

After frying chicken, pour all but 2 tablespoons of oil from skillet. Add the flour and stir over medium heat scraping the pan until the mixture is blended and beginning to brown. Slowly, add the milk or cream and stir until thickened. Add salt and pepper to taste. Pour over fried chicken or serve separately. Yield: 1 cup.

CHICKEN LIVER SAUTÉ WITH MUSHROOMS

4 slices bacon, minced
18 chicken livers
3 tablespoons flour
salt and pepper
½ cup minced onion
12 mushrooms, sliced

1 pint stock
2 tablespoons cornstarch
4 tablespoons water
2 tablespoons sherry
4 slices bread, toasted

Fry bacon until crisp. Remove bacon from pan. Roll the livers in flour and salt and pepper. Brown the livers, onions, and mushrooms in the bacon fat. Add the stock and simmer for 15 minutes. Thicken the sauce slightly with cornstarch mixed with water; add bacon and sherry. Serve the livers on thin slices of toast. Yield: 4 servings.

PRESSED CHICKEN

1 large hen, cooked, deboned
2 envelopes unflavored
   gelatin
2 cups chicken stock
1 small bottle Durkee sauce
4 tablespoons mayonnaise

4 tablespoons celery, chopped
   fine
salt to taste
pepper to taste
6 eggs, hard cooked

Separate light and dark meat and grind separately. Dissolve gelatin in hot chicken stock. Add to meat mixtures. Mix next 5 ingredients; add half of this mixture to white meat and half to dark meat. Congeal white mixture, then cut ends off hard cooked eggs and place end to end, then pour dark mixture over all and congeal. Yield: 8 servings.

ROQUEFORT CHICKEN

6 half-breasts chicken
1 teaspoon salt
1 teaspoon pepper
2 tablespoons butter

4 ounces Roquefort cheese
1 garlic clove, minced
1 cup sour cream

Season chicken with salt and pepper. Brown in butter. Place in a shallow baking dish. In the skillet in which you have browned the chicken, mix the cheese, garlic and sour cream. Heat and pour over the chicken. Cook in covered dish at 350° F for 1 hour. Yield: 6 servings.

LUM CHICKEN

8-10 large chicken breasts,
  deboned
2 cloves garlic
2-3 eggs, beaten

1 cup flour
salt and pepper
butter
lemon juice

SAUCE:
1 quart whipping cream
3 tablespoons dry mustard

2 tablespoons Worcestershire
  sauce
1 tablespoon paprika

Rub chicken with garlic. Dip in eggs, then flour seasoned with salt and pepper. Pack breasts closely together in a pan and cover liberally with chunks of butter about 1 to 1½ inches apart. Squeeze lemon juice over chicken and put in a slow oven to let butter melt. Mix the sauce ingredients. Pour sauce over chicken, return to oven and cook at 350° F for about 1 hour. Serve with wild rice cooked in chicken broth and mushrooms. Yield: 8 servings.

CHICKEN TROPICAL

1 (3 pound) fryer or your
  choice of chicken pieces
flour, seasoned
½ cup shortening
1 teaspoon salt
1 teaspoon basil
1 cup orange juice

2 tablespoons brown sugar
2 tablespoons cider vinegar
¼ teaspoon nutmeg
½ cup peach juice
1 can small whole potatoes
1-2 cans peach halves

Skin chicken, coat with flour and sauté in shortening until golden. Discard remaining shortening and return chicken to frying pan. Sprinkle with salt. Combine basil, orange juice, brown sugar, vinegar, nutmeg and peach juice (taken from can of peaches) and pour over chicken. Drain potatoes and place in pan with chicken. Cover and cook over medium heat for 25 minutes. Add peaches and cook 5 minutes. Garnish with parsley.

CHICKEN MARENGO

SAUCE:

¼ cup butter
2 celery stalks, chopped
1 carrot, peeled and chopped
1 cup chopped onions
1 strip lean bacon, sliced
1 mushroom, chopped
1 tomato, quartered
sprig parsley

bay leaf
salt and pepper
¼ cup flour
1 (2½ ounce) can tomato
    puree
1 pint chicken stock
1 tablespoon sherry

To make sauce, melt butter and sauté next 9 ingredients until golden brown. Add flour and stir well. Add tomato puree. Remove from heat. Slowly add stock and sherry. Bring to a boil then simmer 1 hour.

3½ to 4 pounds cooked
    chicken sauce

8 ounces mushrooms,
    chopped or sliced

Cut chicken in bite size pieces; place in a 2-quart casserole. Add mushrooms. Cover with sauce. Bake uncovered for 1½ hours at 350° F. Serve with rice. Yield: 6 to 8 servings.

CHICKEN CONTINENTAL

4 large chicken breasts
½ to ¾ cup water
2 teaspoons salt
2 packages frozen broccoli
1 recipe Hollandaise sauce
    (see recipe)

1 recipe rich Cream Sauce (see
    recipe)
¾ cup finely chopped pecans
¼ cup butter
½ cup Parmesan cheese,
    grated

Cook chicken breasts and 1 teaspoon salt in water. When chicken is tender, remove from liquid. Cool. Slice each breast in several pieces. Cook broccoli with 1 teaspoon salt. Drain. Place broccoli stalks in bottom of greased baking dish. Arrange chicken slices over the broccoli and cover with the Hollandaise sauce. Spread the cream sauce over the Hollandaise sauce. Brown the pecans in the butter or margarine and sprinkle over top of white sauce. Place in oven. Bake at 400° F for 20 to 25 minutes. Remove from oven, sprinkle with Parmesan cheese. Place under broiler until top is brown, about 5 minutes. Yield: 8 servings.

127

CHICKEN CURRY

1 (2½ pound) fryer or
    chicken breasts
celery tops
parsley sprigs
4 tablespoons butter
1 onion, chopped
2 stalks celery, chopped
1 tart apple, peeled and
    diced

2 tablespoons curry powder
2½ tablespoons flour
1¼ cups chicken broth
salt and pepper to taste
½ cup golden raisins
1 tablespoon lime juice
1 cup half and half
2 tablespoons chopped
    chutney

To cook chicken, cover with water, add salt, celery tops and few sprigs parsley. Bring to boil, reduce heat, cover and simmer about 1 hour or until tender. Strain broth and reserve. Remove chicken from bones and chop to measure 2 cups. Melt butter in skillet and sauté onion, celery and apple until soft. Add curry powder and flour and mix well. Slowly add chicken broth and stir until blended. Check seasonings. Add raisins and lime juice, then cream and continue to stir over low heat until sauce is smooth and thickened. Add chicken and chutney. Serve hot over cooked rice with a variety of condiments; or may be refrigerated and reheated for next day.

CONDIMENTS
Chutney
Chopped peanuts
Crumbled cooked bacon
Chopped tomatoes

Chopped banana
Sliced black olives
Grated coconut
Chopped hard-cooked eggs

Yield: 4 to 6 servings.

CHICKEN BREAST FILLETS WITH LEMON SAUCE

3 whole chicken breasts,
*   halved and deboned*
1 tablespoon vegetable oil
4 tablespoons butter

⅓ cup lemon juice
½ cup dry white wine
3 tablespoons chopped
*   parsley*

Slice each chicken breast into three fillets; heat oil and three tablespoons butter. Flour chicken fillets lightly and sauté over high heat for 30 seconds on each side. (Do not overcook). Remove fillets to platter; add lemon juice, wine, parsley and one tablespoon butter to sauté. Simmer 5 minutes, scraping up the brown bits from the pan, or until sauce has thickened and reduced. Add fillets, turn over once to warm them. Serve with a little sauce and lemon slice. Yield: 4 to 6 servings.

MINCEMEAT GLAZED CHICKEN BREASTS

½ cup margarine
12 whole chicken breasts,
*   deboned*
1½ teaspoons salt
1 teaspoon pepper
1 tablespoon curry powder

2 cups water
2 tablespoons vinegar
1 cup prepared mincemeat
2 tablespoons cornstarch
2 tablespoons water

Heat margarine in skillet over medium heat. Add chicken breasts; brown on both sides. Season with salt and pepper. Sprinkle with curry powder. Place chicken breasts skin side up in large shallow baking dish (about 17 × 12 × 2). Add water, vinegar and mincemeat to skillet drippings. Bring to boil and pour over chicken. Cover and bake at 350° F for 30 minutes. Uncover and bake 30 minutes longer. Blend cornstarch and 2 tablespoons water; stir into pan juice, after removing chicken to platter, stirring until thickened and pour sauce over chicken. Yield: 12 to 24 servings.

"This is an award winning recipe."

CHICKEN HEARTS OF PALM

8 half chicken breasts,
    skinned and deboned
8 hearts of palm
½ cup butter, softened

salt and white pepper
Hollandaise Sauce
parsley, chopped

Pound chicken breasts until very thin. Wrap each around a heart of palm. Spread with butter and sprinkle with salt and pepper. Place in a shallow baking dish and bake for 30 to 40 minutes at 350° F. Serve with Hollandaise Sauce and sprinkle with parsley. Yield: 4 to 6 servings.

CALIFORNIA STUFFED CHICKEN BREASTS

1 bunch small green onions
8 ounces cream cheese,
    softened
4 whole chicken breasts,
    skinned and deboned

8 strips bacon
1 can cream of mushroom
    soup

Chop onions, using some green. Mix well with cream cheese. Stuff chicken breast with mixture and encase with bacon. Secure with picks. Bake at 350° F for 1 hour. Heat soup and pour over chicken. Yield: 8 servings.

CHINESE CHICKEN

1 chicken, cut up
1 clove garlic, crushed
1 small piece fresh ginger,
    finely chopped
3 tablespoons oil

½ pound mushrooms, sliced
4 tablespoons sherry
4 tablespoons soy sauce
½ teaspoon salt

Brown chicken, garlic and ginger in oil. Add mushrooms, cover and cook 5 minutes. Add sherry, soy sauce, and salt. Cover and cook gently 30 to 35 minutes. Remove cover and cook until all liquid has evaporated before serving. Yield: 3 to 4 servings.

ANN COSTA'S CHICKEN RATATOUILLE

¼ cup Mazola corn oil
2 whole broiler-fryer chicken
    breasts, skinned, boned,
    and cut into 1-inch pieces
2 small zucchini squash,
    unpared and sliced thin
1 small eggplant, peeled and
    cut into 1-inch cubes
1 large onion, thinly sliced
1 medium green pepper,
    seeded and cut into
    1-inch pieces

½ pound mushrooms, sliced
1 (16 ounce) can tomato
    wedges
2 teaspoons garlic salt
1 teaspoon Accent flavor
    enhancer
1 teaspoon dried sweet basil,
    crushed
1 teaspoon dried parsley
½ teaspoon black pepper

Heat corn oil in large frying pan. Add chicken and sauté about 2 minutes on each side. Add zucchini, eggplant, onion, green pepper and mushrooms. Cook, stirring occasionally about 15 minutes or until tender. Add tomatoes with juice, stirring carefully. Add garlic salt, flavor enhancer, basil, parsley, and pepper. Simmer about 5 minutes or until fork can be inserted in chicken with ease. Serve chicken on large platter with mound of rice in center. Yield: 4 servings.

"Winner of the National Chicken Cooking Contest, July, 1977."

CHICKEN AND ARTICHOKES

4 whole chicken breasts,
   deboned and skinned
1 teaspoon salt
½ cup butter
½ cup chopped onion
2½ teaspoons paprika
3 tablespoons flour
1 chicken bouillon cube

½ cup water
¾ cup sour cream
1¼ cups white wine
1 (14 ounce) can artichoke
   hearts, drained
5 strips bacon, cooked and
   crumbled
½ cup chopped pecans, toasted

Sprinkle breasts with salt, sauté in butter until golden. Remove from pan and drain. In remaining butter, sauté onion sprinkled with paprika. Stir in flour until smooth; cook 1 minute. Dissolve bouillon cube in water. Gradually add to skillet mixture, stirring until thick. Add sour cream and wine. Stir and heat. Put chicken in a 3-quart casserole and top with artichoke hearts. Cover with sauce. Cover and bake at 350° F for 1 hour. Garnish with bacon and pecans. Yield: 4 servings.

CHICKEN-SHRIMP CASSEROLE

8 whole chicken breasts,
   cooked and cut into large
   cubes
4 pounds shrimp, boiled and
   peeled
3 (14 ounce) cans plain
   artichoke hearts,
   quartered

3 pounds fresh mushrooms,
   sautéed in butter
6 cups medium White Sauce
   (see recipe)
2 tablespoons Worcestershire
   sauce
1 cup sherry or white wine
½ cup Parmesan cheese,
   finely grated

Divide chicken, shrimp, artichokes, and mushrooms equally in two greased three-quart (9″ × 13″) casseroles. Prepare white sauce adding Worcestershire sauce and wine. Pour over casseroles. Top with cheese. Bake uncovered at 375° F for 40 minutes until bubbly. Can be prepared in advance. If refrigerated, allow extra cooking time. Serve with long grain or wild rice. For variation, use as filling for crepes. Yield: 18 to 20 servings.

ROAST CHICKEN

3 pound roasting chicken   *1 small carrot, sliced*
¾ teaspoon salt   *1 small onion, sliced*
2 tablespoons butter

BASTING SAUCE:

2 tablespoons butter, melted
1 tablespoon good cooking oil

Wash and dry chicken. Sprinkle the inside of the chicken with ¼ teaspoon salt and smear with half the butter. Truss the chicken. Rub the chicken with the remaining butter. Place chicken in uncovered roasting pan with breast side up. Add carrot and onion. Place in oven and brown the chicken for 5 minutes; rotate chicken with left side up for 5 minutes; then brown on the right side for 5 minutes, basting after each turn.

Leaving chicken on its side reduce oven to 350° F and continue to baste every 10 minutes with BASTING SAUCE and dripping in pan. Reduce heat if fat is burning. Halfway through cooking time, add ¼ teaspoon salt and turn chicken to its other side. Continue to baste. Fifteen minutes before the end of the estimated roasting time, add ¼ teaspoon salt and turn breast side up; basting.

Chicken is done when the drumstick is tender and will move in its socket and the juice is clear yellow from its vent when the chicken is lifted, or meat thermometer reads 190° F.

Cooking time for an unchilled chicken: 35 to 45 minutes for less than 4 pounds; 30 to 35 minutes per pound for 4 to 5 pounds. If stuffing is used, increase cooking time 10 to 13 minutes.

Before serving, remove trussing strings and let chicken stand for 5 to 10 minutes.

Yield: 4 to 6 servings.

SAUCES FOR ROASTED CHICKEN

BUTTERED SAUCE:

2 tablespoons fat in roasting
  pan
½ tablespoon minced green
  onion

1 cup canned chicken broth
salt and pepper
1-2 tablespoons butter,
  softened

Add onion to fat in roasting pan. Cook slowly for 1 minute. Add broth and cook rapidly until liquid is reduced by half. Stirring constantly, add salt and pepper to taste. Remove from heat and stir in butter. Makes ½ cup sauce.

TARRAGON SAUCE:

½ teaspoon dried tarragon
1 tablespoon fat in roasting
  pan
1 cup canned beef bouillon

1 cup canned chicken broth
1 tablespoon cornstarch
2 tablespoons port
1 tablespoon butter

Sprinkle ½ teaspoon tarragon inside chicken before roasting. Add bouillon and broth to fat in roasting pan. Simmer for 2 minutes; stirring. Blend cornstarch and port. Add cornstarch mixture to pan. Cook until sauce is thickened. Taste. Correct seasoning. Strain and stir in butter. Makes 2⅓ cups sauce.

SHERRY-GINGER SAUCE:

1½ cups chicken broth
2 tablespoons sherry
¼ teaspoon salt

4 teaspoons cornstarch
1 teaspoon soy sauce
½ teaspoon ground pepper

In a small saucepan, combine all ingredients. Cook over medium heat, stirring constantly until mixture thickens and begins to boil. Boil 1 minute longer. Remove from heat and serve. Makes 1⅔ cups sauce.

GARLIC-FRIED CHICKEN

2 (2½ pound) fryers, cut up
1 cup sour cream
2 tablespoons lemon juice
¼ teaspoon Worcestershire
  sauce

½ teaspoon paprika
½ teaspoon garlic
½ teaspoon salt
¼ teaspoon pepper
¼ teaspoon celery salt

Mix above ingredients and pour over chicken. Cover and let stand in refrigerator overnight. When ready to fry, drain, dredge in flour and fry in the usual manner. Yield: 8 servings.

CHICKEN CASSEROLE IN BEER

3-4 pound frying chicken,
    cut up
flour
3 tablespoons butter or
    margarine
1 clove garlic, minced

½ cup minced celery
2 cups beer
2 bay leaves
2 teaspoons parsley
1½ teaspoons salt
½ teaspoon pepper

Roll chicken in flour to coat. Sauté in butter until golden. Transfer to Dutch oven. Add seasonings. Cover and bake at 350° F. for 1½ hours. Serve with juices poured over French or Italian bread. Yield: 6-8 servings.

CREOLE OVEN-FRIED CHICKEN AND RICE

½ cup flour
1½ teaspoons salt
1 teaspoon paprika
¼ teaspoon poultry
    seasoning
¼ teaspoon pepper
2½ to 3 pound fryer, cut up
¼ cup butter, melted
1 cup raw rice
½ cup chopped onion

1 cup chopped celery
¼ to ½ cup chopped green
    pepper
1 clove garlic, crushed
2 tablespoons chopped
    parsley
2½ cups well-seasoned
    chicken broth
2 cups canned tomatoes
salt and pepper to taste

Preheat oven to 350° F. Mix flour, salt, paprika, poultry seasoning and pepper; dip chicken pieces in this mixture to coat well. Place chicken, skin side down, in melted butter in roasting pan. Bake, uncovered, for 25 to 30 minutes, or until lightly browned. Remove chicken from pan. Mix rice, onion, celery, green pepper, garlic and parsley and spread in pan. Cover with chicken pieces, skin side up. Combine chicken broth, tomatoes and seasoning; bring to boil and pour over chicken, to submerge rice completely. Return to oven and bake, uncovered, 40 to 45 minutes, or until chicken is tender, rice is fluffy and most of liquid is absorbed. If necessary, add a bit more broth or hot water during baking to prevent dryness. Yield: 6 servings.

SAVORY CRUST CHICKEN BAKE

CRUST:

½ cup butter, softened
1 cup sour cream
1 egg
1 cup flour
1 teaspoon salt

1 teaspoon baking powder
½ to 1 teaspoon thyme
1 cup shredded Cheddar
   cheese

Cream butter, sour cream and egg. Add flour, salt, baking powder and thyme; blend until combined. Grease 9-inch pie pan; spread batter over bottom and up sides of pan. Spoon FILLING into crust; sprinkle with cheese. Bake at 400° F for 25 to 30 minutes.

FILLING:

2 tablespoons butter
½ cup sliced carrots
½ cup chopped onion
½ cup chopped green pepper
   OR celery

½ cup pimento
2 cups chopped chicken OR
   turkey
½ cup mushrooms
1¼ cups cream of chicken
   soup

Melt butter in skillet. Add vegetables and sauté. Add pimento. Add chicken or turkey, mushrooms and soup.

Yield: 6 to 8 servings.

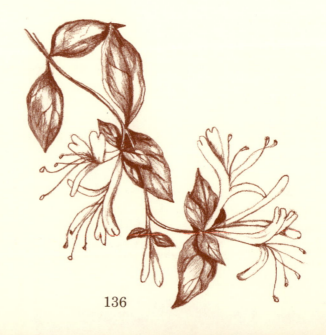

CHICKEN FRICASSEE

1 frying chicken, cut up
10 pearl onions
3 tablespoons butter
1/4 cup flour
1 cup white wine

1 cup chicken stock
1/4 teaspoon thyme
1 bay leaf
salt and pepper to taste
4 ounces mushrooms, sliced

Brown chicken and onions in butter until light brown. Remove from frying pan and set aside. In the drippings, make a roux with the flour. Add wine and stock. Add seasonings. Cook for 1 hour over medium heat. Add mushrooms 15 minutes before serving. Serve with mashed potatoes, noodles or rice. Yield: 4 servings.

The figures below are amounts of chicken to buy for each serving:

Broiling   1/2 of small broiler
Frying   3/4 pound
Roasting   3/4 pound
Stewing   3/4 pound

ROSY CHICKEN STROGANOFF

2 (3 pound) chickens,
    quartered
salt and pepper to taste
1/4 cup butter
1/4 cup oil
1 onion, chopped

2 cloves garlic
2 tablespoons tomato paste
1 teaspoon sugar
2 cups dry white wine
1 cup sour cream (1/2 pint)
2 egg yolks, well beaten

Salt and pepper chicken. Brown in a mixture of butter and oil. Remove chicken, brown onion and garlic. Drain excess oil and return chicken to skillet. Mix tomato paste, sugar and wine; pour over chicken. Cover and simmer for 45 minutes, or until chicken is tender. Remove chicken to a warmed platter. Boil pan drippings only until 1 cup remains. Mix sour cream and egg yolks; stir into pan drippings. Stir until thickened, but do not boil. Pour sauce over chicken. Garnish with parsley. Good with rice or noodles. Yield: 8 servings.

SPINACH-CHICKEN SOUFFLÉ ROLL

SOUFFLÉ:

4 tablespoons butter or
   margarine
½ cup flour
2 cups mulk
½ cup Parmesan cheese,
   grated
½ cup shredded Cheddar
   cheese

¼ teaspoon salt
4 egg yolks, slightly beaten
4 egg whites, room
   temperature
SPINACH-CHICKEN
   FILLING
4 slices Cheddar cheese, cut
   in triangles

In a medium saucepan over moderate heat, melt butter or margarine. Stir in flour. Cook and stir until blended, about 2 minutes. Slowly add milk, stirring constantly with a whisk. Stir over moderately high heat until batter comes to a boil and thickens. Stir in cheeses and salt. The batter will be very thick. Remove from heat. Add a small amount of batter to egg yolks. Mix well and add egg yolk mixture to saucepan. Beat egg whites until stiff but not dry. Gently fold batter into egg whites. Preheat oven to 325° F. Grease jelly-roll pan and line with wax paper, leaving a little extra paper at each end; grease and flour wax paper. Pour batter onto prepared wax paper; spread evenly. Bake in lower third of oven 40 to 45 minutes until golden brown and surface springs back when lightly pressed. Prepare SPINACH-CHICKEN FILLING; set aside. Remove soufflé from oven. Spread SPINACH-CHICKEN FILLING evenly over top of soufflé. Roll up lengthwise using the wax paper to help roll. Roll onto heavy duty foil to help handle. Soufflé may crack. Slide roll seam side down onto greased baking sheet. Preheat oven to 375° F. Cover soufflé roll with foil and reheat 20 minutes or until hot. Remove foil. Overlap triangles of cheese down center of roll. Place under broiler until cheese melts and is lightly browned. Slide a spatula under each end of roll and lift onto a platter. Yield: 8 servings.

(Recipe continued on next page.)

SPINACH-CHICKEN FILLING:

2 tablespoons butter or
  margarine
½ cup chopped onion
¼ pound mushrooms,
  chopped
2 (10 ounce) packages frozen
  chopped spinach, thawed
  and squeezed dry

1 cup diced cooked chicken
1 (3 ounce) package cream
  cheese
⅓ cup sour cream
2 teaspoons Dijon mustard
dash nutmeg
salt and pepper to taste

In a medium saucepan, melt butter or margarine. Sauté onion and mushrooms until tender. Stir in spinach, chicken, cream cheese and sour cream. Cook and stir until cheese is melted. Add mustard, nutmeg, salt and pepper.

CHICKEN ROLL

1 package (of 8) Crescent
  dinner rolls
2 cups chopped, cooked
  chicken
½ cup chopped mushrooms
1 (3 ounce) package cream
  cheese
½ cup water chestnuts, sliced
1 teaspoon lemon pepper

2 tablespoons softened butter
3 tablespoons melted butter
½ cup Pepperidge Farm
  Seasoned Dressing
½ cup finely chopped pecans
1 can cream of mushroom
  soup
1 (8 ounce) carton sour
  cream

Press crescent rolls gently to flatten. Mix chicken, mushrooms, cream cheese, water chestnuts, lemon pepper, and 2 tablespoons soft butter. Put approximately ¼ cup mixture in each roll. Fold to completely cover mixture. Dip rolls in 3 tablespoons melted butter, roll in seasoned dressing mix (crushed fine) then in chopped nuts. Bake 15 to 20 minutes in 375° F oven until lightly brown. Serve topped with mixture of mushroom soup and sour cream. Yield: 8 servings.

Game

    Historians record that in the early days of this section bears were killed throughout the year in the immediate vicinity of Albany. The town was never without venison in season Turkeys were more plentiful and in the winter the residents "fairly reveled in every species of game." A turn of the century cookbook gives these casual directions for broiling birds: "Grease a 'spider' thoroughly, salt birds and season with pepper, place them in cold 'spider,' cover and weight, cook until brown, add water gradually until they are tender, season with Worcestershire sauce." Today's cooks will be thankful to have the more definitive directions in these tested recipes.

DUCK, OYSTER AND SAUSAGE GUMBO

3 large wild ducks, cleaned
2 stalks celery with leaves,
　cut into 2-inch pieces
1 medium onion, sliced
1 tablespoon salt
chicken broth
1 pound hot smoked sausage,
　cut into 1-inch pieces
½ cup vegetable oil
½ cup all-purpose flour

¾ cup finely chopped celery
1 large onion, finely chopped
salt and pepper to taste
6 green onions with tops,
　finely chopped
2 tablespoons finely chopped
　fresh parsley
1 pint oysters, undrained
hot cooked rice
Gumbo filé

Combine first 4 ingredients in large Dutch oven; cover with water, and bring to a boil. Reduce heat; cover and simmer 1 hour or until ducks are tender. Remove ducks from stock; reserve stock. When ducks cool, remove meat from bones; cut meat into bite-size pieces and set aside. Return skin and bones to stock; cover and simmer an additional hour. Strain stock; add enough chicken broth to make 2½ quarts liquid. Set aside.

Cook sausage over medium heat about 5 minutes, stirring occasionally. Drain on paper towels and set aside. Heat oil in 5-quart heavy iron pot; stir in flour. Cook over medium heat at least 30 minutes or until a dark roux is formed, stirring constantly. Add celery and onion; cook for 10 minutes. Remove from heat and gradually stir in reserved hot stock.

Bring mixture to a boil; then reduce heat and simmer 20 minutes. Add duck, sausage, salt and pepper to stock mixture; simmer 20 minutes. Stir in green onion and parsley. Add oysters; simmer an additional 10 minutes. Serve Gumbo over hot cooked rice. Thicken each serving with Gumbo filé. Best made a day ahead. Yield: 8-10 servings.

WILD DUCK CASSEROLE

2 large Mallard ducks or 4
    large wood ducks
3 stalks celery, cut in 2-inch
    pieces
1 onion, halved
1½ teaspoons salt
¼ teaspoon pepper
1 (6 ounce) package long
    grain and wild rice mix

1 (4 ounce) can sliced
    mushrooms
½ cup chopped onion
½ cup melted margarine
¼ cup all-purpose flour
1½ cups half-and-half
1 tablespoon chopped fresh
    parsley
½ cup pecans

Combine first 5 ingredients in a large Dutch oven; cover with water and bring to a boil. Reduce heat; cover and simmer 1 hour or until ducks are tender. Remove ducks from stock; strain stock and reserve. When ducks cool, remove meat from bones; cut into bite-size pieces and set aside. Cook rice mix using duck stock instead of water as directed on box. Drain mushrooms; reserve liquid. Add enough stock to mushroom liquid to make 1½ cups. Sauté chopped onion in margarine until tender; add flour, stirring until smooth. Add mushrooms; cook 1 minute, stirring constantly. Gradually stir in mushroom liquid-stock mixture; cook over medium heat stirring constantly until thickened and bubbly. Stir in duck, rice, half-and-half and parsley; spoon into a greased two-quart shallow casserole. Sprinkle pecans on top. Cover and bake at 350° F for 15 to 20 minutes. Uncover and bake 5 to 10 minutes or until thoroughly heated. Yield: 6-8 servings.

VARIATION:

Substitute 3 cups cubed chicken for duck.

142

WILD DUCK

4 whole ducks
bacon drippings
salt and pepper to taste
4 small onions
1 apple
4 celery stalks

2 cans consommé or bouillon
1 cup sherry
6 green onions, chopped
½ bunch parsley, chopped
1 small can water chestnuts
½ pound fresh mushrooms

Wash and dry ducks thoroughly. Rub inside and out with bacon drippings. Salt and pepper to taste. Insert a small onion, a quarter section of apple and a stalk of celery in each carcass for cooking and remove before serving. Place ducks in Dutch oven or roaster. Cover ducks with water to which has been added 1 can of consommé or bouillon and ½ cup sherry. Sprinkle green onions, parsley, water chestnuts and mushrooms over the top. Cover and cook at 300° F until half the liquid has evaporated. Add second can of consommé and remaining sherry. Cook until ducks are completely tender, about 4½ to 5 hours. Yield: 8 servings.

NOTE: The ducks brown themselves in the long, slow cooking.

DOVE OR QUAIL A L'ORANGE

1 large onion, chopped
2 apples, chopped
8 birds
¾ cup butter
flour
2 cups water

3 chicken bouillon cubes
¾ cup orange juice
¼ cup brandy
onion salt to taste
salt and pepper
1 teaspoon sugar

Combine the onion and apple and stuff the birds. Brown the birds in butter and remove. Add to the skillet a little more butter, enough sifted flour and a little water to make a thick gravy. Then add water, bouillon cubes, orange juice, brandy, onion salt, pepper, salt and sugar. Place birds in a baking dish. Pour gravy over birds and bake at 200° F for 3 hours or until fork tender. Serve with wild rice. Yield: 4 servings.

BAKED DOVE

10 doves
salt
pepper

3 apples
5 bacon slices, halved
½ cup chicken broth

Sprinkle doves with salt and pepper. Core apples and cut into 10 slices. Cut bacon slices in half. Arrange the apple slices in a 6″ × 10″ baking dish; place one dove on each apple slice. Cover each dove with one-half of a bacon slice; add the chicken broth and cover with foil. Bake at 325° F for 1 hour or until doves are tender. Remove foil during the last 15 minutes. Yield: 3-4 servings.

VARIATION:

Onion slices may be placed on top of the apple slices before placing the doves.

SMOTHERED DOVES

10 to 12 doves
salt and pepper
6 tablespoons butter or bacon
    drippings

1 onion, chopped
3 tablespoons flour
1 can chicken broth

Season doves with salt and pepper. Brown in butter or bacon drippings and set aside. Brown onions in butter; set aside. Add flour to butter in skillet and stir well. Slowly add chicken broth, salt and pepper. Place birds and onions in casserole and add sauce. Cover casserole and bake at 350° F for 1 hour. Yield: 6 servings.

DOVE

doves
butter or margarine
Worcestershire sauce

bacon slices
cooking sherry

Place doves breast side down in a rectangular pan. Place ½ teaspoon butter in each breast cavity. Sprinkle all doves with Worcestershire sauce. Gently wrap ½ slice of bacon over each dove. Sprinkle each with about 1 tablespoon cooking sherry. Cover tightly with aluminum foil. Bake 2 to 3 hours in low oven (300° F). Serve with grits.

"These doves are very tender and flavorful."

SAUTÉED FROG LEGS

12 medium-sized frog legs
flour
5 tablespoons butter
2 cloves garlic, crushed
juice of ½ lemon

salt and pepper to taste
2 tablespoons chopped
  parsley
2 tablespoons chopped chives
2 ounces dry white wine

Wash frog legs well in lemon juice and water. Dry and dust with flour. Put butter in frying pan and heat until it foams. Add garlic and lemon juice. Cook for 1 minute; then add frog legs. Shake them in a pan until they are golden brown on each side; add salt and pepper, parsley and chives. Cook for another minute and add wine. Let cook for another minute and serve on a very hot dish. Yield: 6 servings.

ERMA'S SQUIRREL AND DUMPLINGS

3 squirrels or 2 rabbits
water and salt
1 cup buttermilk
¼ teaspoon baking powder
2 tablespoons oil

1 teaspoon salt
flour, about 1⅔ cups
butter
pepper

Boil squirrels or rabbits (or some of both) until the meat falls off the bone; set meat aside; reserve broth. Mix buttermilk, baking powder, oil, salt and enough flour to make a stiff dough. Roll paper thin; cut 1-inch by 3-inch strips. Put meat back in pot of broth; bring to rolling boil. Drop dumplings in one at a time, adding dots of butter and pepper. Push them down in the broth; as broth comes up, add more. Put top on pot; simmer 15 minutes. Yield: 6 servings.

VENISON SPAGHETTI

2 pounds venison, ground
2 medium onions, chopped
3 celery stalks, chopped
½ green pepper, chopped
2 cloves garlic, minced
2 (8 ounce) cans tomato
    sauce
2 (6 ounce) cans tomato
    paste
1 (16 ounce) can tomatoes

2 (4 ounce) cans sliced
    mushrooms
3 whole bay leaves
1 teaspoon Worcestershire
    sauce
salt and pepper to taste
1 (12 ounce) box thin
    spaghetti
Parmesan cheese

Brown venison; spoon into large pot, leaving juice in frying pan. Sauté onions, celery, pepper and garlic in juice from venison. Mix all sautéed ingredients with venison. Add tomato sauce, tomato paste, tomatoes and mushrooms. Add seasonings. Cook over medium heat for 1 hour. Cook over low heat 1 hour, uncovered. Serve over thin spaghetti and sprinkle with Parmesan cheese. Yield: 4 to 6 servings.

VENISON PEPPER STEAK

2 tablespoons oil
1 pound venison, cut in thin
    strips
medium to small onion, cut
    in rings
1 clove garlic, minced
2 green peppers, cut in thin
    strips

1 cup beef bouillon
1 cup tomatoes
1½ tablespoons cornstarch
2 teaspoons soy sauce
¼ cup water
salt and pepper to taste

Place oil in skillet. Sauté venison, onion and garlic. Add peppers and bouillon; cover and cook about 30 minutes. Add tomatoes and cook 5 minutes more. Combine cornstarch, soy sauce and water. Add to skillet and cook 5 more minutes, stirring constantly. Salt and pepper to taste. Serve over rice. Yield: 4 servings.

FRIED VENISON

venison roast, cut in chunks
salt
pepper
milk

2 cups pancake batter (use a
    complete mix)
flour

Salt and pepper meat. Soak in milk in refrigerator for 2 hours. Remove from milk; dip in pancake batter. Shake in paper bag with flour, seasoned with salt and pepper. Fry in deep grease which is 350° F and maintain 350° F. It doesn't take long.

"A great hors d'oeuvre for men."

VENISON CUTLETS

2 pounds venison chops
1½ tablespoons dried dill
    weed
salt
pepper

2 eggs
1 cup milk
1½ cups bread crumbs
½ pound salt pork, sliced

Pound chops to ¼ inch in thickness. Sprinkle both sides of chops with the dill weed, salt and pepper. Beat eggs and milk together. Dip cutlets in egg mixture and then into bread crumbs. Render fat from the salt pork in a frying pan. Fry cutlets in the hot pork fat. Yield: 4 servings.

NOTE: Use very dry bread crumbs for crispy cutlets.

DEER STEAK MARINADE

½ cup dry red wine
½ teaspoon ground cumin
1 large clove garlic, crushed
⅓ cup olive oil

3 tablespoons soy sauce
2 large or 4 small deer
    steaks

Combine ingredients and pour marinade over 2 large or 4 small deer steaks. Marinate steaks at room temperature for 2 to 3 hours, turning occasionally. Drain steaks and broil to desired doneness over charcoal. Brush with marinade while steaks are broiling. Yield: 4 servings.

VENISON CHILI

2 pounds venison, ground
¼ cup vegetable oil
1 cup chopped onions
2 cloves garlic, minced
1 large green pepper,
    chopped
3 tablespoons chili powder

2 teaspoons sugar
3½ cups tomatoes
1 cup tomato paste
1-1½ cups water
1 teaspoon salt
½ teaspoon cumin
½ cup pinto beans, dried

Brown venison in oil. Add onions, garlic and pepper. Cook until onions and pepper are tender, about 5 minutes. Add chili powder, sugar, tomatoes, tomato paste, water, salt and cumin. Simmer 1½ hours. Cook beans according to package directions and add to chili if desired. Yield: 6 to 8 servings.

VENISON ROAST

1 (7 pound) venison roast
3 to 6 slices bacon
1 cup burgundy
½ cup oil
½ cup cider vinegar
2 celery tops
1 medium onion, sliced
4 slices lemon

1 large carrot, pared and
    sliced
1 tablespoon salt
10 whole black peppercorns
2 bay leaves
1 clove garlic, crushed
1 cup water
¼ cup unsifted all-purpose
    flour

Wipe roast with damp towels. Arrange bacon slices over inside surface of meat; roll up and tie or secure with toothpicks. Combine all other ingredients except flour and 2 tablespoons oil. Pour over roast. Cover and refrigerate for 12 to 24 hours, turning occasionally. Remove roast from marinade; coat with flour. Reserve 2 cups of marinade. Brown roast on all sides in hot oil. Add 1 cup of marinade and bring to boil. Reduce heat and simmer covered for 4 hours or until roast is tender. Baste occasionally with pan liquid, adding remaining cup of marinade as needed. Pan juices may be thickened with flour or cornstarch for a gravy. Yield: 12 servings.

PHEASANT

4 pheasant
flour
salt and pepper to taste
oil
½ cup chopped onion
½ cup seedless raisins
1 cup chili sauce

½ cup brown sugar
2 tablespoons Worcestershire
 sauce
¼ teaspoon garlic salt
1 cup sherry
1 (16 ounce) can bing cherries,
 drained

Shake four quartered birds in seasoned flour. Brown birds in oil in skillet. Place birds in roaster. Combine onion, raisins, chili sauce, brown sugar and Worcestershire sauce and garlic salt. Pour over birds; cover and bake 1½ hours in 300° F oven. Remove cover; add sherry and bing cherries. Bake an additional 15 minutes. Yield: 8-10 servings.

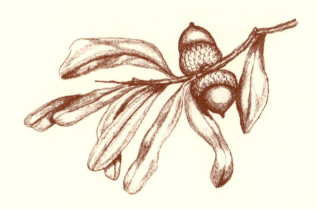

BAKED PHEASANT IN CREAM

2 pheasant, 6 doves or quail
salt to taste
flour
½ cup butter
½ cup dry white wine

2 chicken bouillon cubes
½ cup chives
1 cup sliced fresh
 mushrooms
1 pint sour cream

Salt and flour birds and brown in butter. Save drippings. Mix wine, chicken bouillon cubes, chives, drippings, fresh mushrooms and sour cream. Pour mixture over birds in greased baking dish and bake 1 hour, covered, at 350° F. Yield: 4 servings.

R.D

Meats

"Some hae meat and cannae eat, and some would eat but hae no meat; but we hae meat and we can eat, so let the Lord be thanket" went an old rhyme. The bounty of the meat counter of today offers a variety of choices, but historians, such as Mildred J. Cole of Baconton, recall their grandparents telling of what was available in yester-year. Lamb, goat and kid were on the list along with pork in many forms, hams, spareribs, sausage stuffed in casings or narrow muslin bags, smoked and stored in smoke houses, or sometimes cooked and preserved in jars with fat; souse, pickled pigs feet and beef, fresh or "jerk" (long strips of beef dried in the sun.)

Meats

INDIVIDUAL BEEF WELLINGTON

8 (5 ounce) filets
cooking oil
salt and pepper
1 pound ground sirloin
½ teaspoon salt
½ teaspoon pepper

1 clove garlic, crushed
1 tablespoon snipped parsley
8 Pepperidge Farm pastry
  shells or Pillsbury
  crescent rolls
1 egg white, slightly beaten

Put filets in freezer for 20 minutes. Brush with oil, sprinkle with salt and pepper. Sear filet for 5 minutes on each side. Refrigerate. Combine sirloin, salt, pepper, garlic and parsley. Divide into 8 patties and put one portion of each on filet. Refrigerate. Thaw out pastry shells, roll to 9x5 inch rectangle. Wrap filets in dough, sirloin side down in envelope fashion. Pinch with water to stick. Decorate with remaining dough. Refrigerate until ready to bake. Brush with egg white. Bake on cookie sheet at 450° F for following doneness: 10 minutes for rare; 12 minutes for medium rare; and 15 minutes for medium. Yield: 8 servings.

"Elegance made easy."

POT ROAST PIQUANT

¾ cup port or sherry
¼ cup soy sauce
2 tablespoons water
1 clove garlic, sliced

1 teaspoon ginger
¼ teaspoon oregano
1 tablespoon brown sugar
4 pounds pot roast

Preheat oven to 300°F. Combine wine with soy sauce, water, garlic, ginger, oregano and brown sugar. Place roast in pan; pour wine mixture over top; cover and roast at 300° F for 4 hours. Baste occasionally. Yield: 6 to 8 servings.

GRILLADES AND GRITS

4 pounds boneless round
    steak, ½ inch thick
½ cup bacon drippings,
    divided
½ cup flour
2 cups chopped green onion
1 cup chopped onion
¾ cup chopped celery (stalks
    and leaves)
¾ cup chopped green pepper
2 cloves garlic, minced
2 cups chopped fresh
    tomatoes

½ teaspoon tarragon
⅔ teaspoon thyme
1 cup water
1 cup dry red wine
1 tablespoon salt
½ teaspoon pepper
2 bay leaves
2 tablespoons Worcestershire
    sauce
½ teaspoon hot sauce
3 tablespoons chopped
    parsley sprigs

Remove and discard fat from steak; cut meat into serving size pieces. Pound meat to ¼ inch thickness using a meat mallet. Brown meat well in a dutch oven in ¼ cup bacon drippings; place meat on warm platter and set aside. Add remaining bacon drippings to Dutch oven, stir in flour. Cook over low heat, stirring constantly, until flour is dark brown (cook slowly and do not burn). Add green onion, onion, celery, green pepper and garlic; sauté until onion is transparent. Add tomatoes, tarragon and thyme; cook over low heat 3 minutes. Stir in next 7 ingredients.

Place meat in sauce; cover and simmer 2 hours. Discard bay leaves, stir in chopped parsley. Cool several hours at room temperature or chill overnight. Heat Grillades thoroughly before serving, adding water or beef broth if needed. Garnish with parsley sprigs. Serve over grits. Yield: 8-10 servings.

Note: If available, 4 pounds veal round, ¼ inch thick, cut into serving pieces may be used.

"Creole time in South Georgia."

By searing beef first, the juices are kept in.

MANDARIN BEEF TERIYAKI

½ cup soy sauce
½ cup sherry
2 tablespoons oil
¼ teaspoon powdered ginger
1 clove garlic, crushed
2 pounds flank steak, cut
    into strips
2 tablespoons oil

1 small onion, chopped
1 green pepper, cut into
    strips
¾ cup pineapple juice
2 teaspoons cornstarch
2 cups mandarin oranges,
    drained

Marinate flank steak in first five ingredients for 1 to 2 hours. Remove meat and drain. Heat 1 tablespoon oil in wok or 12 inch skillet. Brown ½ of beef. Repeat with the rest of the beef. Remove beef from wok or skillet; add 1 tablespoon oil. Cook onion and green pepper over high heat about 3 minutes. Return beef to onion mixture and pour ½ cup marinade over all. Simmer 5 to 7 minutes. Pour pineapple juice mixed with cornstarch into wok. Cook until thick. Spoon in oranges and heat through. Serve on rice. Yield: 4 to 6 servings.

BEEF SCALOPPINE MARSALA

2 (¾ pound) beef top round
    steaks, each cut ¼ inch
    thick
1 egg
3 tablespoons milk
1¼ cups dried bread crumbs
¼ cup grated Parmesan
    cheese
1 teaspoon salt

⅛ teaspoon pepper
¾ cup butter
1 garlic clove, sliced
¾ cup water
2 teaspoons flour
½ cup Marsala wine
¼ cup minced parsley
1 beef-flavor bouillon cube

With meat mallet pound each beef top round steak to ⅛ inch thickness. Cut steaks into about 4" by 2" pieces. Beat egg with milk. On waxed paper, combine bread crumbs, Parmesan cheese, salt and pepper. Dip meat in egg mixture, then coat with crumb mixture. In 12-inch skillet over medium-high heat, melt 2 tablespoons butter. Cook garlic and ⅓ of meat until meat is lightly browned; remove to platter; keep warm. Repeat with remaining meat, using ½ cup butter in all. Mix water with flour. Discard garlic; melt remaining butter in skillet. Add water mixture, Marsala, parsley, bouillon. Cook, stirring until thickened; pour over meat. Yield: 4 servings.

ENGLISH STANDING RIB ROAST WITH HORSERADISH SAUCE

6 pound standing rib roast

Preheat oven to 500°F. Place roast, fat side up, on rack in roasting pan. Cook in oven for 20 minutes, reduce heat to 350° F and continue to cook for 1 hour or until beef is cooked to your taste. Transfer beef to heated platter and let stand for at least 15 minutes for easier carving. Serve with its own juices and a HORSERADISH SAUCE. Yield: 12 servings.

HORSERADISH SAUCE:

1/4 cup drained horseradish
1 tablespoon white wine
   vinegar
1 teaspoon sugar
1/4 teaspoon salt
1/4 teaspoon white pepper
1/2 cup heavy cream

Combine all ingredients except cream until well blended. Beat cream with whisk until stiff. Pour horseradish mixture over cream and fold together. Serve with Yorkshire pudding.

EMPRESS BEEF

2 pounds sirloin
salt to taste
6 stalks celery, sliced
   diagonally
2 medium onions, sliced
2 small cans button
   mushrooms or equal
   amount fresh mushrooms
1 can water chestnuts,
   chopped
1 (16 ounce) can French cut
   green beans or 1 box
   frozen snow peas
2 teaspoons cornstarch
10 teaspoons soy sauce
1 teaspoon sugar
1/2 cup water

Slice meat into thin strips. Quickly brown beef in oil and salt in large heavy frying pan. Add celery, onions, mushrooms, water chestnuts, and beans and stir slowly over hot fire for few minutes. Cover pan, turn down heat and simmer for about 3 minutes. Just before serving, stir in thickening made with cornstarch, soy sauce, sugar and water. Serve immediately with fluffy rice. Yield: 5 to 6 servings.

"Quick, easy, and delicious."

FRENCH BEEF AND VEGETABLE CASSEROLE

6 slices bacon
2 pounds lean chuck or
   sirloin tips
½ cup flour
1 teaspoon salt
1 cup dry red wine
2 tablespoons parsley
½ garlic clove
½ teaspoon thyme

1 (10½ ounce) can
   condensed beef broth
6 medium potatoes, peeled
   and halved
12 small onions, peeled
3 carrots, sliced lengthwise
1 (4 ounce) can mushrooms,
   finely chopped

Cook bacon until crisp. Drain on paper towels. Reserve drippings. Cut beef into cubes. Shake a few cubes at a time in bag containing flour and salt. Brown cubes on all sides in bacon drippings. Remove to 2-quart casserole dish. Pour wine into blender. Add parsley, garlic, thyme and beef broth. Blend until solid ingredients are puréed. Pour over meat in casserole. Cover and bake at 350° F for an hour. Stir potatoes, onion and carrots into casserole. Replace cover. Bake 1 hour longer or until vegetables are done. Stir in mushrooms. Crumble bacon and scatter on top with additional chopped parsley. Yield: 5 to 6 servings.

BEEF STROGANOFF

1½ pounds lean beef chuck
   cubes
2 tablespoons flour
½ teaspoon salt
¼ teaspoon pepper
2 tablespoons oil
1 (10½ ounce) can beef
   consommé

3 tablespoons Worcestershire
   sauce
3 tablespoons catsup
2 tablespoons dry mustard
1 (4 ounce) can mushrooms
½ pint sour cream

Dredge beef cubes, seasoned with salt and pepper, in flour. In skillet carefully brown cubes in oil over medium high heat. Add next four ingredients. Cook over low heat, covered, for 2 hours. Add mushrooms the last 15 minutes. Just before serving, add sour cream. Serve over cooked white rice. Yield: 6 servings.

TENDERLOIN BRADSHAW

3 to 4 pounds tenderloin,
    trim fat
garlic salt
1 cup burgundy

¼ cup soy sauce
6 tablespoons butter
lemon pepper

Season meat with garlic salt and sear in 425° F oven for 10 minutes. Warm burgundy. In separate pan warm soy sauce, butter and lemon pepper. Pour over, first the soy sauce then the burgundy. Continue to baste every 10 minutes at 350° F to 400° F for about 40 minutes. Yield: 4 to 5 servings.

EGGPLANT SPAGHETTI SAUCE

2 garlic cloves
4 tablespoons olive oil
3 pounds peeled, diced
    eggplant
1 (1 pound) can whole
    tomatoes
1 (15 ounce) can Hunt's
    tomato sauce with tomato
    bits

1½ pounds ground beef
1 teaspoon salt
½ teaspoon pepper
½ teaspoon oregano
2 large green peppers, sliced
½ to ¾ cup sliced ripe olives

Sauté garlic cloves in olive oil in large frying pan. Remove and discard. Add eggplant; sauté; add tomatoes and tomato sauce. Cover and simmer, stirring occasionally. In separate skillet, brown ground beef. When eggplant is tender, add ground beef to mixture along with salt, pepper and oregano. Simmer about 5 minutes. Add green peppers and olives. Simmer 15 minutes longer. Best made ahead so flavors have time to blend. Yield: 8 servings.

MEAT-MUSHROOM SAUCE
ITALIAN STYLE

1 pound pork sausage
2 pounds ground round or
 chuck
4 very large onions, chopped
4 to 6 large cloves garlic,
 minced or mashed
1 cup chopped parsley
¾ pound fresh mushrooms,
 thinly sliced
3 (15 ounce) cans tomato
 sauce

1 fifth dry red wine
2 teaspoons salt
1 teaspoon ground sage
1 teaspoon dried rosemary,
 crumbled
½ teaspoon dried marjoram,
 crumbled
½ teaspoon thyme, crumbled
coarsely ground black
 pepper

In large kettle or Dutch oven, slowly brown sausage, add ground beef and brown. Add onions and sauté until transparent. Add garlic, parsley and mushrooms and stir to coat with meat drippings. Stir in remaining ingredients. Cover loosely and simmer, stirring occasionally, 3 hours, or until reduced to thick sauce consistency. Skim off any excess fat. Serve over spaghetti. Yield: 3 quarts.

SICILIAN MEAT LOAF

2 eggs, beaten
¾ cup soft bread crumbs
½ cup tomato juice
2 tablespoons parsley, dried
½ teaspoon oregano, dried
¼ teaspoon salt
¼ teaspoon pepper

1 small clove garlic, minced,
 or ⅜ teaspoon garlic
 powder
2 pounds lean ground beef
8 thin slices boiled ham
1½ cups mozzarella cheese,
 shredded

Preheat oven to 350° F. Combine first 8 ingredients. Stir in ground beef, mixing well. On foil or waxed paper, flatten beef mixture to about 10 inches × 12 inches rectangle. Lay ham over, leaving edges free. Spread shredded cheese over ham. Roll long edges toward center, overlapping slightly. Pat firmly all edges to seal in cheese. Invert on cookie sheet or pan so sealed edges are down. Pat again firmly to make sure no holes remain. Bake at 350° F for 1 hour. Meat remains pink from ham. Let set 15 minutes before cutting. Reheats beautifully. May be frozen cooked or uncooked. Yield: 6 to 8 servings.

SPAGHETTI FOR COMPANY

1/4 pound butter
1 tablespoon olive oil
3 large onions, chopped
1 clove garlic
3 (1 pound) cans tomatoes
2 (15 ounce) cans Hunt's
    tomato sauce with tomato
    bits
1 (12 ounce) can tomato paste
water
1/4 teaspoon celery salt
1 tablespoon Worcestershire
    sauce

1/4 teaspoon Tabasco
1 tablespoon A-1 sauce
dash of cinnamon
dash of allspice
1 teaspoon basil
1 teaspoon oregano
salt and pepper to taste
1 pound mushrooms, chopped
    (fresh or canned)
1 (4 to 5 pound) rump roast
3 (1 pound) boxes spaghetti
    noodles
Parmesan cheese

Melt butter and olive oil in a large kettle; add onions, brown; chop garlic fine and add to onions. Add tomatoes, tomato sauce and tomato paste. Add one can of water for each can of tomato sauce and paste. Add spices, salt and pepper, mushrooms and rump roast. Cook 30 minutes covered. Uncover and let cook slowly until sauce coats spoon, (about 6 hours). Stir often as tomatoes tend to stick. Chill overnight. Slice roast paper thin. Cook spaghetti noodles. Toss with additional olive oil or butter after draining. Place 1 layer of spaghetti, roast and sauce until you have a large casserole filled. Heat in oven at 325° F until bubbly. Serve with Parmesan cheese. Yield: 12 to 15 servings.

Gift Idea: Line a basket with a red bandana. Fill it with a jar of your favorite homemade spaghetti sauce. Put a box of spaghetti, Parmesan cheese and bottle of red wine with it.

ROAST CROWN OF PORK

1 crown roast of pork, made
    from 12 to 14 ribs
3 tablespoons butter
3 tablespoons chopped onion
3 tablespoons chopped celery
8 oranges, sectioned
1½ cups cooked rice

2 cups bread crumbs, toasted
1 tablespoon leaf sage,
    crumbled
1 teaspoon salt
¼ teaspoon pepper
1 teaspoon grated orange
    rind

Preheat oven to 450° F. Protect ends of rib bones with pieces of aluminum foil. Put pork on rack in a roasting pan. Place in oven and reduce oven temperature to 350° F. Roast for 40 minutes per pound. Melt butter and sauté onion and celery until tender. Add orange sections and remaining ingredients to onions and celery and toss to mix. One hour before the roast is done, fill center with the stuffing. Baste twice during the last hour with drippings in the pan. Garnish with additional orange sections and preserved crabapples, if desired. Yield: 6 to 8 servings.

"Beautiful dish for holiday dinners."

MARINATED SPARERIBS

4 cloves garlic, finely
    chopped
juice of 4 lemons
¼ cup soy sauce
½ cup honey

2 teaspoons basil
1½ teaspoons black pepper
¼ cup chopped parsley
6 pounds sparefibs

Combine garlic, lemon juice, soy sauce, honey, basil, pepper and parsley to make marinade. Place two sides (5½ to 6 pounds) of spareribs in the mixture. Let the ribs marinate for at least 2 hours, turning them frequently. Refrigerate overnight. Wind the ribs on spits or put them in a roasting pan. Grill on medium heat or cook in a 350° F oven for about 1 hour. Brush occasionally with marinade. The ribs should be nicely glazed when done. Yield: 4 servings.

ROAST SUCKLING PIG

1 suckling pig, 10 to 15
    pounds
2 tablespoons thyme
1 teaspoon salt
1 teaspoon pepper
½ cup melted bacon fat

½ cup chopped onions
¼ cup chopped celery
2 chopped carrots
1 bay leaf
½ cup apple cider
1 red apple

Wash suckling pig inside and out. Dry and sprinkle thyme, salt and pepper in cavity. Refrigerate overnight or 12 hours. With skewers and string, lace opening closed. Cover snout, ears and tail with foil to prevent burning. Put bacon fat in bottom of roasting pan. Make a bed of the onions, celery and carrots. Set pig in vegetables. Roast at 350° F for 5 hours, basting every 10 minutes with pan drippings. When done, remove pig to a large platter and place the apple in the mouth. Drain fat from pan drippings. Pour drippings into a sauce pan; add cider; bring to a boil; season with salt and pepper to taste. Serve sauce as a side dish. Yield: 8 to 10 servings.

"The ultimate answer to outdoor entertaining."

PORK LOIN WITH RED PLUM SAUCE

5 to 8 pound pork loin
garlic salt
onion salt
2 tablespoons butter
¾ cup chopped onion
1 cup red plum preserves
½ cup brown sugar, packed

⅔ cup water
2 tablespoons lemon juice
⅓ cup chili sauce
¼ cup soy sauce
2 teaspoons prepared
    mustard
3 drops Tabasco

Preheat oven to 325° F. Sprinkle pork generously with garlic and onion salts; place fat side up in roasting pan. Roast at 325° F, 25 minutes per pound. If you prefer, place roast on rack and add water to roasting pan. Melt butter, add onion and cook until tender. Add remaining ingredients, simmer 15 minutes. Pour fat off pork; pour about half the sauce over meat. Cook about 20 to 30 minutes longer, basting often. Serve extra sauce on side. Yield: 4 to 6 servings.

"Sauce is delicious on any cut of pork."

161

BRUNSWICK STEW

1 hog head
1 large hen
1 Boston butt
juice of 4 lemons
3 pounds onions, chopped
1 small bottle Worcestershire
    sauce
6 (1 pound) cans tomatoes

¼ cup vinegar
2½ (32 ounce) bottles catsup
4 or 5 large potatoes
1 quart stock
6 cans white cream corn
salt and pepper to taste
Tabasco sauce to taste

Cook hog head, hen and Boston butt until tender. Remove meat from bones. Mix all ingredients. Cook slowly at low heat, for several hours. Stir often. Yield: 30-50 servings.

"Real true South Georgia recipe!"

EASY BRUNSWICK STEW

1 (24 ounce) can Castleberry's
    Brunswick Stew
1 small can Castleberry's pork
1 small can Castleberry's beef

1 can creamed corn
¼ cup Kraft barbeque sauce
juice of 2 lemons
1 tablespoon Worcestershire
    sauce

Combine all ingredients in large sauce pan and heat until bubbling. Stir occasionally to keep from sticking. Yield: 12 servings.

SMITHFIELD HAM

Smithfield ham   *6 cups cold water*

Soak ham in cold water to cover overnight. Scrub ham with stiff brush to remove the pepper coating and any mold that may be present. Place ham in covered roaster with water. Close all vents. Bake ham in preheated 500° F oven 20 minutes. Turn off oven. Allow to remain in oven without opening oven door for 3 hours. Turn heat to 500° F and leave for 15 minutes. Turn off heat and allow ham to remain in oven for at least 3 hours. May be left overnight. Remove ham from roaster and cut off the rind. Ham is ready to serve or may be glazed if desired. Smithfield ham may be served hot or cold. It should be sliced quite thin and always on the bias. Place the fat end (butt) of ham toward you and slice slantwide down toward the bone. Ham trimmings are excellent for appetizers, sandwich fillings and casserole dishes. Yield: A 12 to 14 pound ham yields 24 to 28 servings.

TENNESSEE HAM

Tennessee ham

Cover with water and soak overnight. Pour off water. Cut off wire, if necessary. Cover with fresh water and bring to boil. Then simmer 2½ to 3 hours or until meat slides away from the bone. Cool in its juices. Pour off juice; remove outer skin. Slice thin. Slices easier if chilled. Yield: A 12 to 14 pound ham yields 24 to 28 servings.

RED EYE GRAVY

After frying ham, pour off most of fat from skillet. Be sure to leave the scraps of ham and residue remaining in skillet. To this add a cup of water or more depending on amount of ham fried, and bring to a boil. Do not thicken. Good served over fried ham, biscuits, grits, potatoes, etc. For a change in making red gravy, use coffee instead of water.

BAKED HONEY HAM

1 (10 pound) ham
6 whole cloves
½ cup cider vinegar
1 jar pickled peaches
1 cup honey
1 cup brown sugar

1 cup diced mandarin
  oranges
1 cup diced pineapple
1 cup seeded white grapes,
  cut

Wash ham and place fat side up in roaster. Stick in the 6 cloves. Pour the vinegar and peach juice over the ham (reserve the peaches for garnish). Rub with honey and then the brown sugar. Bake at 300° F, uncovered for 1 hour. Cover and bake 2 hours. Baste the ham every 30 minutes. Add the diced fruits and bake 1 hour or until ham is tender. Serve the sliced ham with the fruit sauce from the roaster. Garnish with peaches. Yield: 20 servings.

COUNTRY HAM IN APPLE CIDER

1 (12 to 14 pound) country
  ham
2 quarts apple cider
1 tablespoon whole cloves

½ cup firmly packed brown
  sugar
2 tablespoons prepared
  mustard
fresh parsley sprigs
  (optional)

Place ham in a very large container; cover with cold water, and soak overnight. Scrub ham thoroughly with a stiff brush. Place ham, skin side down, in a large roasting pan. Pour cider over ham, and sprinkle with cloves. Cover and bake at 325° F for 6 to 7 hours (allow 30 minutes per pound). Carefully remove ham from pan juices; remove skin. Place ham, fat side up, on a cutting board; score fat in a diamond design. Return ham to roaster, fat side up. Combine brown sugar and mustard, stirring well. Coat exposed portion of ham with sugar mixture. Continue baking, uncovered, for 30 minutes. Remove ham from roaster; discard pan drippings. Cool ham thoroughly; place on a carving board or serving platter. To serve, thinly slice ham; garnish with parsley, if desired. Yield: 24 to 28 servings.

HAM RING

1 cup bread crumbs
1 cup milk
1 tablespoon minced onion
2 tablespoons butter
2 eggs, slightly beaten

½ teaspoon salt
½ teaspoon pepper
1 tablespoon minced parsley
1 cup ground cooked ham

Preheat oven to 350° F. Soak bread crumbs in milk, combine with onion, which has been sautéed in butter. Cook together for 5 minutes. Add eggs and other ingredients. May be baked in individual ring molds or casserole. Place mold in a pan of hot water to bake for 30 minutes at 350° F. Serve with a creamed mushroom sauce. Yield: 6 servings.

To prevent sausage and bacon from shrinking, give them a light coating of flour before frying.

HAM AND SPINACH ROLLS

1 (10 ounce) package frozen,
    chopped spinach, cooked
    and drained
1 cup packaged cornbread
    stuffing mix
1 cup sour cream
12 thin slices cooked ham

3 tablespoons butter
3 tablespoons flour
1½ cups milk
¼ cup shredded Cheddar
    cheese
2 tablespoons Parmesan
    cheese

Combine spinach, stuffing mix and sour cream in medium bowl. Spread on ham slices. Roll up and arrange seam side down in one layer in a shallow baking pan. In separate pan, melt butter. Stir in flour, cook 1 minute. Stir in milk slowly and continue to cook, stirring until sauce thickens and bubbles. Add Cheddar, remove from heat and continue stirring until cheese is melted. Pour over ham rolls, sprinkle top with Parmesan cheese. Cover and bake 15 minutes at 350° F. Uncover and bake 15 minutes more. Yield: 6 servings.

SPIESEBRATEN

4-5 pound shoulder pork
    roast, deboned and
    butterflied, 1 to 1½
    inches thick
6 tablespoons salt
6 tablespoons pepper

½ cup mustard
¼ cup garlic salt
3 onions, chopped
string
can of beer

Preheat oven to 325° F. Salt and pepper both sides of roast heavily. Rub mustard on side that you intend to be the inside. Sprinkle garlic salt on mustard. Place chopped onion on top of mustard. Roll roast and secure with string—use blanket stitch to tie securely. Roast for 2½ hours at 325° F or until done. Baste with beer. Make gravy with drippings. Yield: 6 to 8 servings.

MARINATED BUTTERFLIED LEG OF LAMB

6 pound leg of lamb
3 cups dry red wine
½ cup oil
2 onions, thinly sliced
1 carrot, thinly sliced
1 tablespoon thyme

6 parsley stems
2 bay leaves, crumbled
⅛ teaspoon garlic powder
2 teaspoons salt
½ teaspoon pepper

Have the leg of lamb boned, butterflied, and pounded an even thickness. In a large ceramic or glass dish, combine all ingredients, except lamb. Add the lamb and let it marinate, covered, and chilled, turning occasionally, for 1 to 2 days. Drain the lamb, pat it dry with paper towels and fit into a basket grill (which will keep it flat and of even thickness). Broil the lamb under a preheated broiler 3 inches from the heat for 20 minutes on each side. Transfer to a cutting board, let it stand for 10 minutes, and cut it diagonally into ½ inch slices. Yield: 6 servings.

"Lamb takes on new meaning cooked in this fashion."

ROAST LEG OF LAMB

1 (5 to 6 pound) leg of lamb	*¼ teaspoon black pepper*
2 teaspoons salt	*melted butter*
1 teaspoon Accent	

Do not remove thin papery covering from leg of lamb. Rub lamb with a mixture of the salt, Accent and black pepper. Place lamb, skin side down, on rack in a shallow roasting pan and brush surface with melted butter. Insert roast meat thermometer in center of thickest part of meat, being sure that bulb does not rest on the bone or in the fat. Roast lamb uncovered at 300°F for 2½ to 3½ hours, allowing 30 to 35 minutes per pound. Brush surface with melted butter frequently during roasting. Meat is medium done when thermometer registers 175°F, well done at 180°F. Serve lamb with DILL SAUCE.

DILL SAUCE:

3 tablespoons butter	*1¼ teaspoons dill weed*
1 tablespoon flour	*¼ cup finely chopped parsley*
1 cup chicken broth	*1 teaspoon lemon juice*
¼ cup chopped chives	

Heat butter in small sauce pan. Blend in flour and cook mixture until it bubbles. Remove from heat and add chicken broth gradually, stirring constantly. Bring chicken broth to boiling and cook, stirring constantly until thickened, about 3 minutes. Stir in remaining ingredients and heat thoroughly. Serve warm with roast lamb. Yield: 6 servings; 1½ cups sauce.

Garnishes in beautiful colors, varied flavors and interesting shapes give personality and beauty to your table.

Be creative with garnishes but keep it simple!

Edible garnishes are the most appropriate.

At least ⅓ of a dish should be left free of garnish.

A garnish should not interfere with food service.

LAMB SHANKS IN RED WINE

3 slices bacon
4 lamb shanks
flour
salt
pepper
1 (1 pound) can
   tomatoes
1 cup chopped celery
½ cup chopped parsley

2 medium-sized onions,
   chopped
1 clove garlic, chopped
1 teaspoon Worcestershire
   sauce
1 tablespoon grated
   horseradish
1 cup dry red wine
½ pound fresh mushrooms

Render 3 slices of bacon, diced, and remove bacon. Coat 4 lamb shanks thickly with seasoned flour. Brown slowly in bacon fat, turning until nicely browned. Use a deep iron kettle, Dutch oven. When shanks are browned, add tomatoes, bacon bits, celery, parsley, onions, garlic, Worcestershire sauce, horseradish and wine (Burgundy is preferred). Cover and simmer for 2 hours. Add mushrooms, separating stems from tops and, if large, halve or quarter them. Cook for ½ to ¾ hours longer. If gravy has not thickened, just before serving add flour paste (flour and small amount of water). Yield: 4 servings.

GRILLED LAMB WITH ROSEMARY

leg of lamb, 6½ to 7½
   pounds
1 teaspoon salt
¼ cup chopped parsley
3 teaspoons dried rosemary

2 garlic cloves, pressed
2 teaspoons coarse ground
   pepper
2 tablespoons olive oil

Set meat out for 4 hours. Skin leg of lamb, removing all fat. Combine remainder of ingredients and rub mixture into meat. Smoke meat on grill, not directly over coals. Add coals as needed. Use meat thermometer when you think meat is almost done. Should register 185° F on meat thermometer. Approximately 2½ to 3½ hours. Yield: 6 to 8 servings.

LEMON VEAL SCALLOPS

4 veal scallops
paprika
flour

4 tablespoons butter
¼ cup lemon juice
1 tablespoon chopped parsley

With mallet or side of cleaver, pound trimmed veal scallops to ⅛ inch thick, approximately. Coat with paprika and lightly flour. Brown veal in butter and remove to warm platter. Add more butter to skillet along with lemon juice and chopped parsley. Deglaze pan and return scallops to heat thoroughly. Yield: 4 servings.

VEAL SCALLOPS AMANDINE

6 veal scallops
salt and pepper
2½ cups stale bread crumbs
1½ cups sliced almonds,
    lightly toasted
⅓ cup minced parsley

3 tablespoons grated lemon
    rind
3 egg whites
¾ cup clarified butter
lemon slices (for garnish)

Flatten 6 veal scallops, each weighing about 6 ounces, between sheets of wax paper until about ¼ inch thick and sprinkle them with salt and pepper. In a shallow bowl combine stale bread crumbs, almonds, parsley and lemon rind. In another bowl, beat egg whites lightly. Dip the scallops into the egg whites and then into the crumb mixture, pressing the mixture into them. Chill the scallops on a baking sheet for 30 minutes. In a large skillet, sauté the scallops in ¾ cup clarified butter for 1 to 2 minutes on each side, or until they are just cooked and golden. Transfer the scallops to a heated platter and garnish them with slices of lemon. Yield: 6 servings.

Veal scallops can be bought in the store already cut, but you can buy the veal round roast cut ⅛ inch thick and cut the scallops by the natural division of the roast and trim away all membrane and muscle. Cut the large side into 2 scallops, and the small side will probably make 2 smaller scallops. The round roast is cheaper than already cut scallops and just as good. (One slice of the round roast will usually serve 2 people.)

VEAL SCALLOPINI

8 veal scallops
salt and pepper
1 egg
bread crumbs
4 tablespoons butter
½ pound fresh mushrooms

4 tablespoons oil
1 can onion soup
½ cup dry Vermouth
cooked noodles
Parmesan cheese

Salt and pepper veal. Dip in egg, then bread crumbs. Refrigerate at least 30 minutes. Brown fresh mushrooms in butter in large skillet and remove. Brown veal in half butter and half oil. Add onion soup and dry Vermouth. Return mushrooms to pan, cover and simmer about 20 to 30 minutes. Serve on noodles and sprinkle with Parmesan cheese. Yield: 4 servings.

NOTE: This can be prepared ahead of time. Just reheat and serve.

HUNTER SCHNITZEL

2 pounds veal
salt and pepper
3 cups self rising flour
5 eggs

½ cup milk
3 cups cracker meal
cooking oil
onions

Slice veal and pound with a mallet to ⅛-inch thickness. Season with salt and pepper; flour thoroughly. Beat eggs and milk together. Dip veal into egg and milk batter. Coat with cracker meal. Brown on both sides in oil on hot grill or fry in pan. Serve with BROWN GRAVY with sliced onions on top. Yield: 12 servings.

BROWN GRAVY:

1 package brown gravy mix
dash dry white wine

1 (4 ounce) can mushrooms

Follow directions on package adding white wine and mushrooms.

Han's Restaurant

VEAL CHOPS MOZZARELLA

1 extra-large egg
salt, freshly ground white
   pepper
3/4 cup fine bread crumbs
2 tablespoons finely grated
   Parmesan cheese
3 tablespoons butter
3 tablespoons oil
4 rib chops, about 1/2 inch
   thick, well-trimmed

1 tablespoon finely minced
   shallots
4 slices red-ripe tomatoes, 1/8
   inch thick
4 teaspoons finely minced
   fresh basil
4 slices mozzarella cheese
1 cup dry white wine

Preheat oven to 350°F. Beat egg with salt and pepper. Place bread crumbs and Parmesan cheese in a shallow bowl. In large skillet, heat the butter and oil. Quickly dip the veal chops first into the beaten egg, then into the bread crumbs. Sauté over medium heat 5 to 6 minutes on each side, until coating is golden. Transfer chops to a shallow ovenproof dish. Sprinkle shallots over the chops. Lay a slice of tomato over each chop, sprinkle with basil and top with a slice of mozzarella cheese. Pour the white wine over all and bake for 20 minutes. Yield: 4 servings.

Marinades and Sauces

BEEF TENDERLOIN MARINADE

½ cup olive oil
½ cup soy sauce
1 tablespoon sugar
1 teaspoon powdered thyme

salt and pepper
1 bunch spring onions,
  chopped

Combine all ingredients and use as beef tenderloin marinade. Meat should be marinated at least 2 hours.

Excellent for flank steak or other cuts of beef that are to be broiled.

TERIYAKI STEAK MARINADE

¼ cup salad oil
¼ cup soy sauce
3 tablespoons catsup

1 tablespoon vinegar
¼ teaspoon pepper
2 cloves garlic, crushed

Mix all ingredients thoroughly. Pour over steak to coat all sides. Marinate in sauce at least 3 to 4 hours.

BROWN SAUCE

1½ tablespoons butter
1½ tablespoons flour

2 cups beef broth

In a saucepan melt butter. Blend in flour; stir until smooth paste. Stir in beef broth; bring to boiling and cook 3 to 5 minutes. Simmer uncovered for 30 minutes, stirring occasionally until sauce is reduced to 1⅓ cups. Use sauce on beef or in recipes calling for brown sauce. Yield: 1⅓ cups.

MINT SAUCE FOR LAMB

1 cup white wine vinegar
¼ cup sugar
pinch of salt

pinch of pepper
¼ cup crushed mint leaves,
  fresh or dried

Mix all ingredients. Bring to a boil and then cool. Serve with hot or cold lamb. Yield: 1½ cups.

SAUCE ROYALE

½ cup sour cream
½ package dry onion soup
  mix
1 egg yolk

1 teaspoon lemon juice
½ teaspoon Worcestershire
  sauce
salt and pepper to taste

Blend sour cream and soup mix. Add egg yolk, lemon juice and Worcestershire sauce and seasonings. Cook over low heat stirring constantly until sauce starts to thicken slightly. Do not boil. Remove from heat and stir occasionally as sauce continues to thicken on cooling. Serve at room temperature with beef fondue. Yield: ½ cup.

BÉARNAISE SAUCE

¼ cup dry white wine
¼ cup tarragon vinegar
1 tablespoon finely chopped
  green onion
1 teaspoon chopped parsley
¼ teaspoon tarragon

¼ teaspoon thyme
⅛ teaspoon black pepper
2 egg yolks
butter at room temperature
  (⅓) cup)

Add onions, parsley and seasonings to wine and vinegar and boil rapidly until reduced to half volume. Strain. Beat 2 egg yolks in top of double boiler. Slowly add liquid. Add a few tablespoons butter to egg yolks; place over hot (not boiling) water. Cook and stir until butter melts and sauce starts to thicken. Continue adding butter and stirring until sauce is smooth as thick cream. Serve cold. Yield: 1 cup.

CALIFORNIA RAISIN SAUCE

½ cup seedless raisins
½ cup water
⅓ cup port wine or sherry
½ teaspoon orange rind,
  grated (optional)

⅓ cup orange juice
¼ cup brown sugar, packed
1 tablespoon cornstarch
dash of salt
dash of allspice (optional)

Rinse raisins. Place in medium saucepan. Add water, wine, orange rind and juice. Heat until boiling. Blend sugar with rest of dry ingredients. Stir into orange mixture. Cook, stirring until clear. Serve hot. Use over thick slices of warm baked ham. May be prepared ahead of time. Yield: 1½ cups.

R. DIVINE ©

Seafood

Man-made ponds have joined creeks and rivers as sources of fresh fish in this area. Refrigerated trucks bring the harvest of the sea to local stores. All this makes it possible to have crisp fried catfish or oysters on the half shell. The selection is wide and varied enough to please the most discriminating palate.

Fish fries are a delightful informal way to entertain and a good way to use the abundance from a successful fishing trip. Be sure there are plenty of hot hushpuppies.

Seafood

SHRIMP AND WILD RICE CASSEROLE

½ cup thinly sliced onion
¼ cup thinly sliced green
   pepper
½ cup fresh mushrooms,
   sliced
½ cup butter
1 tablespoon Worcestershire
   sauce

1 teaspoon curry powder
2 cups cooked wild rice
2 pounds cooked shrimp,
   peeled
2 cups CREAM SAUCE

CREAM SAUCE:

3 tablespoons butter
3 tablespoons flour

2 cups chicken broth

Sauté onion, pepper and mushrooms in butter. Add seasonings, rice, shrimp and sauce. Mix. Place in 2-quart casserole and bake at 325° F for 35 minutes. Yield: 6 servings.

SHRIMP CURRY WITH SOUR CREAM

½ cup finely chopped onion
2 cloves garlic, finely
   chopped
2 tablespoons butter
¼ teaspoon salt
pepper to taste
1 can cream of mushroom
   soup

2 teaspoons curry powder
1 pound cooked shrimp,
   shelled and deveined, or
   1 pound cooked lobster
¼ cup seedless grapes or
   raisins
4 tablespoons sour cream
few drops lemon juice

Sauté onion and garlic in butter. Add to onion mixture in skillet, soup, seasonings, shrimp, grapes and heat thoroughly. Just before serving, stir in sour cream and a few drops of lemon juice. Serve over cooked rice. Yield: 4 to 5 servings.

BUTTERFLY SHRIMP

16 jumbo shrimp, shelled,
    deveined, uncooked
garlic powder
salt

Accent
soy sauce
sherry
8 slices bacon, cut in half

BATTER:
½ cup flour
½ cup water
1 egg
¼ teaspoon salt
¼ teaspoon Accent

¼ cup soy sauce
¼ teaspoon vinegar
green onion, chopped
½ teaspoon sugar
pinch prepared mustard

Season shrimp with spices. Wrap each shrimp with one-half slice of bacon. Set aside. Coat each bacon wrapped shrimp with flour. Prepare BATTER but do not stir very vigorously. Dip each piece in the slightly lumpy batter and deep fat fry at 375° F for 1 minute or less. Drain and serve hot. Serve with soy sauce. Yield: 4 servings.

One pound of raw shrimp equals 2 cups cooked and peeled shrimp.

SHRIMP AND GREEN NOODLES

1 (8 ounce) package spinach
    noodles
2 pounds shrimp, peeled and
    deveined
½ cup butter, clarified
1 can cream of mushroom
    soup

1 cup sour cream
1 cup mayonnaise
½ teaspoon Dijon mustard
1 tablespoon chives, chopped
4 tablespoons sherry
½ cup grated sharp Cheddar
    cheese

Cook noodles as directed on package. Line a casserole with noodles and make into a nest. In a large frying pan sauté the shrimp in clarified butter until pink and tender, about 5 minutes. Cover noodles with shrimp. Combine soup, sour cream, chives and mayonnaise. Add mustard and sherry. Pour sauce over shrimp and sprinkle Cheddar cheese over all. Bake until heated through and cheese is melted. Yield: 6 servings.

SHRIMP PIE

1 pound shrimp, shelled and
   deveined
½ cup chopped onions
3 tablespoons butter
1½ cups chopped tomatoes
½ cup sliced mushrooms

salt and pepper to taste
flour to thicken
1 recipe for 2-crust pastry
1 boiled egg, chopped
12 black olives, sliced
1 egg, beaten

Simmer shrimp in water covered for 5 minutes. Remove and
drain, reserving ¾ cup stock. Chop shrimp and sauté with
onions in butter until tender. Add tomatoes, mushrooms,
stock, salt, pepper and flour. Simmer for 15 minutes. Prepare
pastry and line 8-inch pie pan. Fill with shrimp and sprinkle
with egg and olives. Weave a lattice crust, brush with egg.
Bake 15 to 20 minutes at 400° F. Yield: 4 servings.

SHRIMP NEWBURG

2 tablespoons butter
1½ tablespoons flour
2 tablespoons water
1 cup half and half
3 tablespoons catsup

2 tablespoons sherry
1 pound shrimp, cooked and
   cleaned
salt and pepper to taste

Make white sauce with butter, flour, water and half and half,
stirring constantly. Blend in catsup, sherry and cooked
shrimp. Serve over rice. Yield: 3 to 4 servings.

GRILLED SHRIMP

½ cup butter
1 cup oil
½ cup white wine
2-3 teaspoons garlic, minced
¼ teaspoon oregano
3-4 bay leaves

2 tablespoons Worcestershire
   sauce
1 tablespoon soy sauce
1 tablespoon salt
2 teaspoons pepper
2 pounds large shrimp,
   unpeeled

Melt butter, add remaining ingredients except for shrimp.
Mix well, then add shrimp. Leave in marinade for at least 3 to
4 hours in refrigerator. Grill until bright orange, then brush
with marinade again. Grill 5 additional minutes, then serve
hot. Yield: 4 servings.

NOTE: For easier turning, place shrimp in a wire cooking
basket.

SHRIMP HARPIN

2½ pounds raw shrimp
1 tablespoon lemon juice
3 tablespoons salad oil
¾ cup uncooked rice
2 tablespoons margarine
¼ cup minced green pepper
¼ cup minced onion
1 teaspoon salt
⅛ teaspoon pepper

⅛ teaspoon mace
dash of cayenne
1 (10 ounce) can cream of
    mushroom soup,
    undiluted
1 cup heavy cream
½ cup dry sherry
¾ cup slivered almonds

Cook shrimp in boiling water. Drain. Clean, peel and devein. Sprinkle with lemon juice and oil. Cook rice and sauté green pepper and onion in the margarine, then combine all of the above ingredients. Bake uncovered in a 2-quart casserole dish at 350° F for 55 minutes. Top casserole with a few shrimp, some almonds and a sprinkling of paprika during last 15 minutes of baking. Yield: 6-8 servings.

"Elegant enough for company."

SHRIMP AND CRABMEAT AU GRATIN

1 pound lump crabmeat
1 pound shrimp, boiled
3 tablespoons melted butter
2 teaspoons sherry
3 ounces sharp American
    cheese

3 cups Medium Cream Sauce
salt and pepper to taste
½ cup crushed Ritz crackers
½ cup Romano cheese, grated
1 tablespoon paprika

Pick over crab, removing any shell. Peel, clean and devein shrimp. Sauté shrimp and crabmeat in butter. Add sherry, American cheese and hot cream sauce. Season with salt and pepper. Pour into individual oven-proof dishes. Sprinkle tops with crumbs, romano cheese and paprika. Dot with butter and bake until heated at 350° F. Yield: 4 to 6 servings.

SHRIMP SCAMPI

2 pounds fresh shrimp　　　　*¼ cup butter, melted*
3 cloves garlic, finely minced　*⅛ teaspoon ground pepper*
¼ teaspoon salt　　　　　　*2 tablespoons lemon juice*
2 tablespoons fresh parsley,　*¼ cup olive oil*
　chopped

Shell and devein shrimp, leaving fantail on. Combine all remaining ingredients; mix well. Dip shrimp in mixture, place in shallow pan in single layer. Pour remaining sauce over shrimp. Broil 6 to 8 minutes, 3 inches from heat. Yield: 4 servings.

"Quick and easy."

SEAFOOD CASSEROLE

2 (6 ounce) packages wild　　　*½ onion, grated*
　and long grain rice mix　　*1 cup chopped green pepper*
1 pound lump crabmeat,　　　*1 cup chopped celery*
　cleaned or 3 (6 ounce)　　*1 (14 ounce) jar pimento,*
　cans white crabmeat　　　　*chopped*
1 pound fresh shrimp,　　　　*2 tablespoons lemon juice*
　cooked or 4 (4½ ounce)　　*1 (8 ounce) can button*
　cans shrimp, drained　　　　*mushrooms*
3 cans cream of mushroom　　*1 (14 ounce) can artichoke*
　soup　　　　　　　　　　*hearts, drained well*

Cook rice as label directs. Remove any cartilage from crab. Rinse shrimp in cold water and drain well. Preheat oven to 325° F. Mix all ingredients and place in a greased 4-quart casserole. Bake for 1½ hours, or use two 2-quart dishes and bake for 45 minutes. Yield: 14 servings.

SHRIMP VERMOUTH

water
1 cup white Vermouth
4 to 5 lemons, halved
1 teaspoon garlic salt
1 tablespoon coarse ground
    black pepper

2½ cups butter (no
    substitute)
5 pounds shrimp, raw in
    shell, rinsed

In large boiler place enough water to cover bottom, about ½ inch in depth. Add Vermouth, juice and ungrated rinds of lemon halves, seasonings and butter. Bring to boil, add shrimp. Simmer until shrimp are pink. Cover pot and remove from heat; let stand 5 to 10 minutes before serving. Retain sauce to dip with French bread. Yield: 8 to 10 servings.

SHRIMP BOIL SEASONINGS

3 tablespoons salt
15 to 20 whole allspice
⅛ teaspoon black pepper
15 cloves
6 to 8 peppercorns
2 pinches thyme
pinch red pepper

6 garlic cloves, sliced
3 small onions, sliced
2 bay leaves
2 sprigs of parsley
2½ quarts water
2½ pounds raw headless
    shrimp

Place all ingredients except shrimp into a large kettle. Bring to a boil. Add shrimp. Bring to a boil again. Cook 3 minutes or until shrimp turns to bright pink. Remove shrimp immediately from liquid. Drain. Cool. Shell and devein shrimp for use in other recipes.

SAUTÉED SCALLOPS

½ cup butter
1 clove garlic, quartered

1½ pints Bay scallops,
    drained and patted dry

Put butter in skillet. Add garlic. When butter is melted and bubbly, remove garlic and add dried scallops. Cook for 5 to 6 minutes. Yield: 4 servings.

BAKED SEAFOOD SALAD

1 cup canned or fresh
  crabmeat
1 cup canned or cooked
  shrimp
1 cup chopped green pepper
½ cup chopped onion
1 cup chopped celery

1 cup mayonnaise
½ teaspoon salt
pepper
1 teaspoon Worcestershire
  sauce
buttered crumbs
paprika

Combine the crabmeat and shrimp with vegetables and mayonnaise. Add salt, pepper and Worcestershire sauce. Mix well. Place in individual shells or 2-quart baking dish. Cover with buttered crumbs. Bake 30 minutes at 350° F. Serve with lemon slice covered with paprika. Yield: 4 servings.

COQUILLES ST. JACQUES WITH SHRIMP

1 pound scallops
½ pound shrimp, peeled
½ pound mushrooms, sliced
3 green onions, sliced
2 or 3 tablespoons butter
2 tablespoons fine bread
  crumbs

1 cup dry white wine
1 tablespoon finely chopped
  parsley
salt to taste
fine bread crumbs
Parmesan cheese, grated

Sauté scallops, shrimp, mushrooms and onions in 2 or 3 tablespoons hot butter for about 3 minutes. Add bread crumbs and dry white wine. Simmer for 8 to 10 minutes, or until sauce is slightly thickened. Add parsley and salt to taste. With slotted spoon, divide scallops, shrimp and mushrooms into 4 ramekins. Divide sauce over each. This may be set aside until ready to serve. When ready to serve, top with fine bread crumbs and Parmesan cheese, moderately, not too thick. Reheat under broiler until bubbly and lightly browned. Yield: 4 servings.

"A real gourmet delight."

SCALLOPS SAVANNAH

1 pound scallops, cut in
    bite-size pieces
2 tablespoons melted butter
½ cup vegetable oil
2 egg yolks, beaten
2 tablespoons instant minced
    onion
2 tablespoons fresh parsley,
    chopped
1 tablespoon chives, chopped
2 tablespoons lemon juice

2 tablespoons sour cream
1 teaspoon dill weed
1 teaspoon Dijon mustard
½ teaspoon salt
½ teaspoon tarragon leaves
½ teaspoon anchovy paste
1 (2 ounce) jar diced pimento
4 stalks celery, chopped
parsley sprigs (optional)
cherry tomatoes (optional)

Sauté scallops in butter for 2 minutes. Cool, drain and spoon
into a shallow dish. Combine remaining ingredients except
parsley sprigs and tomatoes. Stir well and pour over scallops.
Cover and chill overnight. Spoon scallops onto serving plate.
Garnish with parsley sprigs and tomatoes, if desired. Yield:
6 to 8 servings.

ESCALLOPED OYSTERS

1 pint oysters, drained
dash Tabasco
½ cup finely chopped celery
1½ cups Ritz crackers,
    crumbled

¼ cup butter, melted
6 tablespoons cream plus
    oyster liquor

Pick over oysters removing any shell. Place in small bowl.
Add Tabasco. Line quart casserole bottom with oysters, then
layers of celery, crumbs and butter. Repeat layers and end
with crackers on top. Pour liquids over. Bake at 350° F for 30
minutes. Yield: 3 servings.

FRIED OYSTERS

oysters
salt and pepper

egg
cracker meal

Select large oysters, drain and dry. Sprinkle lightly with salt
and pepper. Dip into beaten egg, then into cracker meal. Put a
few at a time in a wire frying basket. Fry in deep hot fat.
Brown well and allow to drain on paper.

LYNNHAVEN OYSTER POT PIE

1 quart oysters
4 tablespoons butter
2 tablespoons finely chopped
    shallots
2 tablespoons flour
1 cup coffee cream
2 egg yolks
¾ tablespoon salt
2 tablespoons Worcestershire
    sauce

1 teaspoon chives
1 teaspoon Monosodium
    Glutamate
1 tablespoon lemon juice
few drops Tabasco sauce
½ cup dry white wine
½ cup Ritz cracker crumbs
paprika

Poach the oysters. Drain the liquid and set to one side. Sauté
shallots in 2 tablespoons butter until they attain a little color.
Add the flour. Stir and cook for about 5 minutes. Add 1 cup
oyster liquid and 1 cup coffee cream to flour. Stir with wire
whisk. Cook until smooth and add the oysters. Bring to a boil
and keep stirring for a few more minutes. Put in a bowl the
yolks of eggs, salt, Worcestershire sauce, chives, Monosodium
Glutamate, lemon juice, Tabasco sauce and wine. Beat this
well and add to the oyster mixture. Mix together well. Do not
bring to a boil. Put the oysters into a 2-quart casserole or a
shallow pan. Sprinkle with the cracker crumbs, 2 tablespoons
butter and paprika. Put this in hot oven to brown, or under
broiler. You can add a cup of diced boiled salt pork and/or a
cup of mushrooms to the ingredients for variety. Also you can
cover the pie with pie dough instead of the cracker crumbs
and bake until dough is done. Yield: 4 servings.

The Cloister, Sea Island, Georgia.

OYSTERS LAFETTE

4 tablespoons butter
¼ cup chopped green onions
1 clove garlic, minced
2 cups chopped fresh
    mushrooms
¼ cup chopped parsley
2 cups cooked shrimp

½ teaspoon salt
¼ teaspoon dry mustard
1 cup half and half
¼ cup flour
2 dozen oysters and liquor
½ cup sherry

TOPPING:
fine bread crumbs
2 tablespoons butter, melted

1 cup Mozzarella cheese

Sauté vegetables in 4 tablespoons butter. Add shrimp, salt, and dry mustard. Simmer 5 minutes. Add this to cream sauce made from half and half, flour, oyster liquor and sherry. Place 3 or 4 oysters in ramekins and cover with sauce. Top with bread crumbs mixed with butter. Top with grated cheese. Bake for 15 to 20 minutes at 325° F. Yield: 6 servings.

To freeze shellfish: Shrimp, oysters and clams should be frozen raw either in the shell or shelled. If shrimp and oysters are cooked first, they toughen during the freezing period. Crab and lobster should be cooked and the meat removed from the shell before freezing.

WILD RICE AND OYSTER CASSEROLE

1 package Long Grain and
    Wild Rice mixture
2 pints oysters
salt and pepper
Tabasco sauce
1 can cream of celery soup

½ cup light cream
1 tablespoon chopped parsley
1 teaspoon onion powder
½ teaspoon thyme
1 teaspoon curry powder

Cook rice according to directions. Place half in bottom of baking dish; cover with the oysters after seasoning with salt, pepper and Tabasco. Add remaining rice. Heat soup; add cream and remaining ingredients. Pour soup mixture over rice and bake at 325° F for 45 minutes. Yield: 12 servings.

CRAB IMPERIAL

2 tablespoons butter
½ cup diced green peppers
1 tablespoon chopped green
  onion
1 tablespoon chopped parsley
½ pound fresh mushrooms,
  minced
1 pound crabmeat
½ cup mayonnaise

2 tablespoons capers
¼ cup white wine
1 tablespoon horseradish
2 tablespoons Worcestershire
  sauce
1 tablespoon grated lemon
  rind
dash Tabasco sauce
½ cup bread crumbs

Sauté peppers, onion, parsley and mushrooms in butter. Add crabmeat. In a bowl combine mayonnaise, capers, wine, horseradish, Worcestershire sauce, lemon rind and Tabasco. Mix sautéed vegetables and crab with mixture in bowl. Place all ingredients into a 1-quart baking dish. Top with bread crumbs. Bake in a preheated 375° F oven for 25 minutes. Serve immediately. Yield: 6 servings.

"Pretty baked and served in seashell bakers."

CRABMEAT ST. JACQUES

½ cup chopped onion
½ cup chopped green pepper
½ cup minced mushrooms
butter
2 cups Medium White Sauce
salt, pepper, paprika to taste

1 teaspoon Worcestershire
  sauce
1 pound crabmeat
¼ cup grated sharp Cheddar
  cheese
¼ cup buttered bread
  crumbs

Sauté onion, pepper and mushrooms in butter; cook until tender. In another pan combine white sauce, salt, pepper, paprika and Worcestershire sauce. Add to sautéed vegetables. Add crabmeat. Put in 2-quart buttered casserole. Sprinkle with cheese, crumbs and paprika. Bake in 450° F oven for 15 minutes. Yield: 6 to 8 servings.

One pound of lump crabmeat serves 6 persons.

TERIYAKI FLOUNDER

2 cups soy sauce
4 cups water
2 tablespoons ginger

6 cloves garlic, minced
2 teaspoons salt
8 flounder fillets

Combine the soy sauce, water, ginger, garlic and salt in shallow pan. Add the fillets and cover. Marinate for 2 to 4 hours. Grill the fillets over hot coals until golden brown. Cooking time varies according to size of fillets. Yield: 8 servings.

FLOUNDER FLORENTINE

2 (10 ounce) packages frozen
  leaf spinach
½ pound fresh mushrooms
2 tablespoons butter
3 pounds flounder fillets
½ pint oysters
1 tablespoon chopped green
  onion, including top

1 tablespoon chopped fresh
  parsley
1½ cups dry white wine (or
  dry vermouth)
1 tablespoon butter
1 tablespoon flour
½ cup grated Swiss cheese

Cook spinach; drain well. Place in bottom to cover greased baking dish. Sauté mushrooms in 2 tablespoons butter. Set aside. Place fish fillets, oysters, onion and parsley in frying pan. Cover with wine. Cover pan and poach fish about 10 minutes. Fish should flake; oysters should just curl. Remove fish and oysters with a slotted spoon and arrange on the spinach. Add mushrooms. Boil fish liquid until reduced to one-half. Thicken with 1 tablespoon butter and flour blended. Season to taste. Pour sauce over fish; top with grated cheese. Put under broiler until cheese melts and slightly browns. Yield: 6 servings.

FLOUNDER AU GRATIN

1 pound flounder fillets
¼ cup mayonnaise
¼ cup bread crumbs

¼ cup grated Parmesan
  cheese
1 lemon, sliced

Brush the flounder with mayonnaise. Coat with a mixture of bread crumbs and Parmesan cheese. Place fillets in shallow baking dish and bake at 375° F for 20 to 25 minutes. Garnish with lemon slices. Yield: 4 servings.

STUFFED BAKED FISH

4 flounder fillets
salt and pepper to taste
1/2 cup chopped onion
1/2 cup chopped green pepper
2 tablespoons butter
1/2 pound crabmeat, flaked
    fish OR 1 pound shrimp,
    cooked, peeled and
    chopped

1/2 cup chopped mushrooms
2 tablespoons bread crumbs
1 egg
1 teaspoon dry mustard
1 teaspoon parsley flakes
1 teaspoon celery seed

SAUCE:

1 1/2 cups melted butter
1/3 cup lemon juice

2 teaspoons garlic salt
dash Worcestershire sauce

Place two fillets in lined baking pan, sprinkle with salt. Sauté onions and green pepper in butter and combine with all other ingredients. Mound stuffing on fillets and cover with other fillets, skin side up. Score top fillets 3 times and sprinkle with paprika. Bake in 350° F oven approximately 1 hour. Baste frequently with SAUCE. Transfer to serving platter and garnish with parsley and lemon slices. Yield: 4 servings.

VARIATION: Snapper, bass or trout may be substituted for flounder.

LEMON CROWNS: (seafood garnish)

Slice off stem ends. Hold lemon on its side and make a diagonal cut into the core. Remove blade; cut at a 30 degree angle to the first cut. Continue cutting in a zigzag pattern around equator of fruit. Plan ahead so points will meet. Pull 2 halves apart. Place a sprig of parsley in center of crown.

Seafood Sauces

CAPER SAUCE

½ cup butter (no substitute)   half of a (3½ ounce) jar
                                          capers

Melt butter in a small saucepan and pour over pre-cooked fish. Spoon capers over fish, using both capers and juice as seasonings.

TARTAR SAUCE

1 cup mayonnaise
1 tablespoon finely chopped
   dill pickle
1 teaspoon grated onion

1 teaspoon chopped parsley
1 teaspoon chopped pimento
juice of 1 lemon

Combine ingredients; chill. Serve with seafood or fried fish. Yield: 1 cup.

COCKTAIL SAUCE

¾ cup chili sauce
¾ cup catsup
2 heaping tablespoons hot
   horseradish to taste

3 tablespoons lemon juice
½ teaspoon celery salt
1 tablespoon Worcestershire
   sauce

Mix all ingredients. Age in refrigerator a day or two. Recipe secret is good fresh horseradish. A new unopened bottle is best. Yield: 1¾ cups.

LEMON CHIVE SAUCE

⅔ cup butter
3 tablespoons chopped chives
2 tablespoons lemon juice

2 teaspoons grated lemon
   rind
½ teaspoon salt
⅓ teaspoon pepper

Melt butter in saucepan. Add remaining ingredients. Mix thoroughly and pour over baked or broiled fish. Yield: 1 cup.

Serve seafoods in scallop shells; garnish with parsley, lemon or lime slices.

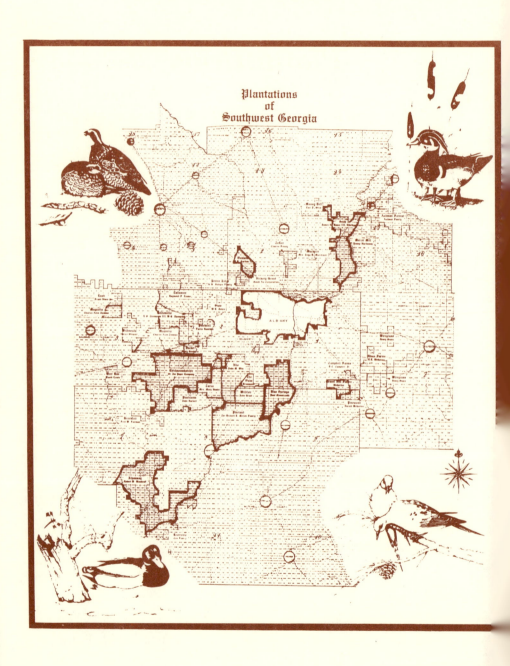

Plantations
of
Southwest Georgia

Plantations

"They come to shoot quail and eat pecan pie" was one succinct comment about visitors who came from all over the world to enjoy the ambience of area plantations. Most of these visitors come during "quail season" to enjoy the sport of quail shooting.

These plantations all have in common the beauty of the surrounding acreage and a pleasant climate. Varying in size, some are old, some newly developed. Although plantations are basically agricultural, some acres are usually set aside for shooting. Just as the owners apply the latest technical knowledge to growing crops, they apply new scientific methods to increase the quail population, not only for shooting, but for preservation. "Quail season" is a time of much social activity for plantation owners. Visitors enjoy a unique experience in a stay at a plantation. There are still mule-drawn wagons for some or horses to be ridden into the fields. No matter what the method of conveyance, hunters follow highly trained bird dogs.

Great pride is taken in making guests comfortable. They are waited on hand and foot and fed well. Lunch in the field may be followed by more quail shooting or a dove shoot. Dinner is a leisurely affair at the "big house."

Menus that fit the lifestyle of the owners and their guests have become modern day tradition. Earlier plantation owners had to rely mostly on what they grew in their own gardens, but today they have available to them a wide variety of foods unknown in times past.

Blue Springs Plantation

PRESIDENT EISENHOWER'S QUAIL HASH

2 stewing hens
20 to 24 quail
onion

salt and pepper to taste
flour (for gravy)

Cook a couple of stewing hens and save broth. (Save chicken for another use.) Cook quail in enough of the chicken broth to cover quail for about 15 minutes. Strip quail of meat and cut into small pieces. Return to pan and cover with broth. Put in small amount of onion. Salt and pepper to taste. Take rest of the broth and make a good rich gravy. Serve with grits. Yield: 6 servings.

President Dwight D. Eisenhower was a guest of W. Alton Jones (a former owner of Blue Springs Plantation) several times. This recipe is copied from the one written by him for John M. Hinson, Sr., Manager of the plantation (1957-1969). President Eisenhower and Mr. Hinson were avid amateur cooks and exchanged quail recipes during a hunter's picnic at Blue Springs.

STUFFED ARTICHOKES

6 cooked artichokes
12 slices bacon
6 chopped green onions
½ pound chopped
    mushrooms
2 tablespoons butter
1 teaspoon beef glaze

½ teaspoon salt
¼ teaspoon pepper
1 tablespoon chopped parsley
2 tablespoons bread crumbs
1 beaten egg
3 tablespoons cooking oil

Remove the chokes from the artichokes and fill with the following stuffing: cook 6 slices of bacon, drain and crumble. Sauté lightly in butter the onions and mushrooms. Add beef glaze, salt, pepper, parsley, bread crumbs, bacon and egg. Mix well and stuff into artichokes. Wrap each with a slice of bacon; tie with a string and place in deep casserole with 3 tablespoons of oil. Bake covered at 300° F for 20 minutes. Remove bacon and string and serve. Yield: 6 servings.

SHRIMP REMOULADE

6 scallions (or green onions),
    chopped
2 tablespoons chopped hard
    boiled eggs
1 tablespoon chopped parsley
1 cup French dressing

3 to 4 tablespoons Louisiana
    Creole mustard
salt and pepper to taste
1½ pounds shrimp, cooked
    and peeled

Combine all ingredients except shrimp and mix well. Marinate the shrimp in the sauce for several hours in the refrigerator. Serve on chilled lettuce. Yield: 8 servings as appetizer, 4 servings as entrée.

BLENDER CHEESE SOUFFLÉ

8 ounces sharp Cheddar
    cheese
10 slices buttered bread,
    crust removed

4 eggs
2 cups milk
1 teaspoon salt
½ teaspoon dry mustard

Put one-half of cheese, bread, eggs and milk in blender (it is not necessary to grate cheese). Turn on high speed until thoroughly mixed. Blend remainder of cheese with salt and mustard. Combine. Cook in greased uncovered casserole (1½ quart) for 1 hour at 350° F. This is not only delicious, but it absolutely never fails. It can be either mixed a day ahead or at the last minute. Yield: 6 to 8 servings.

CUMBERLAND SAUCE FOR HAM

3 finely chopped shallots
1 orange
1 lemon
A little confectioners' sugar
A little cayenne pepper

6 tablespoons melted currant
    jelly
5 tablespoons port wine
½ teaspoon prepared
    mustard (optional)

Parboil shallots in water 1 or 2 minutes, drain. Remove the zest—that is the thinnest peel possible—from the surface skin of the orange and lemon. Cut in fine julienne strips and parboil in water for 10 minutes; drain well. Put shallots, orange and lemon rind in bowl, add the juice of the orange and juice of ½ of the lemon and all the remaining ingredients. Add mustard if a sharper sauce is desired. Yield: 1 cup.

Byron Plantation

CRAB ROLLS

1 pound Velveeta cheese
1 pound butter
2 cans crab meat (or 1 pound
    fresh crab meat)

1½ loaves thin sliced bread
2 cups sesame seeds

Melt cheese and ½ pound butter in double boiler; cool. Add crab meat, stir until cool and spreadable. (Butter and cheese will separate but continue stirring). Remove crusts from bread and roll out with rolling pin until flat. Spread cheese mixture on one side of bread and roll up. Melt remaining butter and add sesame seeds. Roll bread in butter-seed mixture. Lay seam side down on shallow baking dish and freeze. To serve, cut in thirds and broil, about 3 to 5 minutes. Watch closely. Yield: 6 dozen rolls.

HOT CHICKEN SALAD

1 cup slivered almonds
1 cup saltine cracker crumbs
3 cups chopped chicken
2 cups chopped celery
4 tablespoons minced onion
½ cup chicken broth

1 cup mayonnaise
2 cans cream of chicken soup
1 teaspoon lemon juice
1 teaspoon pepper
1 teaspoon Accent

Combine almonds and cracker crumbs; add remaining ingredients and mix well. Place in greased baking dish. Bake at 350° F until bubbly and lightly browned. Yield: 6 to 8 servings.

CURRIED PECANS

1 pound pecans
5 tablespoons vegetable oil
3½ teaspoons sugar

1 teaspoon salt
1½ teaspoons curry powder

Place pecans on baking sheet; sprinkle with oil and spices. Bake at 275° F for about 30 minutes, stirring every 10 minutes. Will keep for 2 to 3 weeks. Do not store in refrigerator. Yield: 1 pound pecans.

Ducker Plantation

Garlic Butter Lamb Chops
Potato Cream Casserole
Honey-Glazed Carrots
Pecan Ice Cream Crunch

GARLIC BUTTER LAMB CHOPS

6 tablespoons butter, softened
4 tablespoons finely chopped
   parsley
4 garlic cloves, finely
   chopped

2 teaspoons lemon juice
8 thick lamb chops
watercress or parsley for
   garnish

Combine butter, parsley, garlic and lemon juice and form into 8 balls. Set aside. Broil lamb chops 5 to 6 minutes on both sides. Season to taste with salt and pepper. Place a butter ball on top of each chop. Put chops on serving platter and garnish with watercress or parsley. Yield: 8 servings.

POTATO CREAM CASSEROLE

2½ cups whipping cream
2 tablespoons butter
3 cloves garlic, finely
   chopped

7 large boiling potatoes,
   peeled
salt and pepper to taste
⅓ cup grated Parmesan
   cheese

Preheat oven to 350° F. Simmer cream, butter and garlic in a saucepan for 15 minutes, until cream has reduced to two-thirds the original quantity. Slice potatoes very thinly and dry on a towel. Butter casserole and make layers of potatoes, salt and pepper and a sprinkle of cheese. Cover potatoes with cream. Add more cream if the potatoes are not covered. Bake uncovered for 1¼ hours. Yield: 8 servings.

HONEY-GLAZED CARROTS

24 baby carrots
6 tablespoons butter

2 tablespoons brown sugar
2 tablespoons honey

Peel carrots and cook in salt water until tender. Drain. Melt butter; add sugar and honey. Stir until blended. Add carrots, turning until well glazed. Cook over low heat about 10 minutes. Use a heavy iron skillet, if possible. Yield: 8 servings.

PECAN ICE CREAM CRUNCH

1 cup chopped pecans
½ cup brown sugar
2 cups Rice Krispies cereal,
  crushed

4 tablespoons butter, softened
½ gallon vanilla ice cream,
  softened

Combine all ingredients except ice cream. Spread crumb mixture on cookie sheet and brown in 375° F oven for 12 minutes. Press crumb mixture in bottom of 9 × 12-inch pan; spread softened ice cream on top. Place in freezer until serving time. Yield: 12 servings.

Fair Oaks Plantation

NARVELLA HADLEY'S CHICKEN DELIGHT

4 whole chicken breasts
1 cup chopped celery
1 cup chopped onions

½ cup chopped bell pepper
1 can cream of chicken soup
parsley and paprika

Put chicken breasts in the bottom of a pyrex dish. Mix the celery, onions and bell pepper and pour over the chicken; add the chicken soup, undiluted. Bake in a 350° F oven about 1 hour until chicken is done. Sprinkle the top with chopped parsley and paprika. Yield: 4 servings.

Holly Plantation

NECTARINE PRESERVES

4 cups finely chopped
  nectarines
2 tablespoons lemon juice

1 box Sure-Jell
5½ cups granulated sugar

Peel and pit nectarines and chop fine. Add lemon juice. Stir Sure-Jell into fruit. Bring this to a full boil over high heat. Stir constantly. Stir in sugar at once. Bring to a rolling boil that cannot be stirred down. Boil hard for several minutes. Remove from heat. Skim off foam with a large metal spoon. Put in hot, sterilized jars immediately and seal. Store preserves in a cool, dry place. Yield: 9 half pints.

GRANNY'S BARBECUE SAUCE

1 (32 ounce) bottle catsup
1 (14 ounce) bottle Kraft
  Barbecue Sauce
juice of 2 lemons
1 teaspoon vinegar

1½ cups sugar
1 tablespoon salt
1 tablespoon pepper
hot sauce to taste

Combine all ingredients and simmer for 30 minutes. Pour over meat. Especially delicious on pork. Yield: approximately 6 cups.

Gillionville Plantation

Grilled Quail

Cheese Grits

Spinach Salad

Homemade Ice Cream

GRILLED QUAIL

12 quail
18 slices bacon
½ cup butter, melted

juice of ½ lemon
12 slices bread, toasted

Stuff each quail with ½ bacon slice. Wrap each quail with a slice of bacon and secure with toothpicks. Mix butter and lemon juice and brush over quail. Let stand about 30 minutes. Roast skewered over coals for 20 to 25 minutes. Trim edges of bread slices and brush each with melted butter or pan drippings. Top with the grilled quail and serve. Yield: 6 servings.

CHEESE GRITS

1 cup grits
4 cups water
¼ cup butter
2½ cups sharp cheese, grated
3 egg yolks mixed with small amount of cream

1 tablespoon Worcestershire sauce
1 clove garlic, crushed (optional)
dash Tabasco sauce
3 stiffly beaten egg whites

Add grits to boiling salted water and cook until thick, about 20 minutes. Stir frequently. While hot, add butter, 2 cups cheese, egg yolks and cream, Worcestershire sauce, garlic and Tabasco. Cool mixture. Fold in stiffly beaten egg whites. Sprinkle ½ cup grated cheese on top. Bake 30 minutes at 400° F in a greased 2-quart casserole. Yield: 6 servings.

SPINACH SALAD

1 pound fresh spinach
½ cup salad oil
2 tablespoons sugar
2 tablespoons rice vinegar
1 teaspoon finely grated
    onion

¼ teaspoon salt
¼ teaspoon dry mustard
6 slices bacon, cooked until
    crisp, drained and
    crumbled

Wash spinach thoroughly in lukewarm water, drain. Chill to crisp. Combine oil, sugar, vinegar, onion, salt and mustard. Beat or blend in blender until dressing becomes thick and syrupy and sugar is thoroughly dissolved. Tear spinach into bite size portions; place in large salad bowl. Add bacon. Pour dressing over all. Let stand about 30 minutes. Toss to thoroughly mix salad. Yield: 6 servings.

BOILED CUSTARD ICE CREAM

4 eggs
pinch of salt
1 cup sugar

1 quart milk or half and half
2 teaspoons vanilla extract

Beat eggs together; add salt and sugar. Mix well and thin with a little of the milk. Pour mixture into milk in a double boiler, cooking until it thickens enough to coat the spoon. When custard thickens, add flavoring. Cool before freezing. Freeze in electric ice cream churn. For chocolate ice cream, add two squares of melted semisweet chocolate. For peach or strawberry ice cream, mash 1 quart of fruit and add to custard. Yield: 12 servings.

Gravel Hill Farms

QUAIL HUNTER'S FIELD PICNIC
Hunter's Consommé
Sliced Rolled Leg of Lamb
Assorted Breads
Marinated Vegetable Salad
Brownie Drops

HUNTER'S CONSOMMÉ

6 cups beef broth	1 clove garlic
3 ripe tomatoes, coarsely chopped	1 small bay leaf
1 onion (stuck with 2 whole cloves)	

Combine all ingredients in a saucepan. Cook covered over low heat for 45 to 50 minutes. Strain through a fine sieve. Serve very hot. For field picnic, place in thermos. Serve in cups, no spoon necessary. Yield: 6 servings.

MARINATED VEGETABLES

1 (1 pound) package carrots	½ cup sugar
1 bunch broccoli	3 cloves garlic
1 head cauliflower	1 tablespoon Dijon mustard
½ pound fresh mushrooms	1 tablespoon salt
1½ cups salad oil	1½ teaspoons pepper
3 cups tarragon vinegar	1 pint cherry tomatoes

Scrape carrots and cut into ¼ inch thick rounds. Blanch in boiling water for 2 minutes. Wash broccoli and cut flowerets into bite size pieces. Wash cauliflower and cut it into bite size pieces. Wash mushrooms and trim stems. Mix oil, vinegar, sugar and spices together. Put vegetables in large bowl or covered container and pour marinade over them. Chill overnight. Add cherry tomatoes about 2 hours before serving. Summer squash, zucchini and sliced cucumbers can be added if used for an appetizer. Serves 8 to 12 as salad.

ROLLED LEG OF LAMB

1 (5 or 6 pound) leg of lamb,
   boned
1 cup chopped parsley
1 teaspoon ground rosemary
   or thyme
4 tablespoons minced green
   onions

2 cloves garlic, finely minced
½ teaspoon powdered ginger
2 teaspoons salt
½ teaspoon pepper

Have butcher bone leg of lamb and supply you with butcher's twine to tie the leg when it is stuffed and rolled. Mix stuffing ingredients together in a bowl. Spread mixture inside the boned leg, carefully filling the pockets left by the bones. Roll up tightly and tie with twine. Roast in a 350° F oven 1¾ to 2 hours for medium rare or 2 to 2¼ hours for well done. (Recommend use of meat thermometer). Chill, slice thinly for sandwiches. May also be served hot for other occasions. Yield: 8 to 10 servings (for sandwiches).

BROWNIE DROPS

2 (4 ounce) bars Baker's
   German Chocolate
1 tablespoon butter
2 eggs
¾ cup sugar
¼ cup flour

¼ teaspoon baking powder
⅛ teaspoon salt
¼ teaspoon cinnamon
½ teaspoon vanilla extract
¾ cup finely chopped pecans

Melt chocolate and butter over hot water. Cool. Beat eggs until foamy; then add sugar, 2 tablespoons at a time. Beat until thickened. Blend in chocolate. Add flour, baking powder, salt and cinnamon. Blend. Stir in vanilla and nuts. Drop by teaspoons onto greased baking sheet. Bake in moderate oven (350° F) until cookies feel "set" when lightly touched, about 8 to 10 minutes. Yield: 3 dozen.

Nilo Plantation

HORS D'OEUVRES
Shrimp Dip

DINNER FOR EIGHT
Corn Soup
Cornish Hens
Brown Rice
Broccoli Casserole
Fabulous Dessert

SHRIMP DIP WITH CRUDITES

1 (4½ ounce) can medium
  shrimp
1 (3 ounce) package cream
  cheese, softened
1 cup sour cream

2 teaspoons lemon juice
1 (0.6 ounce) package Italian
  salad dressing mix
2 tablespoons finely chopped
  green pepper

Drain, rinse and chop shrimp. Beat cream cheese until light and fluffy. Stir in shrimp and remaining ingredients. Chill at least 1 hour. Serve with fresh vegetables. Yield: 1 cup.

CORN SOUP

2½ (16 ounce) cans
  cream-style corn
1 cup milk
½ cup chopped onion
3 tablespoons butter

3 tablespoons flour
1½ teaspoons salt
black pepper to taste
3 cups milk
parsley for garnish

Put corn through sieve or purée in blender. Simmer until tender in 1 cup milk. Sauté onion in butter. Stir flour, salt and pepper into onions making a smooth paste. Add onion mixture to corn, stirring until well blended; add milk. Serve hot with parsley sprinkled on top. Yield: 6 cups.

CORNISH HENS

8 Cornish hens
salt
pepper
tenderizer
2 stalks celery, cut into
    large cubes

2 apples, quartered
2 onions, quartered
1 can chicken broth
2 tablespoons Worcestershire
    sauce
8 slices bacon, cut in half

Clean hens; sprinkle with salt, pepper and tenderizer. Allow to stand for 30 minutes. Place piece of celery, apple and onion in cavity of each hen. Arrange hens in large roaster. Mix broth and Worcestershire sauce together and pour over hens. Place ½ slice bacon in each cavity and one slice on breast of hen. Add enough water to cover bottom of roaster. Cook hens covered in a 350° F oven for 1½ hours, basting often. Remove bacon from breast and cover from roaster to allow to brown about 15 minutes before hens are done. Yield: 8 servings.

BROWN RICE

⅓ cup chopped green peppers
⅓ cup chopped green onions
½ cup sliced mushrooms
2 cups white rice

3 tablespoons butter
1 can chicken broth
1 can water

In a saucepan sauté green peppers, onions, mushrooms, and rice in butter. When just brown, add the broth and water and cook until rice is done. May be served separately or as stuffing for the Cornish hens. Yield: 8 servings.

FABULOUS DESSERT

1 quart coffee ice cream
1 package slivered almonds,
    toasted
1 carton Cool Whip

8 large coconut macaroons,
    toasted and crushed
¼ cup Tia Maria

Mound coffee ice cream by scoops into a tier. Sprinkle with toasted almonds. Cover mound with Cool Whip. Sprinkle with macaroons and then with Tia Maria. Place in freezer to firm before serving. Yield: 8 servings.

BROCCOLI CASSEROLE

1 bunch fresh broccoli or 2
  (10 ounce) packages
  frozen broccoli
2 eggs, beaten
2 tablespoons grated onion
½ cup milk

1 can cream of celery soup
1 cup mayonnaise
1 cup shredded sharp
  Cheddar cheese
buttered Cheese Ritz cracker
  crumbs

Remove tough stems and cut broccoli into 1 inch pieces. Steam in salted water until just tender. Drain. Combine eggs, onions, milk, soup, mayonnaise and cheese. Stir in cooked broccoli. Pour mixture into 2-quart casserole and sprinkle with cracker crumbs and paprika. Bake at 350° F for 30 to 40 minutes. Cool for a few minutes before serving. Yield: 8 servings.

Pebble Ridge Plantation

STUFFED PORK CHOPS

2 cups frozen cut corn
2 cups white bread crumbs
1 teaspoon salt
¼ teaspoon pepper
1 tablespoon chopped onion
2 tablespoons chopped
  parsley
1 tablespoon butter

1 egg, beaten
1 cup chopped fresh apple
½ cup cream
1 teaspoon poultry seasoning
8 (2-rib) pork chops
salt and pepper
1 cup chicken stock or water

Preheat oven to 350° F. Mix corn, crumbs, salt and pepper. Sauté onion and parsley in butter. Add corn mixture with the egg and apple. Stir in cream with a light touch. Add poultry seasoning. Slit pork chops to form pockets. Stuff pockets in pork chops with stuffing mixture and brown on both sides in a heavy skillet. Sprinkle with salt and pepper; pour one cup stock or water in pan, cover and bake at 350° F for 1½ to 2 hours. Add more liquid if necessary. Yield: 8 servings.

PHEBE'S OVEN BEEF STEW

*2 pounds steak, cut in 1 inch
   cubes
1/3 cup flour
1 teaspoon salt
1/4 teaspoon pepper
1 can beef consommé*

*3/4 cup red wine
1/4 cup barbecue sauce
1 cup sliced mushrooms
1 cup sliced carrots
2 cups cubed potatoes
1 dozen small onions*

Dredge steak in flour, salt and pepper. Brown meat 5 minutes in skillet; bake at 350° F for 30 minutes with all liquid (consomme, wine and barbecue sauce). Stir, add seasonings and flour slowly. Add all vegetables. Cover and cook 1½ hours in 350° F oven. Yield: 6 to 8 servings.

GOURMET HAMBURGERS

*1 cup minced yellow onions
6 tablespoons butter
2 pounds ground steak
2 teaspoons salt*

*1/4 teaspoon pepper
1/2 teaspoon thyme
1 cup red wine*

Sauté onions in 4 tablespoons of butter until tender. Mix onions with raw beef, salt, pepper and thyme. Pan fry in equal parts of butter and oil (about 1½ teaspoons each) until patties are medium rare. Remove to hot platter and deglaze the pan with wine. Be sure to scrape up all the pan juices. Reduce wine to at least half. Remove from heat, add 2 tablespoons butter. Stir and pour over hamburgers. Yield: 6 servings.

CREAM CARAMELS

*2 cups sugar
2 cups light corn syrup
1/2 cup butter*

*1/4 teaspoon salt
2 cups evaporated milk
1 teaspoon vanilla extract*

Mix first four ingredients together in a saucepan, bring slowly to boiling point, stirring frequently. Add evaporated milk very slowly so that mixture will not stop boiling. Cook to firm ball stage (248° F), stirring constantly. The candy becomes very thick and will burn easily unless well stirred. Add vanilla. Pour into buttered pan. When mixture becomes cool, mark into squares. When cold, cut and wrap in waxed paper. Yield: 2 pounds.

Pinebloom Plantation

Frozen Daiquiris

Smothered Quail

Consommé Rice

Broccoli with Hollandaise Sauce

Grapefruit and Avocado Salad with Celery Seed
Dressing

Hot Biscuits

Chocolate Luscious Pie

FROZEN DAIQUIRIS

1 quart light rum
1 (48 ounce) can pineapple
juice
1 (48 ounce) can grapefruit
juice

1 (6 ounce) can frozen
limeade
1 (6 ounce) can frozen
lemonade

Mix all ingredients together and put in freezer for several
hours. Serve in short glasses with spoons. Yield: 40 servings.

SMOTHERED QUAIL

16-18 quail
salt and pepper
flour

2 cups chicken broth
white wine

Sprinkle birds with salt and pepper and rub with a little flour.
Brown them in an iron skillet in butter—about 1 to 2 tablespoons butter per each bird. Leave birds in skillet and add 2
cups water and 2 cups chicken broth. Cover and cook slowly in
a moderate 350° F to 375° F oven for about 45 minutes or
until tender. Near the end of cooking, white cooking wine may
be added (this is optional). It is best to baste the birds several
times during cooking to insure that they are not too dry.
Yield: 8 servings.

CONSOMMÉ RICE

½ cup butter	¼ teaspoon pepper
4 tablespoons grated onion	2 cans beef consommé
2 cups raw rice	2 cups water
2¼ teaspoons salt	1 cup mushrooms, sautéed

Melt butter in large frying pan; add onions and cook slightly. Add rice, cook over slow heat, stirring until rice is golden brown. Add salt and pepper, stirring in thoroughly. Place in a 2-quart casserole. When ready to bake, add consommé, water and mushrooms. Mix gently. Cover and bake at 300° F for 1 hour and 15 minutes. Do not stir. Yield: 8-10 servings.

BROCCOLI WITH HOLLANDAISE SAUCE

Cook broccoli until it is tender in hot salted boiling water (try to avoid overcooking). Drain well. Arrange in serving dish. Serve with HOLLANDAISE SAUCE.

HOLLANDAISE SAUCE:

2 egg yolks	½ cup butter
¼ teaspoon salt	1 tablespoon lemon juice
pinch red pepper	

Beat egg yolks with hand mixer (3 to 5 minutes). Add salt and red pepper. Melt butter until bubbly and add very slowly to egg yolks; add lemon juice (or a little more to taste).

GRAPEFRUIT AND AVOCADO SALAD WITH CELERY SEED DRESSING

Arrange grapefruit sections and slices of avocado on chilled Bibb lettuce. Serve with CELERY SEED DRESSING.

CELERY SEED DRESSING:

⅓ cup sugar	¼ cup vinegar or lemon juice
1½ teaspoons dry mustard	1¼ teaspoons grated onion
1½ teaspoons salt	1 cup salad oil
1½ teaspoons celery seed	1 teaspoon paprika

Mix sugar, mustard, salt and celery seed. Add vinegar or lemon juice and onion. Put in a blender and slowly add the oil. Add paprika. When well mixed, pour into container and store in refrigerator. Yield: 2 cups.

CHOCOLATE LUSCIOUS PIE

GRAHAM CRACKER CRUST:

*1½ cups graham cracker
   crumbs
⅓ cup brown sugar*

*½ cup finely chopped pecans
½ cup melted butter*

Combine all ingredients and pack firmly onto bottom and sides of a ten-inch pie pan. Bake at 300° F for 5 minutes. Cool.

FILLING:

*1¼ cups milk
⅓ cup sugar
2 egg yolks
1 envelope unflavored gelatin
¼ cup milk*

*1 square semi-sweet
   chocolate
⅓ cup sugar
2 egg whites
1 teaspoon vanilla extract
1 cup heavy cream, whipped*

Heat 1 cup milk and ⅓ cup sugar just until sugar is dissolved. Beat egg yolks and ¼ cup of hot milk together and slowly add to hot mixture. Cook 2 or 3 minutes, stirring constantly. Soften the gelatin in the remaining ¼ cup milk and add to the hot mixture, stirring until gelatin is dissolved. Chill until partially set (about the consistency of egg white). Cut the square of chocolate with a vegetable peeler. Beat the remaining ⅓ cup sugar with egg whites until quite stiff. Add chocolate, vanilla to partially set mixture. Fold in whipped cream. Fold in the egg whites. Pour all into crust and chill until set. Top with CHOCOLATE SAUCE.

CHOCOLATE SAUCE:

*½ cup chocolate chips
⅓ cup water*

1 tablespoon butter

Heat together to make a smooth sauce and dribble over the top of pie. Return to refrigerator until serving time. Top with dollop of whipped cream. Yield: 8 servings.

Pineland Plantation Lunch in the Field

Charcoal Quail

Macaroni Casserole

Buttered Carrots

Tossed Salad

Blueberry Cobbler

CHARCOAL QUAIL

quail (2 per person)
olive oil or salad oil

CHARCOAL BIRD SAUCE

Marinate quail in oil for at least 2 hours or overnight. Cook over hot charcoal for 20 to 30 minutes basting with CHARCOAL BIRD SAUCE. To serve, pour remaining sauce over quail.

CHARCOAL BIRD SAUCE:

½ cup butter
½ cup evaporated milk
1 tablespoon A-1 sauce

1 tablespoon Worcestershire
  sauce
3 tablespoons sherry

Melt butter; add all other ingredients and heat, stirring constantly until well mixed.

MACARONI CASSEROLE

1 (8 ounce) box macaroni
1 can mushroom soup
¼ cup chopped pimento
¼ cup chopped green pepper

¼ cup chopped onion
½ cup mayonnaise
½ pound Cheddar cheese,
  grated

Cook macaroni according to directions on box; drain and set aside. Heat mushroom soup; add pimento, green pepper, onion and mayonnaise. Mix well. In a casserole dish layer macaroni, sauce, then cheese until all is used up. Top with grated cheese. Bake in 350° F oven until bubbly hot, about 25 to 30 minutes. Yield: 6 servings.

BLUEBERRY COBBLER

½ cup butter
1 cup sugar
1 cup self-rising flour

1 cup milk
1 cup blueberries (sweetened
   to taste)

Melt butter and put in baking dish. Mix sugar, flour and milk. Pour over melted butter. Add blueberries. Do not stir. Bake at 350° F for 25 minutes or until done. Yield: 6 servings.

Other Recipes from Pineland

SPLIT PEA SOUP WITH SHERRY

2 cups split peas
3 quarts water
1 ham bone
1 onion, chopped

1 cup chopped celery with
   leaves
½ cup chopped carrots
1 can consommé
sherry to taste

Cover peas with water and soak for 12 hours. Drain peas, put in kettle with water and ham bone. Cook over low heat for 3 hours; add vegetables and simmer 1 hour. Remove ham bone and purée peas. Add more water for right consistency. Place soup in bowls and stir in sherry in each bowl. Yield: 8 servings.

ASPARAGUS QUICHE

1 (9 inch) deep dish pastry
   shell
½ pound cup finely chopped
   ham
1 (8 ounce) can chopped
   asparagus, drained
¾ cup shredded Cheddar
   cheese

¼ cup chopped onion
¼ cup chopped green pepper
2 tablespoons butter
½ pint whipping cream
4 eggs

Preheat oven to 400° F. Bake pastry shell 8 to 10 minutes. Layer ham, asparagus, cheese, onion and pepper into pastry shell; dot with butter. Beat cream and eggs together. Pour over filling. Bake at 350° F for 45 minutes or until set. Let stand 10 minutes before cutting. Yield: 6 servings.

SHRIMP SALAD SUPREME

2 pounds raw shrimp
1½ tablespoons salt
3 cups diced celery
8 green onions, chopped

3 hard cooked eggs
lettuce
tomato wedges
2 hard cooked eggs, minced

Cook shrimp in salted boiling water until they turn pink, about 5 minutes. Clean under cold water. Combine with celery, onions, eggs and FRENCH DRESSING. Place in covered container and refrigerate at least 4 hours or overnight. Serve on lettuce and garnish with tomato wedges and minced eggs. Yield: 8 servings.

FRENCH DRESSING:

1 can tomato soup
½ cup vinegar
½ cup salad oil
¼ cup sugar
2 tablespoons Worcestershire
   sauce

1 tablespoon prepared
   mustard
1 teaspoon salt
1 teaspoon paprika
½ teaspoon pepper
1 clove garlic, minced

Combine all ingredients. Chill overnight to blend flavors. Yield: Approximately 2½ cups.

CRAB MAIRE

4 green onions, chopped
½ cup chopped parsley
½ cup butter
2 tablespoons flour
1 pint half and half

½ pound Swiss cheese,
   grated
1 tablespoon sherry
salt and pepper to taste
1 pound crabmeat

Sauté green onions and parsley in butter. Stir in flour; add half and half cream to make sauce. Add all other ingredients except crab meat. Cook over low heat until cheese is melted. Add crab meat and heat. Place in chafing dish and serve with melba toast rounds or toast points. Yield: 50 servings.

Pinewood Plantation

FROZEN GRAND MARNIER SOUFFLÉ

1 cup sugar
⅓ cup water
2 tablespoons grated orange
   rind
6 egg yolks, beaten

¼ cup Grand Marnier
2 cups whipping cream
1 sponge cake cut in 1 inch
   cubes

Boil sugar, water and orange rind over moderate heat. Cook this syrup to 220° F on a candy thermometer. Beat egg yolks until thick and lemon colored. Pour the syrup in a stream over the egg yolks and heat until thick. Cool. Beat in Grand Marnier. Beat the cream until lightly whipped and fold into yolk mixture. Fit a 4-cup soufflé dish with a collar of wax paper, 6 inches wide, doubled and oiled to form a collar extending 2 inches above the rim. Tie with a string. Spoon a 2 inch layer of the custard into the dish and top with ½ the cake cubes. Cover the cake cubes with another layer of the custard and add the remaining cake cubes and top with remaining custard. Freeze at least 6 hours. Serve with whipped cream flavored with Grand Marnier. Yield: 6 to 8 servings.

SOUSED APPLE CAKE

4 cups cooking apples
1 cup raisins
brandy
2 cups sugar
½ cup salad oil
2 eggs
2 cups flour

2 teaspoons cinnamon
2 teaspoons baking soda
1 teaspoon nutmeg
1 teaspoon salt
¼ teaspoon mace
1 cup chopped pecans
whipped cream

Peel, core and finely chop apples; put into bowl with raisins and cover with brandy, and soak overnight. Drain apples and raisins. Set aside. Combine sugar, salad oil and eggs. Set aside. Sift together flour, cinnamon, baking soda, nutmeg, salt and mace. Add to oil mixture. Mix in apples, pecans and raisins. Mix well and pour into an oiled 9 × 13 baking dish. Cook in 325° F oven for 1 hour. Cut in squares. Serve topped with sweetened whipped cream. Yield: 15 to 20 servings.

CHOCOLATE RING WITH BING CHERRY SAUCE

CAKE:

1½ squares semi-sweet
   chocolate
2 tablespoons butter
1 cup sugar
2 eggs, unbeaten

½ cup milk
1 cup cake flour, sifted
1 teaspoon baking powder
1 teaspoon vanilla extract

Preheat oven to 325° F. Melt chocolate and butter together in a double boiler. Gradually add sugar, eggs (one at a time), milk, flour, baking powder and vanilla. Mix together. Pour into a buttered 1-quart ring mold. Bake 20 minutes.

SAUCE:

2 cans Bing cherries, pitted
2 tablespoons flour
½ cup sugar
juice of 1 lemon

½ cup chopped pecans
½ pint whipping cream,
   whipped and sweetened
   to taste

Drain cherries reserving juice. Mix flour and reserved cherry juice in double boiler. Add sugar and lemon juice; cook until it thickens. Add pecans and cherries. Pour over chocolate ring. Fill center with whipped cream. Yield: 6 to 8 servings.

RICH PUMPKIN PIE

1 cup pumpkin, steamed and
   strained or canned
   pumpkin
1 cup heavy cream
1 cup sugar
4 teaspoons brandy
3 eggs, slightly beaten

1 teaspoon cinnamon
1 teaspoon nutmeg
¾ teaspoon salt
¾ teaspoon ginger
¼ teaspoon mace
1 (10 inch) pastry shell

Combine all ingredients; mix thoroughly. Pour into unbaked pastry shell. Bake at 350° F for 1 hour or until firm. Butternut squash may be substituted for pumpkin. Yield: 8 servings.

Riverview Plantation

Catfish
Hushpuppies
Green Tomato Pickles
French Fried Onion Rings
Collard Greens
Coleslaw
Vanilla Ice Cream and Sauce

RIVERVIEW PLANTATION'S CHANNEL CATFISH

Select fish no larger than one-half pound. Salt and roll fish in cornmeal. (An easy way is to put cornmeal and fish in paper sack and shake until fish is well-coated with meal.) Deep fry in peanut oil pre-heated to 400° F. Cook 13 minutes. Drain well and serve with hushpuppies and coleslaw.

HUSHPUPPIES

1½ cups yellow cornmeal
   (not self-rising)
½ cup self-rising flour
1 small onion, chopped

½ teaspoon salt
½ teaspoon baking powder
1 egg
1 cup milk

Mix all ingredients to a rather stiff batter consistency. Drop in hot peanut oil pre-heated to 350° F, one teaspoon of batter at the time. Dip spoon in a glass of water after each hushpuppy is dropped. Cook until golden brown. Yield: about 3 dozen.

GREEN TOMATO PICKLES

7 pounds green tomatoes
2 cups lime
4 gallons water
4 ounces alum
2 quarts vinegar

5 pounds sugar
1 (1¼ ounce) box pickling
   spices
cheese cloth

Wash and slice tomatoes. Mix lime with 2 gallons of water. Soak tomatoes in this solution for 24 hours. Drain and wash lightly. Mix 2 gallons of water with alum. Soak tomatoes in this solution for 24 hours. Drain tomatoes and soak for 6 hours in plain water to cover. Mix vinegar and sugar. Soak tomatoes in this solution for 3 hours. Add pickling spices tied in cheese cloth. Cook over medium heat below boiling point for 1 hour. Remove cheese cloth bag. Put into sterilized jars while hot and seal.

FRENCH FRIED ONION RINGS

Cut onion rings ⅛ inch thick. Soak in ice water sweetened with 2 or 3 teaspoons of sugar.

1 cup flour
2 tablespoons salad oil
¼ teaspoon salt

⅔ cup water
1 egg white, stiffly beaten

Mix first four ingredients, fold in egg white. Drain onion rings and pat dry. Dip into batter and fry in deep fat until golden brown.

MISS TEKIE'S COLLARD GREENS

Cook a piece of country ham or bacon in water to cover until tender. Add cleaned and washed collard greens and cook at least 1½ to 2 hours longer. (The secret of good collards is to let liquid cook down low and have plenty of seasonings. You might need to add extra bacon drippings.) Salt to taste. Chop collards well before serving.

COLESLAW

1 head cabbage
2 carrots
1 medium onion

sweet pickle relish
coleslaw dressing

Grate cabbage, carrots and onion. Add sweet pickle relish and coleslaw dressing in desired amounts.

ICE CREAM SAUCE

1 cup dark brown sugar
3 tablespoons white Karo
   syrup

3 tablespoons butter
¼ cup milk
1 cup chopped pecans

Combine all ingredients in a saucepan, bring to a boil and cook 3 minutes. Do not stir. Remove from heat and add chopped pecans. Serve on vanilla ice cream.

Tallassee Plantation

AVOCADO LaRUE

6 avocados
12 teaspoons (heaping) red
   jellied consommé
12 tablespoons sour cream

12 teaspoons (heaping)
   caviar
lettuce or watercress

Cut the avocados in half. Leave the peeling on and remove seed. Top the center of each half with a heaping teaspoon of jellied consommé. Place a tablespoon of sour cream on top of consommé and top with caviar. Serve on chilled lettuce or watercress. Yield: 12 servings.

BEEF OR VENISON STEW

4 pounds boneless beef or
    venison, cut in 1½ inch
    cubes
½ cup flour
6 tablespoons fat
hot water
7 carrots, cut in small
    chunks

4 peeled potatoes, cut in
    small chunks
3 small onions or 4 shallots,
    cut in quarters
salt and pepper to taste
sour cream or chopped
    peanuts

Dredge meat in flour. Add meat to hot fat and brown. Add just enough hot water to cover meat. Cover and simmer for 2 hours until tender. Add carrots, potatoes, onions, salt and pepper. Cook 30 minutes longer. Serve topped with sour cream or chopped peanuts. Yield: 8 servings.

Tolee Plantation

TOLEE'S PECAN BREAD

1 cup corn oil
2 cups sugar
3 eggs
2 cups self-rising flour
1 teaspoon nutmeg

1 teaspoon allspice
1 teaspoon cinnamon
1 jar junior baby food
    prunes
1 cup chopped pecans

Mix sugar and oil. Add eggs and beat at high speed for three minutes. Sift flour and spices and add to mix. Add prunes and mix well. Fold in pecans. Pour into greased and floured tube pan or loaf pan. Bake at 325° F for 1 hour and 20 minutes, or until toothpick pushed into center comes out clean and bread begins to pull away from sides of pan. Pecan breads will freeze well. Yield: 12-15 servings.

BLUEBERRY PECAN TORTE

2 cups graham cracker
  crumbs

½ cup sugar
1 stick butter, softened

Mix together and press into a greased 3-quart rectangular baking dish. Chill.

FIRST LAYER:

8 ounces cream cheese
½ cup sugar

2 tablespoons milk
2 cups chopped pecans

Cream cheese, sugar, and milk together. Spread over graham cracker crust. Top with chopped pecans.

SECOND LAYER:

½ cup whipping cream
2 teaspoons sugar

1 teaspoon vanilla extract

Whip cream, add sugar and vanilla. Spread whipped cream over first layer.

THIRD LAYER:

1 quart blueberries
1 cup sugar

3 tablespoons cornstarch

Combine blueberries, sugar and cornstarch. Cook over medium heat in a saucepan until it starts to boil and thicken slightly. Remove from heat and cool. Spread over whipped cream layer. Refrigerate torte. Cut into squares to serve. Yield: 12 servings.

Wildfair Plantation

HORS D'OEUVRES
Salmon Dip
Pita Crisps

DINNER RECIPES
Chicken Casserole
Artichokes and Peas
Zucchini Bake
Cucumber Aspic
Whisper

SALMON DIP

1 (16 ounce) can red salmon
*1 (8 ounce) package cream
   cheese, softened*
5 teaspoons liquid smoke
2 tablespoons lemon juice
2 tablespoons grated onions
1 tablespoon horseradish
½ cup chopped pecans

Remove bone and skin from salmon. Mix salmon and cheese. Add all other ingredients, reserving ¼ cup pecans. Mix well. Before serving sprinkle with remaining pecans. Best made a day ahead. Serve with wheat thins. Yield: 3 cups.

PITA CRISPS

pita bread loaves
½ cup softened butter
¼ cup Parmesan cheese

Tear pita bread loaves in half. Mix butter with Parmesan cheese. Spread on 6 to 8 flats being very skimpy with mixture. Tear into pieces—about 4 per flat. Heat in 300° F oven until crisp. Watch closely, as they burn easily. This is an excellent hors d'oeuvre if each flat is torn into about 8 pieces.

219

CHICKEN CASSEROLE

6 whole chicken breasts
1 pound vermicelli
1 large can sliced
    mushrooms
1 (4 ounce) package slivered
    almonds

3 cans cream of chicken soup
1 tablespoon onion flakes
½ cup sherry
1 teaspoon curry powder
10 ounces grated cheese

Poach breasts until tender. Remove from bone and cut into bite size pieces. Refrigerate chicken broth. When cold, remove fat. Do this the day ahead if possible. Cook vermicelli according to package directions. Drain and return to cooking pot. Add chicken broth and stir. Mix drained mushrooms, almonds, chicken soup, onion, sherry, and curry powder. Into a large buttered pyrex dish, layer half vermicelli, chicken, soup mixture and cheese. Repeat for second layer. If made day in advance, heat 325° F for 1 hour. If made and served right away heat 350° F until cheese is a golden brown. Freezes nicely in one layer with no cheese. Add grated cheese when thawed and ready to cook. Yield: 10 to 12 servings.

CUCUMBER ASPIC

1 (3 ounce) package lime
    Jello
1 cup boiling water
1 cup shredded cucumbers

½ teaspoon salt
¼ teaspoon grated onion
1 tablespoon cider vinegar

Dissolve Jello in water. When it begins to congeal, stir in remaining ingredients and put in a round mold. Serve on Bibb lettuce; top with mayonnaise. Yield: 6 servings.

ARTICHOKES AND PEAS

1 (10 ounce) package frozen
   artichokes, thawed
3 tablespoons butter
1 (10 ounce) package frozen
   green peas, thawed

½ cup water
1 tablespoon butter
pinch of salt and sugar
1 teaspoon bouquet garni

Quarter artichokes and sauté in butter; add remaining ingredients. Cover and simmer until peas are tender and liquid has evaporated, about 25 minutes. Yield: 4 servings.

ZUCCHINI BAKE

5 medium zucchini, sliced
2 tablespoons minced onion
1 clove garlic, pressed
3 tablespoons olive oil (do
   not substitute)

3 tablespoons butter
5 eggs
½ cup Parmesan cheese

Sauté first 3 ingredients in oil and butter until zucchini is almost done. Transfer to buttered casserole. Mix eggs and cheese. Pour over zucchini. Press lightly so zucchini is covered with egg mixture. Bake at 300° F for 30 minutes. Yield: 8 servings.

WHISPER

brandy
Creme de Cacao

coffee ice cream

Soften ice cream. Place 1 scoop of ice cream, 1 jigger of brandy and 1 ounce of Creme de Cacao in blender; mix all ingredients and pour in parfait glasses. Serve immediately. This dessert takes the place of both coffee and after dinner drink. Number of servings depends on number of scoops of ice cream used. Allow 1 scoop per person.

Willow Oak Plantation

Cold Avocado Soup
Game Pie
Fresh Asparagus with Sieved Egg
Baked Caramel Crème Brûlée
Paul Masson Chablis

GAME PIE

3 wood ducks, cleaned
1 onion, diced
1 apple, diced
2 stalks celery, diced
4 quail, cleaned and split in
*   half*
6 tablespoons butter
1 small can chopped black
*   olives*
1 carrot, shredded

½ pound mushrooms, sliced
4 fresh bay leaves
salt and pepper to taste
3 tablespoons flour
1 can consommé
¼ cup port wine
1 sheet frozen puff pastry
1 egg yolk
1 teaspoon water

The day before, roast duck stuffed with onion, apple and celery for 1 to 1½ hours at 350° F, covered. Remove stuffing and refrigerate. Slice all meat from ducks and refrigerate overnight. Brown quail in 3 tablespoons butter. Cover and cook in oven for about 25 minutes until tender (350° F). Chop reserved stuffing in food processor until puréed. Combine duck meat, quail, olives, carrots, mushrooms, bay leaves and the puréed, cooked stuffing; add seasonings. Divide between 2 one-quart pyrex loaf pans. Make sauce by blending flour and 3 tablespoons butter in food processor. Bring consommé to a boil; blend into flour mixture; add port. Pour over game; let stand several hours (the sauce will thicken while pies bake in oven). Preheat oven to 375° F. Let pastry set at room temperature for 20 minutes, just long enough to handle. On floured board, cut in half and fit over loaf pans, pulling taut. Leave ½ inch overhang. Crimp; brush with egg wash (1 yolk mixed with teaspoon water). Bake 25 minutes until puffy and hot. Yield: 6 servings.

COLD AVOCADO SOUP

3 ripe avocados
2 cups chicken broth (or
    stock)
1 cup sour cream

1 cup cream
1/4 teaspoon chili powder
salt and pepper to taste
3 tablespoons light rum

Peel, remove seed and chop avocados. Mix all ingredients. Process 1/2 of the ingredients in food processor or blender. Set aside. Process second half. Mix together; chill several hours. Serve with shredded almonds, if desired. Yield: 6 servings.

FRESH ASPARAGUS WITH SIEVED EGG

3 pounds tiny, fresh
    asparagus
1/4 cup butter
juice of 1/2 lemon

2 sieved eggs
salt and pepper
paprika

Steam asparagus until barely tender. Place in serving dish. Pour melted butter mixed with lemon juice over vegetable. Sprinkle on egg and seasonings. Yield: 6 servings.

BAKED CARAMEL CRÈME BRÛLÉE

3 cartons heavy cream
5 eggs
1/4 cup white sugar

1 teaspoon Amaretto or
    vanilla extract
brown sugar

Preheat oven to 350° F. In blender mix cream, eggs and white sugar. Add flavoring. Pour into 2-quart oven proof serving casserole. Place in pan of water and bake for 1 hour or until set and top is brown. Cool. On a buttered round of tin foil placed on cookie sheet, pat out a circle of brown sugar the size of the top of the casserole. Heat broiler to very hot. Slip in brown sugar. Watch until it is melted and bubbly (not long). Remove from oven. Cool. Invert on pudding and peel off tin foil. Refrigerate until serving time. This can be served with drained raspberries or fresh strawberries. Yield: 6 servings.

"This is very simple, but elegant."

Vegetables

Not more than one or two varieties of vegetables should accompany a course, advises a 1907 local cookbook, but often there would be more when a hospitable home was open for Sunday dinner following church services. There would be fried chicken from what seemed like a bottomless platter because as one person recalled "if they ran out, there were always more chickens in the yard which could be caught, killed, dressed and cooked." Family members and friends would be invited to "come on for dinner" when church services were over. With the chicken, or other meat, there probably would have been rice, sweet potato soufflé, apple salad with homemade cooked dressing, vegetables from the garden, homemade pickles, biscuits and dessert.

Vegetables

BASIC VEGETABLE COOKING

General directions:
1. Cook in as little water as possible.
2. Cover with a tight fitting lid.
3. Cook only until vegetable is tender.

Seasonings:
Many Southern cooks prefer to use a meat stock to season many vegetables. This seasoning is especially good for use in leafy greens, string beans, peas or lima beans.

To make a stock, boil meat (ham hock, salt pork, or slab bacon) in 2 to 3 cups water for approximately 30 minutes. Cook vegetable in this stock until tender. Season to taste with salt and pepper.

Others may prefer to season with butter or margarine before serving. Lemon juice, dill or other suitable herbs can be a welcome change to season vegetables.

GEORGIA FIELD PEAS

2 cups shelled field peas   1 tablespoon salt
1 piece seasoning meat or
    ham hock (about 1/4
    pound)

Wash peas, removing any faulty ones. Boil with salt and seasoning meat. For 2 cups peas, use 1 quart boiling water which should reduce itself by 1/3. About 1 hour cooking time is needed. Lady peas or crowder peas may be cooked by this method also. Yield: 6 to 8 servings.

"Transplanted southerners return home for these."

Use a garlic press to grate a small amount of grated onion.

Use an egg slicer to cut mushrooms uniformly.

3 teaspoons of fresh chopped herbs = 1 teaspoon of dry.

FRIED GRITS

1 cup grits
4 cups boiling water
2 teaspoons salt

1 cup flour
1 egg
bacon grease

Pour grits into boiling water; add salt. Slowly boil for 10 minutes; stir frequently. While warm, fill jelly glasses with grits to mold. Chill, overnight if possible. When ready to fry, unmold and cut into ½-inch thick slices. Dip into flour then into an egg which has been beaten with 1 tablespoon water. Into a skillet put enough bacon grease to brown circles of grits. Brown on both sides. Serve hot. Yield: 8 servings.

NEW YEAR'S GOOD LUCK PEAS AND JOWLS

1 pound dried black-eyed
   peas
½ pound smoked hog jowl
2-3 cups water
1 cup chopped onion

red pepper to taste
dash of mace
3 cloves garlic, chopped
salt to taste

Wash peas and cover with water; soak overnight. Cook jowl in water until tender. Add peas, onions, red pepper, mace and garlic; cook slowly about 2 hours. Remove jowl; slice and brown in oven. Season peas with salt. Arrange slices of the meat over the bowl of peas. Yield: 6 servings.

"No true Southerner omits this on New Year's Day. A gusta-tory rabbit's foot."

SOUTHERN OKRA AND TOMATOES

1 cup okra, cut in ½ inch
   slices
½ cup chopped onion
¼ cup chopped green pepper
3 tablespoons margarine or
   bacon fat

4 tomatoes, peeled and
   quartered
1 teaspoon salt
¼ teaspoon pepper
1 cup fresh corn (optional)

Sauté okra, onion and green pepper in margarine or bacon fat over low heat. Add tomatoes and seasonings. Cook until tender, stirring as little as possible. One cup fresh corn cut from cob may be added. Yield: 4 servings.

PLANTATION CORN PUDDING

2 cups fresh corn, about 6 to 8 ears
4 eggs, beaten
1 teaspoon sugar

2 cups cream
2 tablespoons butter
1 teaspoon salt

Remove corn from cob; then scrape cob with spoon. Combine corn with eggs and other ingredients. Pour into buttered 2-quart baking dish; set in shallow pan with 1 inch of water in pan. Bake for 40 minutes at 325° F or until knife inserted comes out clean. Yield: 6 servings.

SOUTHERN FRIED CORN

12 ears corn
¼ cup butter

1 cup milk
salt and pepper to taste

Cut corn from cob. Melt butter in a heavy saucepan or skillet, add corn and small amount of milk (1 tablespoon per ear of corn) and simmer until tender. Season with salt and pepper. Yield: 4 to 6 servings.

TURNIP GREENS

1 bunch fresh turnip greens with roots
2-3 cups water

¼ pound salt pork
2 tablespoons salt
1 tablespoon sugar

Turnip greens should be thoroughly washed to be free of all grit. Remove stems and roots. Into a pot, put water, salt pork, salt and sugar; let boil for 30 minutes. Remove salt pork; add turnip greens and boil for 2 hours. About 20 to 30 minutes before greens are done, peel and dice turnip roots. Then add to greens. Serve with cornbread. Yield: 6 to 8 servings.

"French cooking divine, turnip greens sublime."

When cooking greens, place a small tin cup or can half full of vinegar on the stove near the greens and it will absorb all odor from it.

SWEET CORN ON THE COB

6 young ears of corn   salt
1 tablespoon sugar   butter

Select young tender ears; remove husks, silk and bad spots. Wash corn. Place in water to cover, add sugar, bring to boil. Boil 4 minutes. Season with salt and butter to taste. Yield: 4 to 6 servings.

To remove corn silk, dampen a paper towel and brush downward on the cob or corn. All strands should come off.

SPICE 'N BRANDY SWEET POTATOES

½ cup butter   ½ teaspoon nutmeg
1 cup sugar   ½ teaspoon cinnamon
2 eggs, well beaten   ½ teaspoon salt
1 tablespoon milk   ½ teaspoon mace
rind of ½ lemon   1½ cups mashed sweet
1 tablespoon brandy   potatoes

Cream butter, sugar, eggs, milk and lemon rind. Blend in brandy and spices. Add mashed sweet potatoes, blending well. Bake in greased casserole, 350° F approximately 30 to 45 minutes until brown and firm. May use canned mashed sweet potatoes, if desired. Do not use substitutes for butter and brandy. Yield: 6 servings.

"For festive occasions."

SOUTHERN FRIED SWEET POTATOES

3 medium-sized sweet   3 to 4 tablespoons butter or
    potatoes   margarine
flour   sugar

Wash potatoes and place in saucepan with boiling water to cover. Cover pan and cook over moderate heat about 30 minutes or until just tender. Remove potatoes from water, cool and peel. Cut crosswise into ½ inch slices and coat both sides with flour. Melt butter in skillet, add potatoes and cook until lightly browned on both sides. Sprinkle lightly with sugar. Yield: 4 servings.

CANDIED SWEET POTATOES

8 small sweet potatoes
¾ cup brown sugar
½ cup orange juice
2 tablespoons butter

1 tablespoon grated orange
   rind
2 tablespoons dark syrup

Boil potatoes until tender. Peel and slice. Combine other ingredients and simmer to make thin syrup. Add potatoes to mixture and simmer 30 minutes. Yield: 4 servings.

MAGNOLIA'S SWEET POTATO PUDDING

6 medium-sized sweet
   potatoes, finely grated
3 eggs, beaten

2 cups milk
½ teaspoon nutmeg
2 tablespoons butter

Grease 2-quart baking dish. Mix eggs, milk, nutmeg and butter together; thoroughly combine with sweet potatoes. Place in baking dish. Bake at 350° F. for 30 minutes, then at 425° F. for 5 minutes. Yield: 6 servings.

CREAMY CHIVE-STUFFED POTATOES

8 baking potatoes
vegetable oil
½ cup butter, softened
¼ cup chopped chives
2 tablespoons chopped onion

16 ounces sour cream
½ teaspoon salt
¼ teaspoon pepper
paprika

Scrub potatoes and rub skins with oil. Bake at 400° F for 1 hour or until done. Allow potatoes to cool to touch. Slice skin away from top of each potato. Carefully scoop out pulp, leaving shells intact; mash pulp. Combine potato pulp, butter, chives, onion, sour cream, salt and pepper; mix well. Stuff shells with potato mixture, sprinkle with paprika. Wrap in heavy duty aluminum foil and bake at 400° F for 10 minutes. Yield: 8 servings.

PARTY POTATOES

5 pounds potatoes, peeled
½ cup margarine or butter
1 (8 ounce) package cream
 cheese, softened
1 cup sour cream

½ cup Parmesan cheese,
 grated
4 green onions, chopped (tops
 included)
1 tablespoon salt
½ teaspoon pepper

Boil potatoes until tender about 20 minutes. Mash while hot. Stir in butter and cream cheese. Add remaining ingredients and stir just to combine. Spread in 1 large casserole dish or 2 small ones. Bake at 350° F for about 30 minutes to heat. Yield: 10 to 12 servings.

VIDALIA ONION PIE

1 deep dish pastry shell
3 cups thinly sliced Vidalia
 onions or other sweet
 onions
3 tablespoons butter, melted
½ cup milk

1½ cups sour cream
1 teaspoon salt
2 eggs, beaten
3 tablespoons flour
4 strips bacon, fried and
 crumbled

Bake pastry shell. Cook onions in butter until lightly browned. Spoon into pastry shell. Combine milk, sour cream, salt, eggs and flour. Mix well and pour over onion mixture. Garnish with bacon. Bake at 325° F for 30 minutes or until firm in center. Yield: 6 to 8 servings.

Vidalia onions may be kept for months in hydrator if well-wrapped in heavy paper towels.

CREAMED ONIONS

4 cups sliced onions
4 tablespoons butter
1 teaspoon salt

½ teaspoon pepper
White Sauce
bread crumbs

Sauté onions in butter until limp; add salt and pepper. Place onions in casserole. Make white sauce and pour over onions in casserole. Top with bread crumbs. Bake in 375° F oven until browned. Refer to White Sauce recipe. If prepared ahead of time and refrigerated, let warm until bubbly before serving. Yield: 8 servings.

BEER BATTER ONION RINGS

3 cups flour
3 teaspoons salt
3 cups beer
4 teaspoons vegetable oil

½ cup minced parsley
2 pounds onions
oil for frying

Stir flour, salt, beer and oil until smooth. Let mixture stand covered for 2 hours at room temperature. Stir in parsley. Cut 2 pounds onions into ¼ inch slices. Soak in ice water in refrigerator for 2 hours. Drain and pat dry. Dip into batter, coating well. Fry in 375° F oil for 3 minutes, turning them. Yield: 6 to 8 servings.

SWEET AND SOUR ONIONS

4 large Vidalia onions
¼ cup cider vinegar
½ cup melted butter

½ cup boiling water
½ cup brown sugar

Slice onions and arrange in 1-quart baking dish. Mix remaining ingredients and pour over onions. Bake at 300° F for 1 hour. Yield: 6 to 8 servings.

To help in peeling small onions, pour boiling water over the onions and let stand one minute. Drain and cover with cold water.

BUTTERNUT SQUASH CASSEROLE

2 cups cooked butternut
  squash, mashed
3 eggs, beaten
1 cup sugar
½ cup milk

⅓ cup margarine, melted
2 tablespoons coconut
½ teaspoon ginger
½ teaspoon coconut or
  vanilla extract

Combine all ingredients and pour into 1-quart casserole. Bake at 350° F for 1 hour or until set. Sweet potatoes or pumpkin may be substituted for squash. Yield: 5 to 6 servings.

"Good with ham or turkey."

ZUCCHINI STUFFING CASSEROLE

4 medium zucchini, sliced ½
  inch thick
¾ cup shredded carrots
½ cup chopped onions
6 tablespoons margarine or
  butter

2¼ cups HERB STUFFING
  CUBES
1 can cream of chicken soup
½ cup dairy sour cream
herbed stuffing cubes

Cook zucchini in salted water until tender and drain. Cook carrots and onions in 4 tablespoons of margarine until tender. Remove and mix with 1½ cups of HERB STUFFING CUBES. Mix this with soup and sour cream. Gently stir in zucchini and turn into a 1½-quart casserole. To the remaining 2 table-spoons of melted margarine, add remaining stuffing cubes. Toss (enough cubes to cover top of casserole) and add to top of casserole. Bake for 30 to 40 minutes in a 350° F oven.

HERBED STUFFING CUBES:

30 slices bread, cut into ½
  inch cubes
½ cup cooking oil
3 tablespoons instant minced
  onion

3 tablespoons dried parsley
2 teaspoons garlic salt
¾ teaspoon ground sage
½ teaspoon seasoned pepper

Put the ½ inch cubes in a large roasting pan and toast at 300° F for 45 minutes. Remove and cool slightly. In ½ cup of cooking oil, stir in the onion, parsley, garlic salt, sage and pepper. Toss lightly to coat bread cubes. Store in freezer until needed. Yield: 6 to 8 servings.

BOUQUET OF FRESH VEGETABLES

BUTTERED GREEN BEANS:

2 pounds small green beans 1 cup butter
1 tablespoon salt

Wash beans and trim ends. Put in a 4-quart suacepan; cover with boiling water. Add salt; boil uncovered for 10 to 15 minutes. Beans should be crisp. Drain well. Add butter and sauté beans for 2 minutes.

GLAZED ONIONS:

2 tablespoons butter 1 teaspoon salt
2 pounds small white onions, 4 teaspoons sugar
   peeled ½ cup beef bouillon

Melt butter in a skillet. Add onions and sprinkle with salt and sugar. Sauté onions until golden brown. Add bouillon and simmer until bouillon is absorbed by onions.

GLAZED CARROTS:

48 small finger-size carrots 1 teaspoon sugar
1½ cups water 1 teaspoon salt
⅔ cup butter ½ teaspoon white pepper

Place scrubbed carrots in a 2-quart saucepan. Add water, butter, sugar, salt and pepper. Bring to a boil. Cook uncovered for 10 to 15 minutes or until carrots are tender and liquid has evaporated.

SAUTÉED RED POTATOES:

3 pounds small red potatoes 1 tablespoon minced parsley
½ cup butter 1 tablesppon minced chives
2 tablespoons oil 2 teaspoons tarragon
½ teaspoon salt butter, softened

Melt butter and oil in a large skillet. Add potatoes which have been washed then dried in a towel. Shake the skillet back and forth to roll potatoes and to sear them on all sides. Continue this for 5 to 6 minutes. Sprinkle potatoes with salt. Lower heat and cover skillet. Cook potatoes for about 15 minutes. Shake occasionally to prevent sticking. Potatoes are done when a knife pierces them easily. Turn off heat, add softened butter, parsley, chives and tarragon.

HERB-BUTTERED CAULIFLOWER:

1 large head cauliflower   *½ teaspoon white pepper*
½ teaspoon salt   *juice of 1 lemon*
⅓ cup butter   *2 tablespoons minced parsley*

Put cauliflower head down in a 4-quart saucepan. Cover with boiling salty water. Bring water to a boil then reduce to medium heat. Cook for 8 to 10 minutes. Drain and dry cauliflower in a towel. Heat butter in a small saucepan, add pepper and lemon juice. Return cauliflower to large saucepan (head up). Pour butter mixture over cauliflower then sauté for 2 to 3 minutes. Sprinkle with parsley.

Arrange vegetables on a large platter or tray with cauliflower in the center. Garnish with fresh parsley and pimento slices. Yield: 12 to 14 servings.

"This is a beautiful dish for a dinner party."

To release the flavor of dried herbs, crush them gently before using.

Firm herbs such as bay leaves require long slow cooking to bring out their flavor; but ground herbs should be added in the final cooking period.

SQUASH WITH WATER CHESTNUTS

8 small yellow squash   *¼ cup butter, melted*
1 small onion   *1 teaspoon salt*
2 eggs, separated   *½ teaspoon pepper*
½ cup heavy cream   *garlic seasoned croutons*
1 (5 ounce) can water   *made into crumbs*
*   chestnuts, diced*

Simmer squash and onion until tender. Drain and purée in blender. Beat cream into egg yolks and mix with squash, water chestnuts, butter, salt and pepper. Beat egg whites until stiff and fold into squash mixture. Pour into a 2-quart buttered soufflé dish and sprinkle with crouton crumbs. Bake at 350° F for 30 minutes. Yield: 6 to 8 servings.

"Crunchy water chestnuts are nice textural contrast."

ZUCCHINI SAUTÉ

½ cup butter
1 cup sliced onions
8 small zucchini squash

Parmesan cheese
salt to taste
pepper to taste

Melt butter and fry onion slices until soft and golden. Add zucchini, which has been washed and sliced, and fry with the onion. When squash is soft, shake Parmesan cheese heavily over all and let it blend with zucchini. Add salt and pepper. Yield: 4 servings.

ENGLISH PEAS, FRENCH STYLE

2 teaspoons butter
8 very small onions, peeled
2 cups fresh shelled English
  peas
1 heart of Bibb lettuce,
  shredded

1 teaspoon flour
¼ teaspoon salt
½ teaspoon sugar
¼ cup canned chicken broth

Melt butter in a 2-quart saucepan. Add onions and sauté for 3 minutes. Add peas and lettuce and sprinkle with flour, salt and sugar. Mix well. Add chicken broth and bring to a boil. Cover and simmer for 35 minutes. 2 teaspoons fresh mint leaves may be added. Yield: 6 servings.

EGGPLANT WITH CHINESE BATTER

¾ cup flour
¼ cup cornstarch
1½ teaspoons baking powder
¾ cup water (approximately)

1 tablespoon warm oil added
  to batter just before
  frying
1 medium eggplant
2 cups peanut oil heated to
  350° F

Combine all batter ingredients with whisk. Wash eggplant, discard stems, but do not peel. Cut crosswise into ¼ inch slices, cut again into 2 × 2 × ¼ inch pieces. Dip in batter. Fry. Drain and sprinkle with salt. Also for onion rings, zucchini, cauliflower, or mushrooms. Yield: 6 servings.

Many vegetables should not be peeled as the vitamins are located in and just under the skin. Use only a stiff brush to scrub them clean.

EGGPLANT ALLA MARCELLI

1 large firm eggplant
3 tablespoons olive oil
TOMATO SAUCE

¾ cup Romano cheese,
 freshly grated
1 small round mozzarella
 cheese

Wash and slice eggplant in ½ inch slices (do not remove skin). Salt lightly and place in colander. Place piece of waxed paper on top of eggplant slices. On waxed paper, place a heavy object which will weigh down and press out dark, bitter juices of eggplant. Keep under pressure 1 hour. Blot eggplant slices dry. With pastry brush, lightly brush oil onto both sides of eggplant slices. Put slices on cookie sheet and broil on both sides until golden brown. Layer eggplant slices, TOMATO SAUCE mixture and grated cheese, one over the other in a medium-sized baking dish. Repeat layers until dish is filled. Arrange slices of mozzarella cheese on top. Bake in 350° F oven for 20 to 30 minutes until cheese is bubbly and melted. Serve over hot boiled rice or egg noodles. Yield: 5 to 6 servings.

TOMATO SAUCE:
1 clove garlic
¼ cup olive oil
1 (15 ounce) can tomato
 sauce

½ teaspoon sugar
pinch basil OR oregano

Brown garlic in olive oil. Remove when golden brown. Add tomato sauce, sugar and basil or oregano to oil. Simmer 15 minutes.

EGGPLANT SOUFFLÉ

6 small peeled, sliced
   eggplants
4 medium-sized white
   onions, sliced
½ cup butter
4 eggs, beaten with salt and
   pepper

1 pound Cheddar cheese,
   grated
enough plain bread crumbs
   to cover top of casserole
   in which soufflé is baked
½ cup butter

Cook eggplants and onions, in enough water to cover, until tender; and then drain very well. This is important. Place hot onions, eggplant in a mixing bowl. Add eggs, seasonings and cheese. Blend well. Place in a buttered baking dish; cover with bread crumbs; dot with butter. Bake for 2 hours in a 250° F oven. Yield: 8 servings.

TOMATO PUDDING

1 (15 ounce) can Hunt's
   Tomato Sauce with
   Tomato Bits
¼ cup boiling water
¼ teaspoon salt
6 tablespoons brown sugar

3 tablespoons vinegar
1 tablespoon chives, fresh OR
   1 teaspoon dried
½ teaspoon basil
1 cup white bread crumbs
¼ cup melted butter

Place tomato sauce and water in saucepan, bring to a boil. Add salt, sugar and vinegar. Remove from heat, stir in herbs. Butter 1½-quart casserole. Place bread crumbs in casserole and pour tomato mixture and melted butter over all; stir. Cover dish and bake in preheated 375° F. oven for 30 to 35 minutes, or until thickened. Do not remove lid until ready to serve. Yield: 6 servings.

VARIATION:

2 (16 ounce) cans tomatoes
8 whole cloves

8 whole peppercorns
1 bay leaf

Place tomatoes, undrained, in a saucepan. Tie cloves, peppercorns and bay leaf in a cheesecloth bag and put in saucepan with tomatoes. Simmer slowly for 30 minutes, stirring occasionally. Proceed as in above omitting tomato sauce and basil.

VENETIAN RICE AND PEAS

1/4 cup butter or margarine
1 small onion, chopped
1 slice bacon, diced
1 stalk celery, chopped
2 cups fresh shelled green
    peas or thawed frozen
    peas
1/2 cup or more diced cooked
    ham

3/4 cup raw rice
1 3/4 cups chicken stock
1 teaspoon salt
1/4 teaspoon pepper
1 tablespoon grated
    Parmesan cheese
extra cheese for serving

In heavy kettle or electric skillet, melt butter. Add onions, bacon, and celery, and sauté for 5 minutes, or until onion is golden and bacon is cooked. Add peas and ham, cover and braise for about 5 minutes, stirring occasionally. Add rice and cook for 3 minutes, stirring to coat all grains with butter. Add chicken stock, salt and pepper. Bring to a rapid boil, cover and cook slowly over low heat for 30 minutes, or until rice is tender and liquid is absorbed. The rice and peas should remain fairly moist. Stir in 1 tablespoon grated Parmesan cheese. Serve hot with additional grated Parmesan. Yield: 4 to 5 servings.

"Good buffet dish."

TOMATO PIE

12 slices bacon
3 large tomatoes, sliced
    (enough to fill shell)

1 (9 inch) deep dish pastry
    shell, baked
8 green onions, chopped

Fry bacon; drain and crumble. Arrange tomato slices in pastry shell, place chopped onions and crumbled bacon on top. Add TOPPING. Bake at 350° F for 30 minutes. Yield: 6 servings.

TOPPING:

1 1/2 cups grated extra sharp
    Cheddar cheese

1 1/2 cups Hellman's
    mayonnaise

Mix cheese and mayonnaise together. Spread topping evenly over top of pie. Yield: 3 cups.

SPRING ASPARAGUS

36 to 48 fresh asparagus   3 teaspoons salt
    spears

In a large steamer, bring 4 quarts of salty water to a boil. Lay asparagus in steamer, cover. When water boils again, uncover steamer. This helps to keep asparagus green. Boil slowly for 5 minutes. Asparagus should be slightly crunchy yet cooked through. Immediately remove from water. Serve with lemon butter or Hollandaise sauce. Yield: 6 to 8 servings.

"Tastes of springtime in France."

SPAGHETTI PRIMAVERA

2 tomatoes, sliced
3 tablespoons olive oil
1 teaspoon chopped garlic
¼ cup chopped parsley
pinch salt
pinch freshly ground pepper
10 mushrooms, sliced
1 cup sliced zucchini,
    blanced
1½ cups sliced broccoli,
    blanced
1½ cups snow peas,
    blanched
1 cup green peas

6 sliced asparagus spears,
    blanched
1 pound spaghetti
½ cup grated Parmesan
    cheese
⅓ cup butter, melted
1 cup heavy cream, warm
⅓ cup freshly chopped basil
salt to taste
freshly ground pepper to
    taste
whole cherry tomatoes
⅓ cup pine nuts (optional)

Sauté tomatoes in 1 tablespoon olive oil with ¼ teaspoon garlic, parsley, salt and pepper. Set aside (used as topping).

In another pan, sauté lightly in 2 tablespoons olive oil, mushrooms with ¾ teaspoon garlic, then add zucchini, broccoli, snow peas, green peas and asparagus, cooking just long enough to heat vegetables.

Cook 1 pound spaghetti and drain. With a fork, slowly mix spaghetti with Parmesan cheese, butter, cream, basil, salt and freshly ground pepper to taste. Top with vegetables, add sautéed tomatoes and garnish with whole cherry tomatoes. ⅓ cup pine nuts may be added. Yield: 6 servings.

MUSHROOM ARTICHOKE CASSEROLE

4 tablespoons butter
3 cups fresh mushrooms,
    halved
½ cup diced onions
2 tablespoons flour
⅛ teaspoon salt
dash pepper
½ cup water

½ cup milk
1 teaspoon instant chicken
    bouillon
1 teaspoon lemon juice
⅛ teaspoon garlic salt
1 (10 ounce) package frozen
    artichoke hearts

TOPPING:

¾ cup soft bread crumbs   1 tablespoon butter

Melt butter, add mushrooms and onion and cook until onions
are tender. Remove vegetables from butter and set aside.
Blend flour, salt and pepper into butter. Add water, milk,
bouillon, lemon juice, and garlic salt. Cook and stir until it
bubbles and thickens. Add all vegetables and pour into 1-
quart casserole. Combine bread crumbs and butter and place
around edge of casserole. Bake at 350° F for 20 minutes. Yield:
6 servings.

"Something different for dinner parties."

MUSHROOMS BAKED IN CREAM

½ cup butter
1½ teaspoons chopped parsley
1½ teaspoons chopped chives
1½ teaspoons shallots
¼ teaspoon nutmeg

salt and pepper to taste
16 to 20 large mushroom caps
1 cup heavy cream
paprika

Combine softened butter with parsley, chives, shallots, nutmeg, salt and pepper. Stuff mushroom caps with seasoned
butter and set them in a shallow baking dish. Pour 1 cup heavy
cream over mushrooms and sprinkle the dish lightly with
paprika. Bake mushrooms in a 450° F oven for 10 minutes.
Yield: 8 servings.

"Great with beef or lamb."

MUSHROOM MENAGERIE

1 pound fresh mushrooms,
   sliced
1½ bell peppers, slivered
4 spring onions, halved
3 fresh tomatoes, quartered
¼ cup butter
2 tablespoons olive oil

1 tablespoon chopped parsley
1 tablespoon oregano
1 tablespoon minced onion
1 teaspoon salt
1 teaspoon pepper
1 tablespoon soy sauce

Sauté fresh vegetables in butter and olive oil over high heat. Cook only 3 minutes. Add parsley, oregano, onion, salt, pepper and soy sauce. Serve very hot. Yield: 4 servings.

CARROTS AVEC GRAND MARNIER

½ cup butter
¾ teaspoon sugar
½ teaspoon salt

2 bunches very small carrots
¼ cup Grand Marnier

Melt butter in baking dish and stir in sugar and salt. Add very thinly sliced carrots and Grand Marnier. Cover and bake for 45 to 50 minutes at 350° F or until tender, but do not brown. Yield: 6 servings.

CARROT AND SQUASH SOUFFLÉ

1 pound squash
1 pound carrots
1 cup melted butter
4 tablespoons flour

½ cup finely chopped onion
1 teaspoon salt
1 teaspoon pepper
4 eggs, separated

Scrape and boil squash and carrots. Drain and chop in food processor or run through a masher. Melt butter and add flour, blending well. Combine butter and flour sauce with processed carrots and squash and chopped onion, salt and pepper. Beat egg yolks and add to mixture. Beat egg whites and fold into mixture. Bake at 350° F for 30 minutes in a greased casserole dish. Yield: 8 servings.

HAM AND CHEESE BAKED CAULIFLOWER

1 fresh cauliflower
1 tablespoon salt
3 eggs, beaten

1 cup finely minced ham
1 cup grated Cheddar cheese
½ cup butter, melted

In a 2-quart saucepan, boil cauliflower (head down) in salty water for 10 minutes. Drain well. Place in a shallow baking dish (head up), add ½ cup water. Baste cauliflower with ⅓ of egg mixture. Pat ⅓ cup ham and ⅓ cup cheese onto cauliflower. Bake for 5 minutes at 350° F. Now repeat process of basting cauliflower with egg; pat ⅓ cup ham and ⅓ cup cheese on vegetable. Bake again for 5 minutes. Baste with remaining egg, ham and cheese. Once again, bake cauliflower for 5 minutes. Pour melted butter over cauliflower. Serve immediately. Yield: 6 servings.

CAULIFLOWER CASSEROLE

1 large head cauliflower or 2
    (10 ounce) packages
    frozen cauliflower
1½ tablespoons lemon juice
1 (4 ounce) can mushrooms,
    drained
1 green pepper, chopped
3 tablespoons butter

3 cups thick White Sauce
1 (8 ounce) can tiny green
    peas, drained
dash red pepper
dash of Worcestershire sauce
1 cup sharp Cheddar cheese,
    grated
paprika

Cook cauliflower in salted water with lemon juice until tender. Drain. Sauté mushrooms and green pepper in butter. Combine white sauce, peas, red pepper, Worcestershire and half of cheese. Add cauliflower, mushrooms, and green pepper. Pour into 1½-quart casserole. Top with remaining cheese and sprinkle with paprika. Bake at 350° F for 25 minutes or until lightly browned. Serve with ham, turkey or roast beef. For white sauce, see recipe. Yield: 10 servings.

SPINACH SURPRISE

1 (14 ounce) can artichoke
   hearts, quartered
½ cup butter, melted
8 ounces cream cheese,
   softened

1½ teaspoons lemon juice
2 (10 ounce) packages frozen
   chopped spinach or broccoli
Saltine cracker crumbs

Grease 1½-quart casserole. Place artichokes on bottom. Combine butter, cream cheese and lemon juice. Add broccoli or spinach which has been cooked and drained. Pour mixture over artichokes. Top with crumbs. Bake uncovered at 350° F for 25 minutes. For added zip, add Worcestershire sauce, garlic salt and Tabasco (to taste) to cream cheese. Yield: 6 servings.

SPINACH WITH CHEESE SAUCE

4 slices bacon
2 (10 ounce) packages frozen
   spinach, thawed and
   drained
salt and pepper to taste

2 tablespoons butter
2 tablespoons flour
1 cup milk
½ pound sharp Cheddar
   cheese, grated

Fry bacon until crisp and drain on paper towels. Place spinach in a buttered casserole. Sprinkle with salt and pepper. In a saucepan, melt butter and blend in flour. Slowly add milk and more salt and pepper. Stir until smooth and thickened. Add cheese and cook slowly until cheese is melted. Pour over spinach. Sprinkle with bacon and bake for 25 minutes in a 350° F oven. For variations, substitute 1 pound fresh or frozen cooked broccoli. Swiss cheese may be substituted for Cheddar cheese. Yield: 4 to 6 servings.

GREEK CABBAGE

1 cup sugar
1 cup wine vinegar
2 cans cream of tomato soup

2 medium cabbages, chopped
1 pound bacon, chopped,
   fried and drained

In a large saucepan, combine sugar, vinegar and soup. Bring to a boil. Add cabbage and bacon. Cook at low heat until cabbage is tender. Yield: 12 servings.

CELERY CASSEROLE

3 cups diced celery OR
   cauliflower
1/4 cup slivered almonds
1/2 cup water chestnuts, sliced
5 tablespoons butter

3 tablespoons flour
1 cup chicken broth
1/2 cup mushrooms, sliced
1/2 cup Parmesan cheese
1/2 cup bread crumbs

Parboil celery 5 minutes in salted water. Drain and put in casserole with almonds and water chestnuts. Make a sauce with other ingredients. Mix in mushrooms. Combine Parmesan cheese and bread crumbs; put on top. Bake at 350° F until bubbly. Yield: 4 servings.

For your own Bouquet Garni:
The recipe should include at least one fresh herb. If you use only dried herbs, add a few sprigs of fresh parsley.

Place in a small cheesecloth bag:

1 large bay leaf
1/4 teaspoon dried tarragon
6 whole peppercorns
1/4 teaspoon leaf thyme

8 sprigs parsley
3 green celery tops, chopped
clove of garlic, halved

SAUCES FOR VEGETABLES

PARSLEY BUTTER

2 tablespoons minced parsley
1/2 cup butter

lemon juice to taste

Mix all of the above and pour over vegetables.
Also good on fish.

SOUR CREAM CHEESE SAUCE

1 cup sour cream
1/4 cup mayonnaise

1/4 cup grated Parmesan
   cheese

Combine sour cream, mayonnaise and cheese; mix well. Spread mixture over steamed asparagus, broccoli, or cauliflower. Broil until bubbly. Serve immediately. Yield: 1½ cups.

AMANDINE SAUCE

1/8 cup butter
1/4 cup slivered almonds,
    blanched

1/8 cup freshly squeezed
    lemon juice

Heat butter in medium saucepan. Sauté almonds for a few minutes. Remove from heat. Stir in lemon juice just before serving.

SAUCE FOR BAKED POTATOES

1/2 cup butter, softened
1/2 cup sharp Cheddar
    cheese, grated
1/2 pint sour cream

dash of Tabasco
2 tablespoons chopped chives
    (or green onion or pars-
    ley, chopped)

Mix together butter and cheese. Add the sour cream, Tabasco and chives. Yield: 2 cups.

WHITE SAUCE

	BUTTER	FLOUR	MILK	SALT
Thin	1 tablespoon	1 tablespoon	1 cup	1/4 teaspoon
Medium	1 1/2-2 tablespoons	2 tablespoons	1 cup	1/4 teaspoon
Thick	2-3 tablespoons	3 tablespoons	1 cup	1/4 teaspoon
Very Thick	3-4 tablespoons	4 tablespoons	1 cup	1/4 teaspoon

Melt butter in saucepan. Add flour and salt and blend until smooth. Gradually add milk, stirring constantly. When comes to a boil, cook 3 to 5 minutes or until desired thickness.

VARIATIONS:

CHEESE SAUCE: Add 3/4 cup sharp Cheddar or Swiss cheese, grated. Stir until melted.

MUSHROOM SAUCE: Brown 1/2 cup canned button or sliced mushrooms in the butter before making the sauce.

1/4 teaspoon white pepper may be added to sauce.

INSTANT HOLLANDAISE SAUCE

1/2 cup mayonnaise
1/3 cup butter, melted OR 1/2
    cup liquid margarine

juice of 1 lemon

Combine all ingredients; blend well. Yield: 1 cup.

NEVER-FAIL HOLLANDAISE

¾ cup water
salt, red pepper, paprika to
   taste
juice of 1 lemon

1 tablespoon cornstarch
2 egg yolks, beaten
2 tablespoons butter

CONVENTIONAL METHOD:

Heat water in double boiler. Add salt, pepper, paprika and lemon juice. Dissolve cornstarch in a little cold water. Add to hot mixture, stirring constantly. When slightly thickened, add egg yolks and 1 tablespoon butter. Stir, and cook until thickened. Add tablespoon butter just before serving. Can be refrigerated and reheated.

MICROWAVE METHOD:

Heat water in quart size pyrex pitcher. Add salt, pepper, paprika and lemon juice. Dissolve cornstarch in little cold water and add to hot water mixture. Stir well. Return to microwave on "high" for 15 seconds; stir. If not thickened, return to oven for 5 second intervals until slightly thickened. Add beaten egg yolks and 1 tablespoon butter. Stir and return to oven for 15 seconds. Check and stir every 15 seconds until thickened. Add the other tablespoon of butter just before serving. Refrigerate and reheat in microwave. Yield: 1 cup.

BLENDER HOLLANDAISE SAUCE

3 egg yolks
2 tablespoons lemon juice
¼ teaspoon salt

2 drops Tabasco sauce
½ cup butter

Place egg yolks, lemon juice, salt and Tabasco in a warm blender container. Turn motor on and off at medium speed, just enough to blend. Heat butter in small saucepan until bubbling and very hot. Remove blender cover, turn motor to high speed; drizzle in hot butter slowly until all is added. Turn off blender. Serve warm. To keep warm, set blender container in pan of warm water. Just before serving, blend again to freshen. Yield: 1 cup.

Quick and easy vegetable sauce: Use 1 (10¾ ounce) can of cream soup diluted with ¼ cup milk instead of making 2 cups of cream sauce.

247

OVEN FRIED APPLE RINGS

10 Winesap apples, peeled
   and cored
½ cup butter or margarine,
   divided
10 tablespoons sugar

10 tablespoons packed brown
   sugar
2 teaspoons cinnamon
1 teaspoon nutmeg
fresh mint sprigs

Slice apples into rings. Place half in baking dish; dot with ¼ cup butter. Combine sugars and spices; sprinkle half over apples. Repeat the layer. Bake at 350° F for 55 minutes or until apples are tender. Garnish with mint. Yield: 8 to 10 servings.

OVEN BAKED APPLESAUCE

12 medium apples
   (York/Washington)
½ cup sugar
½ teaspoon cinnamon
¼ teaspoon salt

dash of nutmeg
pinch of mace
¼ cup water
2 tablespoons butter

Peel, core and cut apples into chunks. Place in lightly buttered pan. Mix sugar, cinnamon, salt, nutmeg, mace and sprinkle over apples. Add water and dot with butter. Cover and bake at 300° F for 1 to 1½ hours. Yield: 6 to 8 servings.

BRANDIED FRUIT

⅓ cup margarine
¾ cup packed brown sugar
½ cup brandy
10 whole cloves
4 sticks cinnamon
1 (30 ounce) can apricot
   halves

1 (29 ounce) can pear halves
1 (29 ounce) can peach
   halves
1 (20 ounce) can pineapple
   slices
1 (10 ounce) jar cherries

Heat oven to 325° F. Melt margarine; stir in sugar and brandy, cloves and cinnamon. Drain fruits. Layer in large casserole with peaches on top. Pour in butter mixture. Place cherry in center of each peach half. Bake uncovered 1 hour at 350° F. Cool, cover and refrigerate. To reheat for serving, bake in 350° F oven for 20 minutes or until bubbly. Remove cinnamon sticks before serving. Yield: 12 servings.

"Elegant touch to a dinner party."

PINEAPPLE CHEESE CASSEROLE

1 (20 ounce) can pineapple
    chunks
½ cup sugar
3 tablespoons flour

1 cup shredded sharp
    Cheddar cheese
¼ cup butter, melted
½ cup Ritz cracker crumbs

Drain pineapple, reserving 3 tablespoons of juice. Combine sugar and flour. Slowly stir in reserved pineapple juice; add cheese and pineapple chunks, mixing well. Put into greased 1-quart casserole dish. Combine butter and crumbs and sprinkle on top. Bake at 350° F for 20 to 30 minutes. Yield: 4 to 6 servings.

"Marvelously different flavor."

BAKED PINEAPPLE

3 eggs, beaten
1 (20 ounce) can crushed
    pineapple, unsweetened
½ cup sugar

1 tablespoon flour
¼ pound butter, melted
6 slices of bread, cubed

Place eggs in 2½-quart casserole dish. Add pineapple, undrained. Stir in sugar and flour. Melt butter; add bread cubes and coat with the butter. Put on top of ingredients in the casserole dish and bake at 350° F for 30 minutes. Yield: 6 servings.

CURRIED FRUIT BAKE

1 (29 ounce) can cling peach
    halves
1 (20 ounce) can pineapple
    slices
1 (29 ounce) can pear halves

5 maraschino cherries with
    stems
⅓ cup butter
¾ cup light brown sugar,
    packed
4 teaspoons curry powder

Day Before: Preheat oven to 325° F. Drain fruits and dry well on paper towels; arrange in 1½-quart casserole. Melt butter, add brown sugar and curry; spoon over fruit. Bake 1 hour, uncovered. Refrigerate. To reheat 30 minutes before serving, place casserole of curried fruit in 350° F oven for 30 minutes. Serve warm with ham, lamb or poultry. Yield: 12 servings.

Sweet Things

Delectable syllabub and charlotte come to mind when thinking of desserts of an earlier time. Then the recipes often began with the words "take a quart of heavy cream." Of course there was ambrosia which to this day is a traditional Thanksgiving and Christmas dinner dessert in many homes. Custards, too, were popular and often when one is served now there are blissful sighs as memories are stirred of meals at grandmother's house. Church picnic menus often included egg custard pies with deep meringue, sweet potato pie, lemon pie and deep dish fruit pies using either peaches, blackberries or pears from the farm. Cakes included lemon cheese and pound.

Cakes

PECAN ROLL

7 eggs
¾ cup sugar
1½ cups ground pecans
1 teaspoon baking powder

confectioners' sugar, sifted
1 cup whipping cream
vanilla extract and sugar to
taste

Brush a jelly roll pan, 10 × 15, with oil; line with wax paper and oil the paper. Separate the eggs. With an electric mixer or a heavy whisk, beat the yolks with ¾ cup sugar until mixture is pale in color and thick enough to fall in ribbons when beater is lifted. Stir in ground pecans and baking powder. Fold in egg whites, stiffly beaten. Spread batter in the prepared pan and bake the cake in a moderate oven (350° F) for 15 to 20 minutes, or until it is golden. Cool the cake in the pan; cover it with a damp towel and chill it.

Dust the cold cake generously with sifted confectioners' sugar and turn it out on a board covered with two overlapping sheets of wax paper. Carefully strip the paper from the bottom of the cake. Spread the cake with cream, whipped and flavored with sugar and vanilla to taste. Roll up cake, using the paper as an aid, and slide the roll onto a flat serving platter. Sprinkle roll with more sifted confectioners' sugar. Yield: 8 to 12 servings.

"An elegant dessert."

SPONGE CAKE

¾ cup cold water
3 eggs, separated
1¼ cups sugar

1½ cups flour
1 teaspoon baking powder
pinch of salt

Preheat oven to 325° F. Combine water and egg yolks and beat until stiff. Fold in sugar and flour with baking powder and salt. Beat egg whites until stiff and fold into batter. Pour into ungreased tube pan and bake at 325° F for 45 minutes. For a different flavor substitute ¾ cup orange juice and 1 tablespoon grated orange rind for the water.

LANE CAKE

CAKE:

1 cup butter
2 cups sugar
1 cup milk
3 cups flour

4 teaspoons baking powder
¼ teaspoon salt
8 egg whites, beaten

Preheat oven to 350° F. Cream butter and sugar gradually. Add milk and flour with baking powder and salt in flour. Fold beaten egg whites in last. Bake in 3 greased and floured pans at 350° F for 20 to 25 minutes.

FILLING:

½ cup butter
1 cup sugar
8 egg yolks, beaten
¼ cup bourbon

1 cup raisins
1 cup chopped pecans
1 coconut, grated

Cream butter, sugar and egg yolks. Add bourbon to mixture. Cook in double boiler until thick. Cool; add raisins, pecans and coconut. Put between layers.

DIVINITY ICING:

2 cups sugar
½ cup water
¼ cup White Karo syrup

2 egg whites, stiffly beaten
1 teaspoon vanilla extract

Put sugar, water and syrup together; mix and boil without stirring until it gives a long thread. Pour slowly over stiffly beaten egg whites and beat until cool and stiff enough to hold its shape. Add vanilla. Double recipe to completely ice cake.

Always preheat oven for at least 10 minutes unless otherwise stated in recipe.

TO PEEL A FRESH COCONUT, drain milk, place nut in oven until hot to touch; remove and tap all over with a hammer, particularly at the ends; give one hard knock and shell will crack open. Lift shell off; peel brown skin and cool before grating or grinding.

LEMON CHEESE CAKE

CAKE:

2 cups sugar
1 cup Crisco
4 eggs
1 cup milk
3 cups cake flour

3 teaspoons baking powder
½ teaspoon salt
½ teaspoon lemon juice
½ teaspoon vanilla extract

Preheat oven to 375° F. Cream sugar and Crisco together; add eggs one at a time; alternate milk and dry ingredients, blending until batter is smooth. Then add lemon juice and vanilla. Pour batter into 3 (9-inch) greased cake pans. Bake at 375° F for 20 to 25 minutes. Cool on rack before FILLING. Frost with white icing.

FILLING:

1 cup sugar
2 eggs
4 tablespoons lemon juice

1 teaspoon flour
¼ cup boiling water

Combine all ingredients and mix well. Cook in a double boiler, stirring constantly until the mixture thickens and drops from the spoon in a lump. Yield: 12 to 16 servings.

WHITE ICING

2 egg whites
8 marshmallows
1¾ cups sugar

½ cup hot water
pinch salt
1 teaspoon vanilla extract

Beat egg whites until they stand in peaks. Chop marshmallows. Cook sugar and water until syrup threads a long thread when poured from a spoon. Put marshmallows in egg whites and slowly pour in syrup while beating. Add salt and vanilla. When cool and thick, spread on cake. Yield: Frosts 2 cake layers. Use 1½ or twice the recipe for a large cake.

BLACKBERRY CAKE

1 cup margarine
2 cups sugar
3 eggs
3 cups cake flour
3 teaspoons soda
½ teaspoon cinnamon

½ teaspoon allspice
½ teaspoon nutmeg
1 cup buttermilk
1 cup blackberries with juice
1 teaspoon vanilla extract

Preheat oven to 325° F. Cream shortening and sugar. Add eggs one at a time, beating well after each. Sift flour and other dry ingredients; add alternately with buttermilk. Add blackberries and vanilla. Mix well. Bake in a greased pan, 13 × 9 × 2 inches, for 1 hour at 325° F. Yield: 12 to 16 servings.

ICING:

1 cup sugar
½ cup buttermilk

1 tablespoon white corn
    syrup
½ cup butter

Combine all ingredients in a saucepan. Bring to a boil. Pour over warm cake.

CHOCOLATE SHEET CAKE

CAKE:

2 cups sugar
2 cups flour
3½ tablespoons cocoa
½ cup margarine
½ cup Wesson oil

1 cup water
2 eggs
½ cup buttermilk
1 teaspoon soda
1 teaspoon vanilla extract

FROSTING:

½ cup margarine
3 tablespoons cocoa
⅓ cup sweet milk

1 pound confectioners' sugar
1 cup chopped pecans
1 teaspoon vanilla extract

Sift sugar, flour and cocoa into a large bowl. In a saucepan put margarine, oil and water. Bring to a boil. Pour over dry ingredients. Blend well. Add eggs, buttermilk, soda and vanilla. Pour into a 11 × 16 greased pan. Bake at 400° F for 20 minutes. When cake has been in oven 15 minutes, begin preparing frosting. In a saucepan combine margarine, cocoa and milk. Bring to a boil. Remove from heat and add confectioners' sugar, pecans and vanilla. Stir. Pour on warm cake. Yield: 35 servings.

CHOCOLATE MACAROON CAKE

1 egg white	½ cup sugar
1 teaspoon vanilla extract	1 teaspoon soda
½ cup sugar	½ cup sour cream
2 cups (7 ounce package) grated coconut	1¼ cups sugar
	½ cup shortening
1 tablespoon flour	3 egg yolks
½ cup cocoa	1 teaspoon salt
¾ cup hot coffee	1 teaspoon vanilla extract
3 egg whites	2 cups sifted flour

Preheat oven to 350° F. Beat 1 egg white until soft mounds form; add vanilla. Add sugar gradually; beat until stiff. Stir in coconut and flour; set aside. Dissolve cocoa in hot coffee; set aside. Beat 3 egg whites until soft mounds form. Add sugar gradually; beat until stiff peaks form. Add soda to sour cream. Cream sugar, shortening, yolks, salt, vanilla and half of cocoa-coffee mixture until light, about 4 minutes. Blend in flour, sour cream mixture and remaining cocoa-coffee mixture. Fold in beaten egg whites. Turn ⅓ of the chocolate batter into 10 inch tube pan greased on bottom. Place ½ of coconut mixture on top. Cover with ½ of remaining chocolate batter. Top with remaining coconut, then chocolate batter. Bake at 350° F for 55 to 65 minutes. Do not invert. Cool completely; remove from pan. Frost with CHOCOLATE CREAM FROSTING.

CHOCOLATE CREAM FROSTING:

1 cup (6 ounce package) semi-sweet chocolate pieces, melted	1 egg yolk
	1½ cups sifted confectioners' sugar
2 tablespoons butter	¼ cup milk

Combine melted chocolate pieces, butter, egg yolk, confectioners' sugar and milk. Beat until smooth and of spreading consistency.

Yield: 16 to 20 servings.

Cake is done when a toothpick is inserted into the center and it comes out clean.

PERFECT CHOCOLATE CAKE

1 cup cocoa
2 cups boiling water
1 cup butter or margarine,
    softened
2½ cups sugar
4 eggs

1½ teaspoons vanilla extract
2¾ cups flour
2 teaspoons soda
½ teaspoon baking powder
½ teaspoon salt

Preheat oven to 350° F. Combine cocoa and boiling water, blending until smooth; set aside and cool. Combine butter, sugar, eggs and vanilla; beat with electric mixer at high speed until light and fluffy, about 5 minutes. Sift together dry ingredients. Then add to sugar mixture alternately with cocoa mixture, beating at low speed of mixer—beginning and ending with dry ingredients. Do not over-beat. Pour into three greased and floured 9-inch pans. Bake 25 to 30 minutes at 350° F. When baked, cool cakes 10 minutes in pans before removing. Cool completely. Put layers together with FILLING and spread (top and sides) with FROSTING.

FILLING:

1 cup whipping cream,
    whipped

¼ cup confectioners' sugar
1 teaspoon vanilla extract

Combine all ingredients. Chill.

FROSTING:

1 (6 ounce) package
    semi-sweet chocolate
    chips

½ cup half and half
1 cup butter
2½ cups confectioners' sugar

Combine chocolate chips, half and half and butter in saucepan. Place over medium heat. Stir until chocolate is melted. Remove from heat; blend in sugar. Set saucepan in bowl of ice and beat with mixer until it holds its shape.

Yield: 16 to 20 servings.

Use cocoa rather than flour to dust pans for CHOCOLATE CAKES.

BROWNIE REFRIGERATOR CUPCAKES

½ cup butter
1½ (1 ounce) squares
   unsweetened chocolate
1 cup sugar
⅔ cup flour, unsifted

1 teaspoon vanilla extract
2 eggs, well beaten
1 cup coarsely chopped
   pecans

Preheat oven to 350° F. Melt butter and chocolate together in top of double boiler over hot water. Mix remaining ingredients and add chocolate-butter mixture, blending well. Place small size paper baking cups in gem muffin tins (or use petite, bite-size paper baking cups). Fill half full with batter—no more. Bake 12 minutes for small, 10 minutes for petite at 350° F. They may not look done but don't overcook.

ICING:

2 tablespoons butter
1 (1 ounce) square
   unsweetened chocolate

3 cups confectioners' sugar
cold, strong coffee

Prepare icing while cakes are baking: Melt butter and chocolate together. Add confectioners' sugar gradually and enough cold coffee to make smooth mixture. Ice cakes while they are hot, filling to top of paper cups. Store in refrigerator.

Yield: 2 dozen small or 34 petite cupcakes.

For SMOOTHER FROSTINGS, sift sugar.

CARAMEL ICING

2½ cups sugar
1 cup whipping cream

½ cup butter
½ teaspoon vanilla extract

Heat 2 cups sugar and the cream in a saucepan over medium heat. Put ½ cup sugar in an iron skillet over medium heat. Stir constantly so it does not scorch. When sugar has caramellized, add it to the first mixture which should have just begun to boil. Cook until a firm ball forms in cold water (250° F if using a candy thermometer). Add butter and continue cooking until butter melts. Remove from heat and let stand a minute or two. Add vanilla and beat until creamy. Yield: Covers 2 (9-inch) layers.

COCA-COLA CAKE

2 cups flour
2 cups sugar
1 cup butter
3 tablespoons cocoa
1 cup Coca-Cola
1½ cups miniature
  marshmallows

2 eggs, beaten
1 teaspoon soda
¼ teaspoon salt
½ cup buttermilk
1 teaspoon vanilla extract

Preheat oven to 350° F. Mix flour and sugar in large bowl. Bring butter, cocoa, Coca-Cola and marshmallows to a boil. Pour over flour and sugar. Add eggs and mix well. Add soda and salt to buttermilk; then add to mixture. Add vanilla and stir. Pour into greased pan, 13 × 9 × 2 inches. Bake at 350° F for 40 to 45 minutes. Yield: 12-16 servings.

ICING:

2 tablespoons cocoa
½ cup butter
6 tablespoons Coca-Cola
1 pound confectioners' sugar

½ teaspoon vanilla extract
1 cup chopped pecans,
  toasted

Bring cocoa, butter and Coca-Cola to boil. Pour over sugar. Add vanilla and chopped pecans; beat well.

DATE NUT CAKE

4 eggs, separated
1 cup sugar
1 cup flour
2 teaspoons baking powder
¼ teaspoon salt

2 teaspoons vanilla extract
1 pound dates, chopped
4 cups pecans, chopped
1 cup flour

In small bowl, beat egg whites until stiff, but not dry. Set this aside. In another bowl, beat egg yolks and sugar. Add baking powder, salt and vanilla. Set egg mixture aside. In large bowl, mix dates and nuts. Dredge nuts and dates with flour. Set aside. Add yolk mixture to coated dates and nuts. Stir to mix. Fold egg whites into mixture. Line bottom of tube pan with waxed paper. Grease sides and center of tube pan. Pour cake mixture evenly into pan. Bake at 250° F for 1 hour, 20 minutes. Let cool before removing. Yield: 10-12 servings.

CHOCOLATE POUND CAKE

CAKE:

1 cup butter	2/3 teaspoon baking powder
1 cup margarine	1/2 cup cocoa
3 cups sugar	3 cups flour
5 eggs	1 1/4 cups milk
1/4 teaspoon salt	1 teaspoon vanilla extract

Preheat oven to 300° F. Cream butter, margarine and sugar. Add eggs one at a time. Add sifted dry ingredients alternately with combined milk and vanilla. Bake in a greased and floured bundt pan for 1 hour and 25 minutes at 300° F. Cool in pan 10 minutes before removing. Ice when cool.

ICING:

2 cups sugar	2/3 cup milk
1/4 cup cocoa	1/2 cup margarine
1/4 teaspoon salt	1 teaspoon vanilla extract

Combine ingredients except vanilla and bring to rolling boil on high heat. Stir constantly. Boil fast for 2 minutes, stirring constantly. Remove from heat. Add vanilla. Beat until creamy. Yield: 16 to 20 servings.

The finest CONFECTIONERS' SUGAR can be made from granulated sugar by using your blender. Just turn your blender on high, gradually pour the granulated sugar in and cover the top. Result—beautiful confectioners' sugar which can be made as it is needed with no more hard lumps to worry about.

Use medium to large eggs for baking. Extra large eggs may cause cakes to fall when cooled.

OLD FASHIONED POUND CAKE

8 eggs, separated
2⅔ cups sugar
1 pound butter

½ cup half and half
3½ cups flour, sifted
1 teaspoon vanilla extract

Preheat oven to 300° F. Beat whites of eggs; add 6 tablespoons of the sugar. After the eggs foam, continue to beat until peaks form. Set in refrigerator. Cream butter and remaining sugar. Add egg yolks, cream and flour and beat again. Add vanilla and stir. Fold in egg whites. Bake in greased and floured tube or bundt pan for 2 hours at 300° F. Yield: 16 to 20 servings.

Never use oil, butter or margarine to grease a cake pan. Use only shortening.

PINEAPPLE POUND CAKE

½ cup vegetable shortening
1 cup butter
2¾ cups sugar
6 eggs
3 cups sifted flour

1 teaspoon baking powder
¼ cup milk
1 teaspoon vanilla extract
¾ cup crushed pineapple
    with juice

TOPPING:

¼ cup butter or margarine
1½ cups confectioners' sugar

1 cup crushed pineapple,
    drained

Cream shortening, butter and sugar. Add eggs one at a time, beating thoroughly after each addition. Add flour sifted with baking powder alternately with milk. Add vanilla; stir in crushed pineapple and juice; blend well. Pour batter into well-greased 10-inch tube pan. Place in cold oven. Turn oven to 325° F and bake for 1½ hours or until top springs back. Let stand for a few minutes in pan. Run knife around edge and remove carefully to rack. Combine butter, confectioners' sugar and about 1 cup drained pineapple. Pour over cake while hot. Yield: 16-20 servings.

"Freezes well."

CARAMEL NUT POUND CAKE

½ pound butter
½ cup shortening
1 pound light brown sugar
1 cup granulated sugar
5 large eggs
3 cups flour

½ teaspoon salt
½ teaspoon baking powder
1 cup sweet or evaporated
  milk
1 tablespoon vanilla extract
1 cup chopped pecans

Preheat oven to 325° F. Cream butter, shortening and brown sugar and beat well. Add granulated sugar. Beat until light and fluffy. Add eggs, one at a time, beating well after each. Beat 3 minutes. Sift together dry ingredients. Add alternately to sugar mixture with milk. Add vanilla and pecans. Bake in a greased and floured 10 inch tube pan for 1 hour and 30 minutes. Frost or glaze with a caramel icing if desired.

BROWN SUGAR POUND CAKE

1 (1 pound) box light brown
  sugar
1 cup sugar
1½ cups butter
5 large eggs

1 cup milk
3 cups flour, sifted
½ teaspoon baking powder
1 cup chopped pecans
1 teaspoon vanilla extract

Preheat oven to 325° F. Cream sugars and butter. Add eggs one at a time. Beat until mixture is pale in color and thick enough to fall in ribbons. Add milk. Then add flour and baking powder, alternately. Stir in pecans and vanilla. Bake in greased and floured tube pan at 325° F for 1 to 1½ hours. Yield: 16 to 20 servings.

SOUR CREAM POUND CAKE

1 cup butter
2¾ cups sugar
6 eggs
3 cups flour

¼ teaspoon baking powder
¼ teaspoon salt
1 cup sour cream
1 teaspoon vanilla extract

Preheat oven to 325° F. Cream butter and sugar until fluffy. Add eggs one at a time, beating in well. Add baking powder and salt to sifted flour. Stir in flour and sour cream, alternately, to butter-egg mixture in 4 portions, beginning and ending with flour. Add vanilla. Pour in greased and floured bundt pan. Bake for 1 hour and 15 minutes at 325° F. Yield: 20 servings.

CHOCOLATE CHEESECAKE

CRUST:

18 graham crackers   ¼ cup sugar
½ cup butter

Crush graham crackers to make coarse crumbs (packaged crumbs are too fine). Melt butter and mix with sugar and crumbs; mixture should look like wet sand. Butter the sides of a 9-inch springform pan and press graham cracker crumb mixture against bottom and sides of pan. Set aside. Preheat oven to 350° F.

FILLING:

2 (8 ounce) packages cream   ⅔ cup sugar
    cheese   2 tablespoons rum
2 (6 ounce) packages   ⅛ teaspoon salt
    semi-sweet chocolate bits   1 cup whipping cream
½ cup strong black coffee   shaved chocolate
4 eggs, separated

Bring cream cheese to room temperature. Melt chocolate in coffee over low heat. In electric mixer bowl, beat egg yolks; add ⅓ cup sugar and beat until pale yellow and thickened. Gradually beat in cream cheese, a bit at a time, and beat until it looks like whipped butter. This takes 5 to 10 minutes, depending on your mixer. You cannot overbeat this cheese mixture. Beat in rum and salt. In another bowl, beat egg whites until foamy; add remaining ⅓ cup sugar gradually, a tablespoonful at a time, and beat until glossy but not stiff. Set aside. With mixer on low speed, beat the hot coffee chocolate mixture into cheese mixture (batter will be thin). Then fold in egg whites and pour into prepared pan. Place on the middle shelf of a preheated 350° F oven and bake 1 hour. Turn off oven and leave cake in the oven, door closed, until oven is cold. The cake will crack as it bakes and sink as it cools; this is normal. To serve, loosen cake from pan with a small knife; invert on serving plate and remove springform. Whip cream over ice; do not sweeten it. Pack into a pastry bag fitted with a star tube and pipe rosettes of whipped cream all over the top. Decorate with shaved chocolate curls or with cocoa, sieved and sifted over cake with a teaspoon. Yield: 16 servings.

CHEESECAKE

CRUST:

1 cup flour
1/4 cup sugar
1 teaspoon grated lemon peel

1/2 cup butter
1 egg yolk, slightly beaten
1/4 teaspoon vanilla extract

Preheat oven to 400° F. Combine flour, sugar and lemon peel; cut in butter until crumbly. Add egg yolk and vanilla, blending thoroughly. Pat one-third of this mixture on bottom of springform pan. Bake at 400° F for 8 minutes or until golden brown. Butter sides of pan and add remaining mixture to height of 1¼ inches all around.

FILLING:

5 (8 ounce) packages cream
    cheese, softened
1/4 teaspoon vanilla extract
3/4 teaspoon grated lemon
    peel
1¾ cups sugar

3 tablespoons flour
1/4 teaspoon salt
4 or 5 eggs, enough to make
    1 cup plus 2 more egg
    yolks
1/4 cup whipping cream

Beat cheese until creamy. Add vanilla and lemon peel. Mix sugar, flour and salt; add to cheese gradually. Add eggs and yolks one at a time, beating to blend. Fold in whipping cream. Turn into pan. Bake at 450° F for 12 minutes. Reduce heat to 300° F and bake for approximately 55 minutes. Remove from oven and cool. Loosen sides with knife after 30 minutes. Remove sides at end of 1 hour. Allow to cool 2 hours longer. May be topped with cherry or strawberry pie filling or whipping cream and garnished with strawberries. Yield: 12 servings.

Use metal cake pans to insure even browning of cakes.

FRESH COCONUT FILLING FOR CAKE

2 cups sugar
1 cup milk
1 coconut, grated

1/8 teaspoon salt
1 tablespoon butter
1 teaspoon vanilla extract

Bring sugar and milk to boil and add ¾ of the coconut. Add salt, butter and vanilla and blend well. While still warm, spoon onto cake layers. Ice with a white icing; use remaining coconut on top. Yield: 1⅓ cups.

ENGLISH TRIFLE

1 (12 ounce) piece of
 homemade pound cake
4 tablespoons raspberry jam

1 cup almonds
1/4 cup medium dry sherry
1/4 cup brandy

Cut pound cake into 1-inch thick slices and coat with raspberry jam. Place in glass serving dish. Sprinkle almonds on top; add sherry and brandy. Steep for 30 minutes.

CUSTARD:

2 teaspoons cornstarch
3 tablespoons sugar
1 1/2 cups milk
1 egg yolk

2 teaspoons vanilla extract
2 cups whipping cream
2 cups raspberries
1/2 cup almonds

Combine cornstarch, 1 tablespoon sugar and slowly add milk in a double boiler and cook until custard thickens. Beat egg yolk, stir in a small amount of custard. Whisk egg yolk mixture into custard; cook for 1 minute. Remove from heat; add vanilla. Whip cream until thickened, add remaining 2 tablespoons sugar and continue beating until stiff peaks form.
To assemble, scatter raspberries over cake; spread with custard and cover with half of whipped cream. Garnish with raspberries and 1/2 cup almonds; use whipped cream decoratively around the edge. This is best served at once but may be refrigerated for 1 or 2 hours. Yield: 8 servings.

MADELEINES

1 1/4 cups cake flour
1/2 teaspoon baking powder
1/4 teaspoon salt
3 eggs
1 teaspoon vanilla extract

2/3 cup sugar
2 teaspoons grated lemon
 rind
3/4 cup melted butter, cooled
confectioners' sugar

Sift flour, baking powder, and salt. Beat eggs until light; add vanilla and gradually beat in sugar until four times volume. Stir in lemon rind and gradually stir in flour mixture. Pour in melted butter. Brush madeleine pan with melted butter and spoon 1 tablespoon batter in each shell. Bake at 350° F for 12 to 15 minutes. Sift confectioners' sugar over top. Yield: 3 dozen.

BOSTON CREAM PIE

SPONGECAKE:

4 eggs, separated
3 tablespoons cold water
1 cup sugar
1½ tablespoons cornstarch
1 cup sifted flour (less 1½ tablespoons)

1¼ teaspoons baking powder
¼ teaspoon salt
1 teaspoon vanilla extract
½ teaspoon almond extract
2-9 inch cake pans

Preheat oven to 350° F. Do not grease pans. Beat egg yolks and water until thick; add sugar gradually. Sift cornstarch, flour, baking powder and salt together. Add to first mixture. Beat whites of eggs; add flavorings. Fold into yolk mixture. Bake in 2 (9-inch) cake pans at 350° F for 25 minutes.

FILLING:

1 pint milk
⅓ cup flour
2 eggs, beaten

¾ cup sugar
1 cup flavored whipped cream

Mix flour with some milk. Beat eggs, sugar, flour mixture. Scald milk; gradually add to egg mixture. Cook until thick. Split cakes horizontally and fill cooled cakes. Frost top of cake with flavored whipped cream. Yield: 16 servings.

LADYFINGERS

½ cup egg whites (4 eggs)
¼ teaspoon cream of tartar
10 tablespoons sugar
2 egg yolks
⅛ teaspoon salt

1 teaspoon vanilla extract
1¼ cups cake flour, sifted
½ teaspoon baking powder
confectioners' sugar

Beat egg whites to foam. Add cream of tartar. Gradually add 5 tablespoons sugar. Beat until mixture is very stiff. Beat egg yolks, salt and vanilla until light. Gradually add remaining sugar. Beat until pale yellow and thick enough to form a ribbon. Fold egg whites into egg yolk mixture. Gently stir in flour sifted with baking powder. Form 3-inch fingers on well greased cookie sheet. Bake at 350° F for 12 minutes. Sift confectioners' sugar over ladyfingers as soon as taken from oven. Remove from sheet immediately. Yield: 3 dozen.

ORANGE RUM CAKE

1 cup butter
1 cup sugar
2 eggs
2 orange rinds, grated
1 lemon rind, grated
2½ cups flour

2 teaspoons baking powder
1 teaspoon soda
½ teaspoon salt
1 cup buttermilk
1 cup chopped pecans

Preheat oven to 350° F. Cream butter, sugar and add eggs, beating until light and fluffy. Add rinds and sifted dry ingredients alternately with buttermilk. Fold in pecans. Bake in a greased 10-inch tube pan at 350° F for 1 hour.

While cake is baking, combine and boil 1 minute:

1 cup sugar
juice of 2 oranges

juice of 1 lemon
2 tablespoons rum

Pour slowly over cake when you remove it from oven. Yield: 16-20 servings.

FRESH APPLE NUT CAKE

1¼ cups Wesson oil
2 cups sugar
3 eggs
3 cups flour
1 teaspoon soda

1 teaspoon salt
2 teaspoons vanilla extract
3 or 4 apples, finely chopped
1 cup chopped pecans

Mix oil and sugar. Add eggs, beating well. Sift dry ingredients together and add. Stir in vanilla, apples and pecans. Pour into a greased and floured 9 × 13 inch pan. Bake at 350° F for 40 minutes. Pour GLAZE over cake while warm.

GLAZE:

1 cup sugar
½ teaspoon soda
½ cup buttermilk

1 tablespoon Karo syrup
¼ cup margarine
1 teaspoon vanilla extract

Combine sugar, soda, buttermilk, syrup and margarine. Cook until soft-ball stage. (This bubbles up in pan so use a larger pan for cooking—at least two-quart size). Remove from heat. Add vanilla. Beat until cool. Pour over cake and let cool. Yield: 16 servings.

ORANGE DATENUT CAKE

1 cup butter
2 cups sugar
4 eggs
1½ cups buttermilk
1 teaspoon soda
4 cups flour

2 tablespoons orange rind, grated
1 (8 ounce) package dates, chopped
1 cup pecans, chopped

Preheat oven to 325° F. Cream butter and sugar. Add eggs one at a time; beat. Dissolve soda in buttermilk. Continue beating. Add flour and milk alternately while beating. Add orange rind, dates and pecans. Stir well. Pour into greased bundt pan and bake for 1½ hours in 325° F oven. Take from oven and pour ORANGE SAUCE over; let it drain into cake. Remove from pan when cool. Yield: 16 to 20 servings.

ORANGE SAUCE:

1 cup orange juice
1¾ cups confectioners' sugar

2 tablespoons orange rind, grated

Combine orange juice, sugar and orange rind. Beat until smooth.

"A lovely Christmas cake!"

PLUMMY RUMMY CAKE

3 eggs
2 cups sugar
1 cup vegetable oil
2 small jars plum baby food
2 cups self-rising flour

1 teaspoon ground cloves
1 teaspoon ground cinnamon
1 teaspoon rum flavoring
1 cup chopped pecans (optional)

Preheat oven to 325° F. Combine eggs, sugar, oil and baby food. Thoroughly mix in flour, cloves, cinnamon and rum flavoring. Add nuts. Pour into greased and floured bundt pan. Bake at 325° F for 1 hour.

TOPPING:

1 cup confectioners' sugar
¼ cup rum

¼ cup water
2 tablespoons butter, melted

Combine all ingredients and pour over hot cake. Cool. Better the next day after topping soaks in. Yield: 12-14 servings.

CARROT CAKE

4 eggs
2 cups sugar
1½ cups salad oil
3 cups grated carrots

2 cups cake flour
1 teaspoon salt
2 teaspoons baking soda
2 teaspoons cinnamon

Preheat oven to 350° F. Cream the eggs, sugar and salad oil. Add remaining ingredients. Mix well. Bake in 3 greased and floured cake pans at 350° F for 25 to 30 minutes.

ICING:

1 (8 ounce) package cream
    cheese
¼ cup butter

⅔ box confectioners' sugar
1 teaspoon vanilla extract
⅔ cup chopped pecans

Have cheese and butter at room temperature. Mix all ingredients together and frost cake. The food processor can be used for this.

Yield: 12-16 servings.

PRALINE ICE CREAM CAKE

1½ cups flour
⅔ cup sugar
1 cup graham cracker
    crumbs
1 tablespoon baking powder

½ teaspoon salt
½ cup butter
2 eggs, beaten
1 pint vanilla ice cream,
    softened

Combine flour, sugar, graham cracker crumbs, baking powder and salt. Set aside. Melt butter. Combine butter, flour mixture, eggs and ice cream. Stir until smooth. Pour batter into lightly greased 13 × 9 × 2-inch pan. Spoon ⅓ cup TOPPING over batter. Bake at 350° F for 30 minutes. Spread remaining topping over hot cake.

TOPPING:

1 cup firmly packed brown
    sugar
½ cup sour cream
2 tablespoons butter

2 teaspoons cornstarch
½ teaspoon vanilla extract
½ cup chopped pecans

Combine brown sugar, sour cream, butter and cornstarch. Cook over medium heat until thickened. Stir often. Remove from heat; stir in vanilla and pecans.

Yield: 6 to 8 servings.

Candies

SPICED PECANS

2 cups sugar
1/4 cup water
1 teaspoon nutmeg

1/4 teaspoon cinnamon
1/8 teaspoon salt
2 cups pecans

Boil ingredients except pecans until mixture threads. Add nuts, stir until coated. Pour on a cookie sheet covered with waxed paper and separate. Yield: 2 cups.

CANDY COATED PECANS

3 1/2 to 4 cups pecan halves
2 egg whites
1 cup sugar

dash of salt
1/2 cup butter

Toast pecan halves in 300° F oven until light brown, (10 to 15 minutes). Beat egg whites until stiff peaks form. Then fold in sugar and salt. Fold nuts into meringue. Melt butter in large pan. Spread nut mixture over butter. Bake in slow oven 300° F about 30 minutes. Stir every 10 minutes. Yield: 4 cups.

ORANGE PECANS

3 cups sugar
1/2 cup evaporated milk plus
   1/2 cup water
juice and shredded rind of 2
   oranges

1/4 cup butter or
   margarine
1 quart shelled pecans
   (halves or large pieces)

Cook sugar, milk and water to soft ball stage. Add juice and shredded rind. Cook to soft ball stage (238° F). Add butter, remove from heat. Cool, then beat until creamy. Add pecans. Drop by teaspoonfuls on waxed paper. Yield: 4 cups.

PECAN BRITTLE

2 cups sugar
1 cup Karo syrup
1 cup water
pinch of salt

2 cups pecans, coarsely
   chopped
1 tablespoon margarine
1 teaspoon baking soda

Mix sugar, syrup, water and salt in a heavy iron skillet. Bring to a full boil, then pour in pecans. Cook until mixture starts to brown; add margarine and stir. Add soda and stir. Pour on a greased cookie sheet. Let cool. Break up into pieces. Yield: 2 pounds.

PECAN TOFFEE

1 cup butter (no substitute)
1 cup sugar
¼ cup water
½ teaspoon salt

3 squares semi-sweet
   chocolate
1 cup coarsely broken pecans

Combine butter, sugar, water and salt in heavy saucepan. Cook, stirring constantly to hard crack stage (300° F), watching carefully. Immediately pour into ungreased 13 × 9-inch pan. Cool until hard. Melt chocolate over hot, not boiling, water. Spread on toffee, sprinkle with nuts and press them down into chocolate. Let chocolate set 2 to 3 hours. Break into bite-size pieces. Yield: 1 pound.

PRALINES

4 cups sugar
½ cup butter
1 cup light cream
pinch of salt

1 tablespoon vanilla extract
1 cup coarsely chopped
   pecans

Put 3 cups sugar, butter, cream, and salt in heavy saucepan and bring to boil before caramelizing other cup of sugar. Put 1 cup sugar in frying pan over medium high heat and stir constantly until it melts and turns a medium brown. Pour syrup slowly into other mixture stirring constantly. Cook to the soft ball stage (238° F.) on candy thermometer. Cool slightly; add vanilla. Hand beat until it looks creamy and thick. Add pecans and quickly drop by spoonfuls onto waxed paper. Yield: 24 pralines.

PEANUT BUTTER BALLS

1 pound box confectioners'
   sugar
1 (12 ounce) jar peanut
   butter

1 cup margarine, softened
2 (12 ounce) packages
   chocolate chips
1 (1 inch) square paraffin

Combine sugar, peanut butter and margarine. Roll into one-inch balls. Chill. In a saucepan, on low heat, melt chocolate chips and paraffin. Using toothpicks, dip peanut butter balls into chocolate mixture. Place on a cookie sheet covered with waxed paper. Remove toothpick after dipping. Yield: 75 to 100 balls.

PEANUT BRITTLE

1 cup peanuts
1 cup sugar
½ cup white Karo syrup

½ cup water
⅛ teaspoon salt
½ teaspoon soda

Put all ingredients, except soda, in iron skillet. Cook 8 to 10 minutes. Add soda and stir well. Pour on greased marble or a cookie sheet. With a spatula, work over and under mixture to stretch until it becomes thin. Cool a second or so and break into pieces as it becomes crisp. Yield: 1 pound

VARIATION: For chocolate-coated Peanut Brittle, dip each piece in melted dipping chocolate.

COATED PEANUTS

2 cup raw peanuts
1 teaspoon red or green food
   coloring

1 cup sugar
½ cup water

Put all ingredients in boiler and cook stirring constantly, until all liquid is absorbed. Spray cookie sheet with vegetable shortening. Pour contents of boiler into pan. Place pan in oven set at 300° F for 15 to 20 minutes. Peanuts will be coated and each will be separated.

CHOCOLATE CARAMELS

2 cups sugar
¾ cup light corn syrup
⅛ teaspoon salt
3 or 4 squares unsweetened
    chocolate

2 cups light cream
1 teaspoon vanilla extract
½ to ¾ cup chopped pecans

Combine sugar, syrup, salt, chocolate and 1 cup cream in large heavy saucepan. Stir constantly until mixture comes to a full boil. Gradually add remaining cream so that boiling does not stop. Continue cooking, stirring constantly, to firm ball stage (248° F). Remove from heat. Stir in vanilla extract and nuts. Pour into buttered 8-inch square pan. When cold, turn out on cutting board and cut into ¾-inch squares. Yield: 2 pounds.

CHOCOLATE FUDGE

⅔ cup cocoa
3 cups sugar
⅛ teaspoon salt
1½ cups milk

4½ tablespoons butter
1 teaspoon vanilla extract
1 cup chopped pecans or
    pecan halves (optional)

Combine cocoa, sugar and salt in a saucepan. Add milk. Bring to a boil stirring frequently. Reduce heat and cook to soft ball stage (232° F). Remove from heat, drop in butter and let cool to 110° F. Add vanilla. Beat by hand until mixture thickens. Pour into buttered pan. Add chopped nuts or place pecan halves on top of fudge before it cools. Let cool completely. Cut in 1-inch squares. Yield: 64 one-inch squares.

HARD CANDY

3¾ cups sugar
1½ cups light corn syrup
1 cup water
¼ teaspoon food coloring

1 teaspoon of flavoring oil
    (cannot be extract), such
    as clove, cinnamon,
    lemon, orange

Mix first three ingredients in a large saucepan. Stir over medium heat until sugar dissolves. Boil without stirring, until temperature reaches 310° F or until drops of syrup form hard brittle threads in cold water. Remove from heat. After boiling has ceased, stir in flavoring and coloring. Pour onto lightly greased cookie sheet. Cool. Break into pieces. Store in airtight containers. Yield: 2 pounds.

LIGHT CARAMELS WITH PECANS

2 cups sugar
¾ cup light corn syrup
⅛ teaspoon salt
½ cup butter

2 cups heavy cream
1 teaspoon vanilla extract
½ to ¾ cup chopped pecans

Combine sugar, syrup, salt, butter and 1 cup cream in large heavy saucepan. Stir constantly until mixture comes to a full boil. Gradually add remaining cream so that boiling does not stop. Continue stirring to hard ball stage (250° F). Remove from heat. Stir in vanilla extract and nuts. Pour into buttered 8-inch square pan. When cold, turn out on cutting board and cut into ¾-inch squares. Yield: 2 pounds.

TURTLES

1 (14 ounce) package
    caramels
2 teaspoons half and half
    cream
1 (5 ounce) package pecan
    halves

1 (6 ounce) package
    semi-sweet chocolate
1 (1 inch) square paraffin

Melt caramels and half and half in double boiler, stirring occasionally until smooth. Place pecan halves in groups of 3 on buttered baking sheets, arranging a turtle. Spoon caramel mixture over nuts to form turtle back using about 1 table-spoon per turtle. Refrigerate uncovered for 30 minutes. Melt the chocolate and paraffin together and spoon over the caramel. Store cool in single layers in a covered container. Will keep about 3 weeks. Yield: 12 turtles.

CHOCOLATE PECAN BARS

4 (1 ounce) squares
    semi-sweet chocolate
1 (14 ounce) can condensed
    milk
2 cups crushed vanilla
    wafers

pinch of salt
1 cup chopped pecans
1 pinch of cinnamon
1 teaspoon vanilla extract
1 cup confectioners' sugar

Melt chocolate in a double boiler. Add milk, stir until thick. Add all other ingredients except confectioners' sugar. Pour mixture into greased pan and allow to cool. Cut into small bars and roll in confectioners' sugar. Yield: 4 dozen.

SYRUP PULL CANDY

1 quart Georgia cane syrup   1 cup nuts
1 tablespoon vinegar   2 tablespoons butter

Put all ingredients in heavy saucepan. Bring to boil on high heat. Cook to the hard crack stage on medium heat, takes 30 minutes. Pour into buttered platter to cool. When cool enough to handle, pull until bright in color, about 15 minutes. Put in any kind of nuts you like. Put butter on your hands, and break candy into pieces.

Store separately different types of candy. Brittles will soften if stored with creamy candies. Airtight storage in a cool place is the best.

ANGEL BALLS

1 pound dates, chopped   4 cups Rice Krispies
1 (3½ ounce) can coconut   2 cups chopped pecans
1 cup white sugar   1 teaspoon vanilla extract
1 cup brown sugar, packed   confectioners' sugar
½ pound butter or
    margarine

Mix dates, coconut, sugars and butter. Cook 6 minutes. Cool. Add Rice Krispies, pecans and vanilla. Make balls and roll in confectioners' sugar. Yield: 100 balls.

Do not make divinity, peanut brittle or hard candy on a humid or rainy day.

DIVINITY

3 cups sugar   1 teaspoon vanilla extract
¾ cup white Karo syrup   1 cup chopped pecans OR ¾
¾ cup water   cup chopped candied
2 egg whites, beaten   cherries (optional)

Dissolve sugar and syrup in water over low heat, stirring. Cook without stirring to firm ball stage (248° F). Remove from heat. Pour gradually over stiffly beaten egg whites. Add vanilla and continue beating until mixture will hold its shape when dropped from spoon. Add pecans or cherries, if desired. Drop by spoonfuls on waxed paper. Yield: 50 servings.

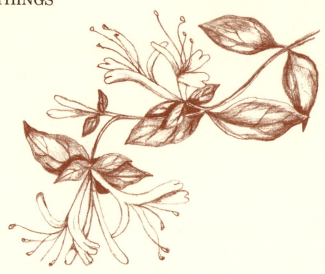

CANDIED GRAPEFRUIT PEEL

2 or 3 grapefruit
1 cup sugar per grapefruit

½ cup water per grapefruit
sugar

Remove pulp and inner skin of grapefruit. Cut peel into long strips, one-half inch wide. Soak peel 24 hours in enough water to cover, changing water several times. Put peel in fresh cold water and boil 5 minutes; repeat twice. The third time, boil peel until tender. Drain and let rest. Make a heavy syrup using the sugar and water measurements for each grapefruit. Cook syrup to soft ball stage (238° F). Add peel and simmer until most of syrup has evaporated — about one-half hour. Watch to prevent peel from sticking. Drain in sieve. Roll peel, a few pieces at a time, in sugar. Cool. Store in covered container. Oranges may be substituted for grapefruit. Yield: 2 to 2½ cups.

COCONUT-ORANGE BALLS

1 pound vanilla wafers,
    finely crushed
1 pound box confectioners'
    sugar
½ cup margarine

1 (6 ounce) can frozen orange
    juice, thawed
1 cup chopped pecans
coconut, grated

Mix all ingredients together. Dampen hands and form into quarter-size balls; roll in coconut. Recipe may be frozen when completed. Yield: 8 dozen.

Cookies

PEARL COOKIES

½ pound butter
1 cup sugar
¼ teaspoon salt
1½ teaspoons vanilla extract

1 egg yolk
2 cups flour
1 egg white, beaten
1 cup chopped pecans

Preheat oven to 225° F. Cream butter and sugar; add salt, vanilla and egg yolk. Add flour to butter and sugar mixture. Pat this mixture onto a greased cookie sheet. Make it fairly thin. Beat egg white, brush over cookie dough with a pastry brush. Press pecans into dough. Bake at 225° F for 2 hours. Cut cookies while warm. They will crispen quickly. Yield: 10 dozen.

STRAWBERRY PRESERVES COOKIES

1 cup margarine
4 tablespoons sugar
2 teaspoons vanilla extract

2 cups flour
2 cups finely chopped pecans
strawberry preserves

Cream margarine, sugar and vanilla. Add flour, then nuts. Roll in ball; place on greased cookie sheet. Make indentation in center. Bake at 300° F about 35 minutes. Put small amount of preserves in center about 10 minutes before done. Yield: 3 to 4 dozen.

SESAME CHERRY COOKIES

1 cup butter, softened
½ cup sugar
1 teaspoon almond extract
2 cups flour

¼ teaspoon salt
⅓ cup sesame seeds
⅓ cup halved, candied cherries

Cream butter and sugar well. Add almond extract, flour, salt. Chill at least 1 hour. Preheat oven to 400° F. Roll dough into 1 inch balls. Roll balls into sesame seeds. Put ½ cherry on each. Bake until lightly browned, about 5 minutes, on ungreased cookie sheet. Let cool on cookie sheet. Yield: 2 dozen.

GINGER-BEER PECAN COOKIES

¾ cup shortening
¾ cup molasses
1 cup firmly packed brown
   sugar
1 teaspoon baking soda
½ cup hot flat Miller High
   Life beer

1¾ teaspoons powdered
   ginger
½ teaspoon powdered
   cinnamon
½ teaspoon salt
4 cups sifted flour
½ cup finely chopped pecans

Preheat oven to 375° F. In a mixing bowl, beat together shortening, molasses, sugar and baking soda. Gradually pour in hot Miller High Life beer and continue beating as you flavor with ginger, cinnamon and salt. Sift in flour and beat until dough is shiny and pliable. On a floured board, roll out dough to ⅛ inch thickness. Cut into cookie shapes with a floured cookie cutter. Sprinkle pecans on each cookie and place on an ungreased cookie sheet, 1 inch apart. Bake for 7 to 10 minutes, or until moderately browned. Yield: 4 dozen.

Miller Brewing Company

BUTTER RICHES

¾ cup butter
½ cup firmly packed brown
   sugar
1 tablespoon sugar

1 egg yolk, unbeaten
1 teaspoon vanilla extract
1¾ to 2 cups flour, sifted
pecan halves

Cream butter. Gradually add brown sugar and sugar. Cream well. Add unbeaten egg yolk and vanilla. Beat well. Blend in sifted flour to form a stiff dough. Shape into balls about the size of a marble; place on greased cookie sheets. Flatten to the size of a fifty cent piece with the bottom of a glass dipped in sugar. Bake at 350° F for 7 to 9 minutes until light golden brown. Cool and frost. Garnish with pecan halves.

BROWNED BUTTER FROSTING:

¼ cup butter
2½ cups confectioners' sugar,
   sifted

1 teaspoon vanilla extract
3 to 4 tablespoons cream

Brown butter. Blend in sifted confectioners' sugar and vanilla. Gradually add cream until of spreading consistency. Yield: 7 dozen.

Y-DEAR'S DANISH BARS

CRUST:

1 cup flour   *⅓ cup butter*

Mix flour and butter; pat in 9 × 13-inch ungreased pan; bake at 350° F for 12 to 15 minutes.

FILLING:

2 eggs   *¾ cup finely chopped pecans*
1 cup brown sugar   *½ teaspoon salt*
¾ cup coconut

Mix filling ingredients thoroughly and spread on hot crust. Bake at 350° F for 25 to 30 minutes. Cool in pan.

ICING:

1½ cups confectioners' sugar   *5 teaspoons orange juice*
2 tablespoons butter, softened   *¾ teaspoon almond extract*

Mix icing ingredients; spread on cool bars, uncut, while still in pan.

When icing firms, cut in squares or bars and remove from pan. Store in sealed container. May be frozen. Yield: 2½ dozen.

DATE PIN WHEELS

FILLING:
1 pound dates   *½ cup water*
½ cup sugar

DOUGH:
½ cup butter   *2 cups flour*
½ cup brown sugar   *½ teaspoon soda*
½ cup granulated sugar   *½ teaspoon salt*
1 egg   *1 cup chopped pecans*

Grind dates; add sugar and water. Cook just until a soft paste. Make dough by creaming butter and sugars; beat in egg. Stir in flour, soda and salt. Blend thoroughly; then add pecans. Roll out dough on pastry sheet. Add filling; roll up. Chill overnight. Cut in rounds. Bake at 325° F for 12 to 15 minutes. Yield: 6 dozen.

OATMEAL CARAMELITE

CRUST:
1 cup flour
1 cup oatmeal
¾ cup brown sugar, firmly
    packed

½ teaspoon soda
¼ teaspoon salt
¾ cup melted margarine

FILLING:
1 cup chocolate chips
½ cup chopped pecans

¾ cup caramel ice cream
    topping
3 tablespoons flour

Mix all crust ingredients. Press ½ of mixture in a 9-inch square pan. Bake at 350° F for 10 minutes. Remove from oven. Sprinkle with chocolate chips and pecans. Blend flour and topping. Spread over all. Sprinkle with remainder of crust mixture; press in. Bake 15 to 20 minutes until golden brown. Chill 1 to 2 hours. Cut into bars. Yield: 3 dozen bars.

COCOA CRISPS

¾ cup butter
¾ cup sugar
1 egg
1½ cups flour
1 teaspoon baking powder

½ teaspoon salt
2 tablespoons cocoa
1 tablespoon water
3 tablespoons chopped pecans
2 tablespoons sugar

Cream butter and ¾ cup sugar. Beat 1 egg slightly; reserve 1 tablespoon of egg. Add remainder of egg to sugar and butter. Blend in dry ingredients. Chill 2 hours. Place dough on slightly floured surface. Divide dough into 4 parts; shape into long rolls. Place 4 inches apart on ungreased baking sheets. Pat into ¼ inch thickness with a fork. Blend water with reserved egg. Brush over dough. Combine pecans and 2 tablespoons sugar; sprinkle over dough. Bake at 400° F for 10 minutes. Cut into strips crosswise. Yield: 3-4 dozen.

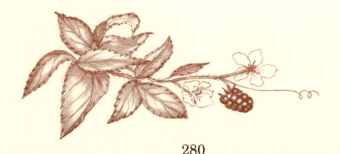

REFRIGERATOR OATMEAL PECAN COOKIES

1 cup butter
1 cup brown sugar
1 cup granulated sugar
2 eggs, well beaten
1 teaspoon vanilla extract

1½ cups flour
1 teaspoon soda
1 teaspoon salt
1½ cups chopped pecans
2 cups oatmeal

Preheat oven to 325° F. Cream butter and sugars. Add eggs, vanilla extract. Sift flour, soda and salt. Add to sugar-egg mixture. Stir in pecans and oatmeal. Shape dough into rolls 1½ inches in diameter. Chill. Slice and place on ungreased baking sheet. Bake at 325° F for 10 minutes. Turn oven off and let cookies crisp for a few minutes. Yield: 4 dozen.

ICE BOX COOKIES

1 cup butter
2 cups brown sugar
2 eggs, beaten
4 cups flour

1 teaspoon soda
1 teaspoon cream of tartar
1 cup chopped pecans
1 teaspoon vanilla extract

Cream butter and sugar; add eggs; sift flour with soda and cream of tartar. Add flour mixture to butter mixture a little at a time; stir in pecans and vanilla. Shape into rolls about 1½ inch round. Wrap in waxed paper; refrigerate 8 hours or overnight. Slice ¼ inch thick and bake in a 350° F oven for 8 to 10 minutes. Rolls of dough may be frozen. Yield: 8 to 10 dozen.

REFRIGERATOR CHOCOLATE CHIP COOKIES

½ cup butter
1 cup brown sugar
1 egg, well beaten
½ teaspoon vanilla extract
1¼ cups flour

½ teaspoon salt
½ teaspoon soda
½ cup chopped pecans
1 cup chocolate chips

Cream butter and sugar. Add egg and vanilla. Mix well. Add flour which has been sifted with salt and soda, a little at a time. Continue stirring until mixed. Add nuts and chocolate chips. Form into two rolls. Wrap in waxed paper. Refrigerate several hours. Slice into cookies. Bake in top part of oven for 10 minutes at 325° F. May be frozen. Yield: 4 dozen.

CHOCOLATE LAYER COOKIES

COOKIE LAYER:
2 squares unsweetened
   chocolate
½ cup sweet butter
2 eggs

1 cup sugar
½ cup almonds, sliced
½ cup flour

Preheat oven to 350° F. Thoroughly grease 9 × 9 × 2-inch pan. Melt unsweetened chocolate and butter. Cool. Beat the eggs and sugar until thick. Add nuts, flour and chocolate mixture and stir until smooth. Pour batter into pan. Bake for 25 minutes and cool on wire rack.

MINT CREAM FILLING:

1½ cups confectioners' sugar
3 tablespoons butter
2 tablespoons heavy cream

¾ teaspoon peppermint
   extract
green food coloring

Beat together all the ingredients until smooth. Add a drop of green coloring. Spread the filling evenly over the cookie layer. Cover and chill until firm, about 1 hour.

CHOCOLATE GLAZE:

3 ounces semi-sweet
   chocolate bits

2 tablespoons butter
1 teaspoon vanilla extract

Melt chocolate bits and butter in saucepan. Stir in vanilla. Drizzle the glaze over the mint topping. Cover and chill until firm. Cut into bite-size squares. Yield: 64 cookies.

REAL SCOTTISH SHORTBREAD

1 cup butter
1½ cups flour, unsifted
½ cup rice flour

⅓ cup sugar
confectioners' sugar

Combine all ingredients except confectioners' sugar until they become a soft dough. Roll out to 1 inch thick. Put into a shortbread mold or bake in a 9-inch pie pan. Decorate edges by marking with a fork. Bake at 325° F until golden brown, about 1 hour. Dust with confectioners' sugar. Rice flour may be purchased at health food stores. Yield: 16 wedges.

BROWNIES

½ cup margarine
½ cup cooking oil
1 cup water
2 cups sifted flour
2 cups sugar
4 tablespoons cocoa

½ teaspoon salt
2 eggs
½ cup buttermilk
1 teaspoon soda
1 teaspoon vanilla extract

FROSTING:

½ cup margarine
1 tablespoon cocoa
6 tablespoons milk

1 teaspoon vanilla extract
1 box confectioners' sugar
1 cup chopped pecans

Preheat oven to 350° F. Grease and flour a 9 × 13-inch pan. In a medium size saucepan, combine margarine, cooking oil and water; bring to a boil. Combine flour, sugar, cocoa, and salt. Combine hot liquid and dry ingredients; beat well. Beat 2 eggs into mixture; add buttermilk. Add soda and vanilla. Pour in pan and bake for 30 minutes. In a saucepan, combine margarine, cocoa, milk and vanilla. Cook to blend. Sift confectioners' sugar. Add sugar a little at a time while beating after margarine is melted. Add pecans. Spread evenly over cool cake. Yield: 36 to 40 squares.

BROWN SUGAR BROWNIES

½ cup butter
1 cup brown sugar
1 egg
1 cup sifted flour
1 teaspoon baking powder

¼ teaspoon salt
1 teaspoon vanilla extract
1⅓ cups chopped pecans
confectioners' sugar

Cream butter and sugar. Add egg and mix until smooth. Sift flour. Measure and sift again with baking powder and salt. Add dry ingredients to sugar mixture; mix. Add vanilla and pecans. Spread batter into greased 9 inch square pan. Bake 30 minutes at 350° F. Cut into bars while still warm. Dust with confectioners' sugar. Yield: 3 dozen bars.

KISSES

3 egg whites
1 cup plus 1 tablespoon
   sugar

1 cup chopped pecans
1 teaspoon vinegar

Beat egg whites until stiff. While still beating, add sugar and vinegar. Fold in nuts. Grease cookie sheet and cover with brown paper. (An open paper sack will do.) Drop mixture onto paper with tablespoon. Cook at 325° F for 20 to 30 minutes until done but not brown. Yield: 3½ dozen.

TOLL HOUSE BRITTLE

1 cup margarine
½ teaspoon salt
1½ teaspoons vanilla extract
1 cup brown sugar

2 cups flour
1 (6 ounce) bag chocolate
   chips
½ cup chopped pecans

Blend margarine, salt and vanilla. Add brown sugar. Blend. Add flour and chocolate chips. Press into 15 × 10 × 1-inch pan. Sprinkle with pecans. Bake at 375° F for 25 minutes. Cool and cut or break. Yield: 4 dozen.

Thoroughly chilled dough is the secret for successful rolled cookies.

ALMOND PENCIL CHRISTMAS COOKIES

½ cup shortening
½ cup butter
⅓ cup sugar
⅔ cup finely chopped
   almonds

¼ teaspoon salt
1⅔ cups flour
1 cup confectioners' sugar
1 teaspoon cinnamon

Cream shortening, butter and sugar together. Add almonds and salt. Work in flour by hand. Chill dough thoroughly. Remove small portion from refrigerator at a time and roll dough to about the thickness of an art pencil. Cut into 2½-inch lengths. Bake at 325° F on ungreased cookie sheet for 14 to 16 minutes. Let stand on sheet to cool (just slightly). Lift off while still warm and roll into confectioners' sugar that has been sifted with cinnamon. Do not use margarine; butter is needed for richness. May be frozen after baking. Yield: 3 dozen.

PECAN CRESCENTS

½ cup butter
¼ cup sugar
1 cup flour

½ teaspoon vanilla extract
1 cup chopped pecans
confectioners' sugar

Mix butter and sugar. Add flour and vanilla. Work in pecans and place in refrigerator to chill. Shape into crescents, balls or fingers and bake in slow oven (250° F to 300° F) for 1 hour or until crisp. Roll in confectioners' sugar; store in boxes to keep crisp. Yield: 2 dozen.

LEMON COCONUT SOURS

⅓ cup butter or margarine, chilled
¾ cup flour, sifted
2 eggs, well beaten
½ teaspoon vanilla extract

1 cup light brown sugar, firmly packed
1 teaspoon lemon peel, grated
¾ cup flaked coconut
½ cup coarsely chopped pecans

GLAZE:

¾ cup confectioners' sugar

2 tablespoons lemon juice

Cut butter or margarine into flour until thoroughly blended; press evenly and firmly into 9-inch square pan. Bake at 350° F for 10 minutes. Meanwhile, beat eggs, extract and brown sugar until creamy. Stir in lemon peel, coconut and pecans. Spread evenly over partially baked layer in pan. Return to oven and bake about 20 minutes. Immediately spread lemon glaze over top. When cool, cut into bars. Yield: 4 dozen.

"Absolutely divine! Nice for a large party."

THE WOOKY COOKY

1 cup margarine
1 cup sugar
1½ cups flour
½ teaspoon baking powder

½ teaspoon baking soda
½ cup chopped pecans
½ cup Rice Krispies
1 teaspoon vanilla extract

Cream butter and sugar. Stir in all other ingredients; do not crush cereal. Cool in refrigerator. Shape into balls; press with fork to flatten. Bake on greased baking sheet at 325° F for 10 to 15 minutes. Yield: 4 dozen.

FORGOTTEN COOKIES

2 egg whites, beaten
2 cups sugar
1 teaspoon vanilla extract

1 cup chopped pecans
1 (6 ounce) package chocolate
  chips

Preheat oven to 350° F. Beat egg whites until stiff. Add sugar
and beat well. Add vanilla. Fold in nuts and chocolate chips.
Line cookie sheet with foil; drop by teaspoonfuls; put in oven
and turn oven off. Leave overnight. Yield: 3 dozen.

CAMEO TEA COOKIES

1¾ cups flour
1 teaspoon baking powder
½ teaspoon salt
¾ cup butter
½ cup sugar
1 unbeaten egg

1 teaspoon vanilla extract
1 square unsweetened
  chocolate, melted
2 tablespoons sugar
1 to 2 tablespoons flour

Sift together flour, baking powder, and salt. Set aside. Cream
butter and sugar; add egg and vanilla. Blend in dry ingredients. Place ¾ cup of the dough in another bowl. Blend in
melted chocolate and 2 tablespoons sugar. Add 1 to 2 tablespoons flour to give desired cookie press consistency. Drop
light dough by teaspoonful onto ungreased baking sheets.
Flatten to ¼ inch with floured bottom of a glass. Place chocolate dough in a cookie press with desired design. Press design
on top of each drop cookie. Bake at 375° F for 10 minutes.
Yield: 4 to 5 dozen.

PECAN MACAROONS

4 egg whites, beaten
2 cups sugar
1½ cups finely chopped
  pecans

¾ cup bread crumbs, sifted
1 teaspoon vanilla or almond
  extract

Beat egg whites until stiff; gradually add sugar, beating constantly. Put half of the meringue in another bowl and add the
pecans and sifted bread crumbs. To the remaining meringue,
add the vanilla or almond extract. Spread mixture ⅛ inch
thick on floured board and cut out rounds with cookie cutter.
Put cookies on oiled baking sheet and spread them with flavored meringue almost to the edges. Bake at 350° F for 20 to 25
minutes, or until very light brown. Yield: 2 dozen.

SUGAR COOKIES

2 cups flour
½ teaspoon salt
½ teaspoon baking soda
½ teaspoon cream of tartar
1 cup sugar

1 cup margarine or butter
1 egg
1 teaspoon vanilla extract
granulated sugar

Sift flour with salt, soda and cream of tartar and set aside. Cream sugar and margarine. Add egg, vanilla and dry ingredients to sugar mixture. Chill dough at least 2 hours before baking. Roll dough in small balls; place on greased cookie sheet and press flat with the bottom of a glass dipped in sugar. Bake at 350° F until lightly browned, about 9 to 10 minutes. BE CAREFUL NOT TO BURN. Yield: 2 to 4 dozen.

CINNAMON FLATS

2 cups butter
2 cups sugar, scant
4 cups flour

2 tablespoons cinnamon
2 egg yolks

TOPPING:
2 egg whites, beaten
1 cup sugar

1 tablespoon cinnamon
2 cups chopped pecans

Cream butter and sugar; add flour, cinnamon and egg yolks. When blended, press lightly into jelly roll pan about ¼-inch thick. Beat egg whites slightly and brush over the surface. Mix sugar and cinnamon and sprinkle over egg whites. Sprinkle chopped pecans over all, pressing in lightly. Bake at 350° F for 20 to 25 minutes. Cut into squares while hot and cool in pan. Nutmeg may be substituted for cinnamon for a unique flavor. Yield: 8 dozen.

PRALINE STRIPS

graham crackers
½ cup butter
½ cup margarine

1 cup light brown sugar
1 cup chopped pecans
1 teaspoon vanilla extract

Line 9 × 13-inch pan with foil and cover bottom completely with graham crackers. Boil butter, margarine and sugar for 2 minutes. Add pecans and pour over crackers; spread evenly. Bake at 350° F for 10 to 15 minutes. Cut while warm. Yield: 4 dozen.

Pies

PECAN FUDGE PIE

½ cup butter
3 squares unsweetened
   chocolate
4 eggs
3 tablespoons white corn
   syrup

1½ cups sugar
¼ teaspoon salt
1 teaspoon vanilla extract
1 cup chopped pecans
1 (9 inch) pastry shell,
   unbaked

Melt butter and chocolate in top of double boiler. Meanwhile, place eggs in mixing bowl and beat until light. Beat syrup, sugar, salt and vanilla into eggs. Add pecans. Add slightly cooled chocolate mixture. Mix thoroughly and pour into pastry shell. Bake at 350° F for 25 to 35 minutes or until top is crusty and filling is set but soft inside. Do not over bake. Pie should shake like custard so it will not be too stiff when cool. May be served plain or with ice cream or whipped cream. Yield: 8 servings.

Mrs. George Busbee

PECAN PIE

3 eggs
½ cup sugar
1 cup light corn syrup
½ teaspoon salt
1 teaspoon vanilla extract

¼ cup butter, melted
1 cup coarsely chopped
   pecans
1 (9 inch) deep dish pastry
   shell, unbaked

Beat eggs slightly; add sugar, corn syrup, salt and vanilla. Blend well, but do not overbeat; add butter. Stir in pecans. Pour into pastry shell. Bake in preheated 350° F oven approximately 50 minutes or until knife inserted comes out clean. Yield: 6 servings.

To make nut meats come out whole, soak nuts in salt water overnight before cracking.

When using pastry cloth, rub flour well into surface so no additional flour is rolled into pastry.

CHOCOLATE CHIP PECAN PIE

1 (6 ounce) bag chocolate
    chips
1 cup sugar
½ cup flour
2 eggs

½ cup melted butter
1 teaspoon vanilla extract
1 cup chopped pecans
1 deep dish pastry shell
Cool Whip or whipped cream

Mix first 7 ingredients and pour into pastry shell. Bake for 45 minutes to 1 hour, or until the top has a light brown crust. Let cool at room temperature. Serve topped with whipped cream. Yield: 6 to 8 servings.

GERMAN CHOCOLATE PECAN PIE

⅔ cup sugar
⅛ teaspoon salt
1 cup light Karo syrup
1 (4 ounce) bar German
    sweet chocolate
3 tablespoons butter

3 eggs, beaten
1 teaspoon vanilla extract
1 cup chopped pecans
1 deep dish pastry shell,
    slightly baked

In medium saucepan, mix sugar, salt and syrup; bring to a boil, stirring constantly. Boil 2 minutes after sugar dissolves; remove from heat. Add chocolate and butter; stir until melted together. Cool this mixture and pour into beaten eggs. Add vanilla and pecans. Pour into slightly baked deep dish crust. Bake at 350° F for about 50 minutes. Yield: 8 servings.

ICE CREAM PIE

CRUST:

3 egg whites
1 cup sugar
1 teaspoon vanilla extract

1 cup vanilla wafer crumbs
½ cup chopped pecans
ice cream (any flavor)

Beat egg whites until stiff. Add ½ cup sugar and vanilla extract. Mix vanilla wafer crumbs with ½ cup sugar and pecans. Fold into egg whites. Put in a greased and floured 9" pie plate. Cook at 325° F for 25 to 30 minutes. Cool. Then fill with ice cream and freeze. Yield: 8 to 10 servings.

NOTE: Butter pecan ice cream is delicious in this recipe.

PECAN TEA TARTS

CRUST:

½ cup butter   1 cup flour
1 (3 ounce) package cream
   cheese

Cream butter and cream cheese; stir in flour. Mix thoroughly; chill dough for 1 hour. Shape into 2 dozen round balls. Press into miniature muffin tins. Do not bake crust first.

CUSTARD:

1 cup chopped pecans   ½ cup Karo syrup
1 egg   1 tablespoon butter
½ cup light brown sugar   1 tablespoon vanilla extract

Put pecans in pie crust. Mix egg, sugar, syrup, butter and vanilla. Spoon over nuts. Bake tarts in 325° F for 25 minutes. Turn out with knife while still warm. Yield: 24 tarts.

VARIATION: Chocolate Fudge Filling

1 cup (6 ounce package)   1 tablespoon butter
   semi-sweet chocolate   1 teaspoon vanilla extract
   pieces   1 egg, beaten
⅓ cup sugar   pecan halves
1 tablespoon milk

Melt chocolate pieces in double boiler. Remove from heat. Stir in sugar, milk, butter, vanilla and egg. Place scant tablespoon of filling in each tart. Top with pecan half. Bake at 350° F for 20 to 25 minutes. Yield: 2 dozen.

PEANUT BUTTER ICE CREAM PIE

1 quart vanilla ice cream   1 (8 ounce) jar crunchy
1 (12 ounce) carton Cool   peanut butter
   Whip   2 graham cracker crusts

Let ice cream soften. Stir all ingredients together and put in 2 graham cracker crusts. Place in freezer until ready to serve. Will keep in freezer several weeks. Yield: 12 servings or 2 pies.

PEANUT BUTTER PIE

1 (8 ounce) package cream
   cheese, softened
2/3 cup crunchy peanut butter
2 cups confectioners' sugar
1 cup milk

1 (9 ounce) package Cool
   Whip
1 (1 ounce) square
   semi-sweet chocolate
2 graham cracker crusts

Mix cream cheese and peanut butter. Add the sugar and milk, stirring until smooth. Add the Cool Whip and mix thoroughly. Pour into pie crusts and freeze. When ready to serve, let thaw for about 10 minutes. Shave chocolate curls onto top. Whipped cream or chopped peanuts may be used instead of chocolate. The filling may be prepared in the food processor using the plastic blade. Yield: 12 servings or 2 pies.

"Make several and leave in the freezer for unexpected company."

MACAROON PIE

FIRST MIXTURE:
20 Ritz crackers, crushed
   very fine
1 cup chopped pecans

1/2 cup sugar
pinch of salt

Mix together.

SECOND MIXTURE:
1/3 cup sugar (scant)
1 teaspoon vanilla extract

3 egg whites

Beat sugar and vanilla into egg whites until stiff peaks form. Fold second mixture into first mixture. Pour into well-buttered 9-inch pie plate. Bake in a 300°F oven for 20 to 25 minutes. Test with toothpick. Cool well.

TOPPING:
3 tablespoons sugar
1 teaspoon vanilla extract

1/2 pint of cream, whipped

Blend sugar and vanilla into whipped cream. Spread over top of cooled pie. Refrigerate for at least 3 hours. Yield: 6 to 8 servings.

CREAM CHEESE PIE

2 eggs
8 tablespoons sugar
2 (8 ounce) packages cream
  cheese, softened

1 teaspoon vanilla extract
1 tablespoon lemon juice
graham cracker crust

Beat eggs until light; add sugar gradually. Add cream cheese to egg mixture. Mix well until smooth. Add vanilla and lemon juice. Pour into cracker crust and bake 20 minutes at 350° F. Remove from oven and cool.

TOPPING:

½ pint sour cream
2½ tablespoons sugar

1 teaspoon vanilla extract

Mix sour cream, sugar and vanilla. Spread on pie and bake for 5 minutes at 350° F. Refrigerate. Yield: 6 to 8 servings.

LEMON PIE WITH PECAN CRUST

CRUST:

1 cup margarine
2 cups flour

2 cups chopped pecans

Cut flour into margarine. Add pecans and mix well. Divide dough and press into 2 (9-inch) pie plates. Bake at 300° F for 30 to 45 minutes.

PIE FILLING:

1 (14 ounce) can sweetened
  condensed milk
1 (9 ounce) carton Cool Whip

1 (6 ounce) can frozen
  lemonade concentrate

Combine condensed milk and lemonade. Blend well. Fold in Cool Whip. Pour into cooled crusts. Garnish with whipped cream. NOTE: The crust is what makes this lemon pie different. The secret is to bake the crust SLOWLY until it begins to brown. Yield: 2 pies or 12 servings.

LEMON ICE BOX PIE

3 egg yolks
½ cup sugar
4 tablespoons lemon juice

3 egg whites
1 cup whipping cream
graham cracker crust

In a saucepan on low heat cook egg yolks, sugar and lemon juice. When mixture coats the spoon, it's done. Cool. Whip cream. Beat egg whites. Fold custard into cream; fold egg whites into mixture. Pour into graham cracker crust. Freeze. Yield: 8 servings.

"Excellent dessert because it is very light and can be made ahead of time."

LEMON TARTS

1 (8 ounce) package cream
    cheese, softened
1 (14 ounce) can sweetened
    condensed milk

⅓ cup lemon juice
6 tart shells or 1 (8 inch)
    pastry shell, baked

Place cream cheese in mixing bowl, slowly add milk. Add lemon juice. Blend well. Fill 6 baked tart shells or 1 (8-inch) baked pastry shell. Decorate with strawberries or mint and lemon slices. Yield: 6 servings.

LEMON MERINGUE PIE

4 eggs, separated
1 cup sugar
juice of 2 lemons
3 tablespoons of cornstarch
1 lemon rind, grated

1 cup hot water
4 tablespoons butter
dash salt
1 (9 inch) pastry shell, baked

Combine egg yolks, sugar, cornstarch, water, butter, lemon juice and rind (this may be done in a blender). Cook in double boiler until thick. Make meringue and fold ⅓ of it into custard; pour into pastry shell and top with remaining meringue. Brown in 300° F oven. Refer to MERINGUE recipe. Yield: 6 servings.

Meringue topping on a pie should touch the edges of the crust; otherwise, it may shrink from sides.

BLACKBERRY COBBLER

Filling:

5 cups fresh blackberries	*3 tablespoons sifted flour*
1 cup sugar	*butter*

Toss fresh blackberries with cup of sugar and pour them into a well-buttered 1½ quart oblong baking dish. Sprinkle flour over the berries; dot with butter, and set aside.

CRUST:

2 cups flour, sifted	*½ teaspoon cream of tartar*
2 tablespoons sugar	*½ cup butter*
4 teaspoons baking powder	*½ cup milk*
½ teaspoon salt	*cream*

Sift flour with sugar, baking powder and salt and cream of tartar. Cut in ½ cup butter until the mixture resembles coarse meal. With a fork, stir in milk and form the mixture into a ball. Roll the dough out ¼ inch thick on a floured board. Cover the blackberries with the dough and trim the edges. Cut a vent in the center of the dough and sprinkle the top generously with sugar. Bake the cobbler in a hot oven (400° F) for 40 minutes, or until the crust is golden. Serve the cobbler warm with cream. Yield: 6-8 servings.

BLUEBERRY CREAM PIE

1 cup sour cream
2 tablespoons flour
¾ cup sugar
1 teaspoon vanilla extract
¼ teaspoon salt
1 egg, beaten

2½ cups fresh blueberries
1 (9 inch) pastry shell,
    unbaked
3 tablespoons flour
2 tablespoons butter, softened
3 tablespoons chopped pecans

Combine first 6 ingredients; beat until smooth. Stir in berries. Pour into pastry shell. Bake at 400° F for 25 minutes. Combine remaining ingredients, stirring well. Sprinkle over top of pie. Bake 10 minutes more. Chill before serving. Yield: 6-8 servings.

STRAWBERRY PIE

1 quart fresh strawberries
1 cup sugar
¼ teaspoon salt
2 tablespoons cornstarch

½ cup boiling water
1 pastry shell, baked
whipped cream

Wash, hull and sort berries, saving perfect berries for placing in the shell. Mash enough berries to make 1 cup. Mix sugar, salt, cornstarch, crushed berries, and boiling water. Cook, stirring constantly, until thickened. Cool thoroughly. Just before serving, place reserved berries in the cooled, baked pastry shell. Pour cooled sauce over berries in the shell. Garnish with whipped cream. Yield: 6 to 8 servings.

APPLE PIE STREUSEL

½ cup sugar
dash of salt
½ teaspoon cinnamon
6 cups pared and sliced
    apples

1 (9 inch) pastry shell,
    unbaked
¾ cup brown sugar
½ cup flour
6 tablespoons butter, softened

Combine sugar, salt and cinnamon; mix with apples. Spoon into pastry shell; combine other ingredients and sprinkle over apples. Bake for 30 minutes at 425° F. Serve warm. Yield: 6 servings.

If the juice from your apple pie runs over in the oven, shake some salt on it; this causes the juice to burn to a crisp so that it can be easily removed.

FRESH PEACH PIE

1½ cups sugar
¼ cup cornstarch OR ½ cup
    flour
2 cups water
1 (3 ounce) package of peach
    Jello

4 cups peeled, sliced fresh
    peaches
2 (9 inch) pastry shells,
    baked

Mix sugar and cornstarch; add water and bring to a boil for 3 minutes. Remove from heat and add package of Jello. Cool. Add 4 cups of peaches and pour into 2 baked, cooled pie shells. May be topped with whipped cream or Cool Whip. Yield: 2 (9-inch) pies.

These are lighter than baked pies.

VARIATION: substitute fresh strawberries and strawberry Jello.

CREAM CHEESE PEACH PIE

1 (9 inch) pastry shell, baked
1 (3 ounce) package cream
    cheese, softened
7 peaches, sliced

1 cup sugar
¼ cup water
2 tablespoons cornstarch
1 teaspoon almond extract

Line pastry shell with softened cream cheese. Place 5 sliced peaches in shell. Combine sugar, water, cornstarch and remaining peaches. Cook and stir until thickened. Cool. Add almond extract; pour over peaches in the pie shell and let set until ready to serve. Top the pie with whipped cream. Yield: 6-8 servings.

PINEAPPLE PIE

1 (14 ounce) can sweetened
    condensed milk
½ cup lemon juice
2 cups canned, crushed
    pineapple, drained

½ cup chopped pecans
1 (8 ounce) carton Cool Whip
2 graham cracker pie crusts

Mix condensed milk, lemon juice, pineapple and pecans. Fold in the Cool Whip. Put in 2 graham cracker crusts. Top with Cool Whip. Refrigerate until set. Yield: 2 pies.

"Quick and delicious and is also good frozen."

PEACH CRISP

8 fresh peaches, peeled,
    sliced
¼ cup water
2 to 3 tablespoons lemon
    juice

¾ cup flour
⅛ teaspoon salt
1 cup brown sugar
2 tablespoons butter
½ teaspoon cinnamon

Place peaches in a greased baking dish and sprinkle with water and lemon juice. Combine flour, salt, sugar, butter and cinnamon using pastry blender. Sprinkle this over peaches. Bake in a moderate oven at 350°F until fruit is tender and top is brown. Yield: 8 servings.

FRENCH FRUIT COBBLER

1¼ cups milk
3 eggs
⅛ teaspoon salt
1 cup flour
⅓ cup sugar

4 tablespoons butter, melted
2 cups fresh sliced peaches,
    dark red cherries, pitted
    or blueberries
1¼ cups cream, whipped

Preheat oven to 400° F. Make a smooth batter of milk, eggs, salt, flour and ¼ cup of sugar. Stir in melted butter. Set aside. Into a greased ovenproof pan, place peaches or cherries in the bottom. Sprinkle with the remainder of the sugar. Pour batter over this. Bake in preheated oven for 30 minutes. Reduce heat to 325° F for 10 minutes. Serve hot, topped with whipped cream. Yield: 6 servings.

CHOCOLATE CHESS PIE

1½ cups sugar
3 tablespoons cocoa
2 eggs
⅔ cup canned evaporated
    milk

1 teaspoon vanilla extract
¼ cup butter
1 (9 inch) pastry shell
whipping cream, whipped
    and sweetened to taste.

Mix sugar and cocoa. Add slightly beaten eggs. Add milk, vanilla and butter. Mix well and pour into prepared uncooked pie shell. Bake at 350° F for 45 minutes. Cool before cutting. Garnish with whipped cream. Yield: 6 servings.

LEMON CHESS PIE

½ cup butter
1½ cups sugar
3 eggs
2 tablespoons cornmeal
1 tablespoon flour

3 tablespoons lemon juice
1 teaspoon vanilla extract
1 (9 inch) pastry shell,
    unbaked

Cream butter and sugar. Add remaining ingredients and mix well. Pour into an unbaked pastry shell. Bake 10 minutes at 400° F, then 30 minutes at 300° F. Yield: 6 servings.

PRALINE CHESS PIE

½ cup butter, softened
1½ cups sugar
3 eggs
¼ cup flour
1 cup buttermilk

1 teaspoon vanilla extract
dash nutmeg
1 (9 inch) pastry shell,
    unbaked

Preheat oven to 425° F. In large mixing bowl, cream butter and sugar until light and fluffy. Add eggs, one at a time, beating well after each addition. Beat in flour. Gradually beat in buttermilk, then vanilla and nutmeg. Pour into pastry shell. Bake at 425° F for 10 minutes. Reduce heat to 350° F; bake an additional 30 to 35 minutes or until filling is set. Sprinkle PRALINE TOPPING over top of hot pie; broil until lightly browned. Yield: 6 to 8 servings.

PRALINE TOPPING:

¼ cup flour
¼ cup firmly packed brown
    sugar

¼ cup butter, softened
¼ cup chopped pecans

In small bowl combine flour and brown sugar. Cut in butter until mixture resembles coarse crumbs. Stir in pecans.

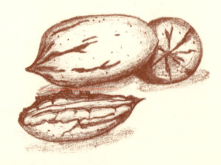

MARBLED CHOCOLATE RUM PIE

1 envelope unflavored gelatin
1 cup sugar
1/8 teaspoon salt
2 eggs, separated
1 cup milk
1/4 cup rum

12 ounces semi-sweet
   chocolate chips
1 cup whipping cream
1 teaspoon vanilla extract
2 graham cracker crusts

In top of double boiler, mix gelatin, 1/4 cup of sugar and the salt. Beat in the egg yolks, milk and rum. Cook over boiling water, stirring constantly, until slightly thickened. Remove from heat and stir in chocolate until thoroughly blended. Chill until thickened, but not set. Beat egg whites until they form peaks; gradually add 1/2 cup sugar and beat until very stiff. Fold into chocolate mixture. Whip cream; add remaining sugar and vanilla. Alternate 2 mixtures in 2 cold graham cracker crusts; swirl with spoon and chill until firm. Yield: 2 pies.

MERINGUE

4 egg whites
1 teaspoon vanilla extract

1/4 teaspoon cream of tartar
6 tablespoons sugar

Beat egg whites with vanilla and cream of tartar until soft peaks form. Gradually add sugar, beating until stiff and glossy peaks form and all sugar is dissolved. Yield: covers 1-9" pie.

PRALINE PASTRY SHELL

1/4 cup margarine or butter
1/4 cup firmly packed brown
   sugar

1/3 cup chopped pecans
1 (9 inch) unbaked pastry
   shell

Combine margarine and sugar in saucepan. Cook and stir until sugar melts and mixture bubbles vigorously. Remove from heat and stir in nuts. Spread over bottom of pastry shell. Bake at 425° F for 5 minutes. Cool before filling. Yield: 1 (9 inch) pastry shell.

"A nice rich pastry for cream pies!"

CRUSTLESS COCONUT PIE

2 cups milk
3/4 cup sugar
1/2 cup Bisquick mix
4 eggs

1/4 cup melted butter
1 1/2 teaspoons vanilla extract
1 cup grated coconut

Place all ingredients except coconut in blender or food processor for 3 minutes. Pour into greased 10-inch pie pan. Let stand for 5 minutes. Sprinkle coconut on top. Bake at 350° F for 40 minutes. Yield: 8 servings.

FROZEN GRASSHOPPER PIE

FILLING:

1 egg white
dash of salt
2 tablespoons sugar
1/3 cup light corn syrup

1/2 pint whipping cream
4 tablespoons green creme de menthe
4 tablespoons white creme de cacao

Beat egg white and salt until peaks form. Add sugar gradually. Beat until smooth and glossy. Beat in syrup slowly until mixture holds stiff, firm peaks. Whip cream until stiff; fold in creme de menthe and creme de cacao. Fold into egg white mixture.

CHOCOLATE CRUST:

1 1/2 cups chocolate cracker crumbs

1/4 cup melted butter
1/4 cup brown sugar

Combine ingredients and press into a 9-inch pan and bake at 400° F for 5 minutes. Cool. Pour in filling. Freeze overnight.

Yield: 6 to 8 servings.

Add 1 tablespoon of water per egg white to increase the quantity of beaten egg whites for meringue.

BRANDY BLACK BOTTOM CHIFFON PIE

GINGER SNAP CRUST:

*1½ cups finely crushed
  ginger snaps
3 tablespoons sugar*

*¼ cup butter
1 tablespoon water*

In a bowl, toss gingersnaps with sugar. Add butter and 1 tablespoon water; mix well. Press mixture evenly on bottom and sides of a 9-inch pie plate. Refrigerate for 30 minutes before filling. Makes 1 gingersnap crust.

FILLING:

*1 envelope unflavored gelatin
5 tablespoons brandy
4 eggs, separated
½ cup dark brown sugar
1¼ tablespoons cornstarch
¼ teaspoon salt
1½ cups milk, scalded*

*1½ squares bitter chocolate
¾ teaspoon vanilla extract
¼ teaspoon cream of tartar
½ cup white sugar
whipped cream
sweet chocolate, shaved*

Soften gelatin in 2 tablespoons water and 1 tablespoon brandy. Beat egg yolks in the top of a double boiler until light. Add brown sugar, cornstarch and salt. Gradually stir in scalded milk and brandy. Cook until mixture is thick and smooth. Stir constantly as it cooks. Remove from heat; stir 1 cup of custard into melted chocolate and vanilla. Cook chocolate custard and pour into crust. To the remainder of the custard, add softened gelatin; mix well; cool slightly but do not set. Beat egg whites until stiff; fold in sugar and cream of tartar. Fold egg whites into custard. Pour this over chocolate pie filling. Chill for at least 3 hours. To serve, spread pie with whipped cream and sprinkle with sweet chocolate. Yield: 6 servings.

A rolling trick: Roll pastry between 2 sheets of waxed paper to desired circumference. Peel off top, flip the bottom into pie pan; then remove paper.

Do not freeze cream or custard pies.

Fruit pies freeze well.

PUMPKIN CHIFFON PIE

1 envelope plain gelatin
¾ cup brown sugar
½ teaspoon salt
2 teaspoons cinnamon
½ teaspoon ginger
½ teaspoon allspice
3 egg yolks
½ cup milk

1⅓ cups canned pumpkin
3 egg whites
¼ teaspoon cream of tartar
6 tablespoons sugar
1 graham cracker pie crust
    or gingersnap crust (see
    recipe)
whipped cream for topping

Combine in saucepan gelatin, brown sugar, salt and spices. Stir in egg yolks and milk; add pumpkin. Cook over low heat until bubbling, stirring constantly. Cool until mixture will mound when dropped from spoon. Beat egg whites and cream of tartar until stiff; add sugar, one tablespoon at a time, beating well. Fold pumpkin mixture into egg whites. Pour into crust. Chill several hours. Top with whipped cream before serving. Dust with a little nutmeg. Yield: 8 servings.

"Folks who do not like pumpkin pie like this."

CHOCOLATE CHIFFON PIE

PIE SHELL:

3 egg whites
⅛ teaspoon cream of tartar
pinch of salt

¾ cup sifted sugar
¾ cup finely chopped pecans
1 teaspoon vanilla extract

Beat egg whites until foamy; add cream of tartar and salt. Gradually add sugar and beat until very stiff. Fold in pecans and vanilla. Put in buttered 10-inch pie plate, nest-like. Bake in a slow 250° F oven for 2 hours.

FILLING:

4 squares of chocolate
½ cup sugar
½ cup milk
1 package unflavored gelatin

3 tablespoons strong coffee
1 tablespoon water
½ pint cream, whipped

Melt chocolate over hot water; add sugar and milk. Soften gelatin in coffee and water. Add to chocolate mixture. Melt gelatin. Remove from hot water. Allow to cool. Fold in whipped cream. Put in pie shell and chill for 2 hours. Yield: 6 to 8 servings.

Desserts

SOUTHERN BREAD PUDDING

2 cups soft bread crumbs
3 eggs, beaten
1/4 to 1/2 cup sugar
1/8 teaspoon salt
1/3 cup raisins

2 cups whole milk
1 teaspoon vanilla extract
1/4 teaspoon ground
    cinnamon

Mix all ingredients well. Place in a shallow 9 × 13-inch pan and bake at 350° F about 30 minutes or until knife inserted in center comes out clean. Serve with whipped cream. Yield: 8 servings.

APPLE PUDDING

1/4 cup butter
1 cup sugar
1 egg
1 cup flour
1/4 teaspoon nutmeg
1/4 teaspoon cinnamon
1/2 teaspoon salt

1/4 teaspoon baking soda
4 or 5 medium size apples,
    cubed
1 cup chopped pecans
whipping cream, whipped or
    Hard Sauce (see recipe)

Cream butter and sugar; add egg and blend. Sift flour, spices, salt and soda together; add to butter and sugar mixture and blend. Add apples and chopped nuts. Bake in a greased oblong shallow pan in 350° F oven. Cut in squares and serve with whipped cream or Hard Sauce. Yield: 6 servings.

EASY RICE PUDDING

2 level tablespoons rice
1 level tablespoon butter
pinch of salt

3 level tablespoons sugar
1 quart milk

Wash the rice well and put it in a 2-quart baking dish with butter, salt and sugar. Pour the milk over the rice and bake at 275° F for 2½ hours, stirring twice during the first hour. Yield: 6 servings.

QUICK ICE CREAM DESSERTS

Take a pint of ice cream and soften. Fold in or swirl through one of the following:

½ cup semi-sweet chocolate bits to coffee, chocolate or vanilla ice cream.

½ cup crushed peppermint candies to fudge ripple or chocolate ice cream.

½ cup grated coconut to strawberry ice cream or pineapple sherbet.

½ cup finely chopped toasted, unsalted pecans to vanilla ice cream.

½ cup chopped maraschino cherries to vanilla, coconut or chocolate ice cream.

½ cup fresh puréed fruit to French vanilla ice cream.

½ cup raisins and pecans to coffee ice cream.

Do not add liqueurs to ice cream as it will never refreeze.

MINT ICE

2 quarts water
2 cups sugar
juice of 6 lemons

1 bunch fresh mint or 1 dozen sprigs
few drops of green food coloring

Add 2 cups water to the sugar to boil and make a syrup. Stir in the rest of the water and let cool. Add the juice of the lemons and enough coloring to make a pretty delicate green. Strip the leaves from the mint and put into a strong cloth; pound until beaten to a pulp. Dip the cloth holding the mint into the lemon water; shake well until as strongly minted as liked. Pour into container and freeze. Serve in iced glasses with tiny tender sprigs of mint on top. Yield: 2 quarts.

"Nice served with a salad course or added to iced tea which is to accompany a salad course."

ORANGE ICE

4 cups water
2 cups sugar
¼ cup lemon juice

2 cups orange juice
grated rind of 2 oranges

Boil sugar and water until syrup forms thread (230° F). Add juices and grated rind; cool. Strain. Pour into freezer trays and stir every 30 minutes during freezing process. Should be flaky but frozen. Serve in sherbet glasses. Yield: 2 quarts.

LEMON ICE

4 cups water
2 cups sugar

¾ cup lemon juice

Boil sugar and water until syrup forms thread (230° F). Add juice; cool. Strain. Pour into freezer trays and stir every 30 minutes during freezing process. Should be flaky but frozen. Serve in sherbet glasses. Yield: 2 quarts.

CHOCOLATE ROLL

5 eggs, separated
1 cup sugar
2 tablespoons flour
2 tablespoons cocoa

½ pint whipping cream
2 tablespoons sugar
½ teaspoon vanilla extract
grated chocolate

Combine egg yolks and sugar; beat until creamy. Fold in flour and cocoa. Beat whites stiff; fold into yolk mixture. Bake in well greased and floured jelly roll pan (15½ × 10½ × 1) in 350° F oven for 20 to 25 minutes. Cool cake in pan covered with a damp towel. Turn out on a board covered with a sheet of wax paper. Whip whipping cream and gradually add sugar and vanilla. Continue beating until stiff. Spread cake with 1 cup whipped cream. Roll up. Slide onto flat serving platter. Ice with remaining whipped cream and garnish with grated chocolate. Yield: 8 servings.

BANANA PUDDING

¾ cup sugar
2 tablespoons flour
½ teaspoon salt
2 cups milk
4 egg yolks, beaten
1 tablespoon butter

1 teaspoon vanilla extract
vanilla wafers
2 to 4 bananas
whipping cream, whipped
  and sweetened to taste

In a double boiler combine sugar, flour and salt. Gradually stir in milk, mixing until smooth. Cook until thickened. Stir half of hot mixture into egg yolks. Return to boiler; cook for 1 minute, stirring. Remove from heat. Stir in butter and vanilla. Cool. Line bottom of 2-quart casserole with vanilla wafers and arrange bananas over wafers. Pour half of cooled filling over bananas. Make a second layer of wafers and bananas, pour on remaining sauce. Top with whipped cream. Refrigerate until ready to serve. Yield: 6 to 8 servings.

"A Southern tradition."

MOCHA BROWNIE TORTE

1 (22 ounce) package Duncan
  Hines Brownie Mix
6 tablespoons water

3 eggs
⅔ cup chopped pecans

Heat oven to 350° F. Grease and flour 3 (9-inch) layer pans. Blend brownie mix (dry), water and eggs; beat 50 strokes. Stir in nuts. Spread in pans and bake 18 minutes. Turn out of pans. Spread FILLING between cake layers and on top. Use chocolate curls as a garnish. Yield: 12 servings.

FILLING:

2 cups whipping cream
  (chilled)
½ cup brown sugar

1½ tablespoons instant coffee
  dissolved in 1 tablespoon
  hot water, cooled

Whip cream; add brown sugar and coffee.

HOT FUDGE SUNDAE CAKE

1 cup flour
3/4 cup sugar
2 tablespoons unsweetened
  cocoa
2 teaspoons baking powder
1/4 teaspoon salt

1/2 cup milk
2 tablespoons salad oil
1 teaspoon vanilla extract
1 cup chopped pecans
  (optional)

TO BE SPRINKLED ON TOP:

1 cup packed brown sugar
1/4 cup unsweetened cocoa

1 3/4 cups very hot tap water

Preheat oven to 350° F. In a 9 × 9 inch ungreased pan stir together flour, sugar, cocoa, baking powder and salt. Add milk, salad oil, vanilla and pecans. Mix with a fork until smooth. Sprinkle brown sugar and cocoa mixture evenly on top. Pour hot water over finished batter. Bake at 350° F for 40 minutes. A delicious cake will be on top and rich fudge sauce on bottom. Spoon into pretty serving bowls. Top with vanilla ice cream or whipped cream. Yield: 8-9 servings.

LEMON CAKE CUSTARD

3 eggs, separated
1 cup sugar
2 tablespoons butter, softened
1/4 cup sifted flour
1/4 teaspoon salt
1 cup milk

grated rind of 1 lemon
1/3 cup lemon juice
whipping cream, whipped
  and sweetened to taste
maraschino cherries

Beat egg whites until stiff. Set aside. Beat the egg yolks, sugar, butter, flour and salt until blended. Slowly add milk. Add the lemon rind and juice. Fold in beaten egg whites. Pour into buttered custard cups. Set cups in a pan of hot water. Bake at 325° F for about 50 minutes. Serve warm or chilled, topped with whipped cream and maraschino cherries. Yield: 6 servings.

"For a summer treat top with fresh strawberries."

STRAWBERRIES ROMANOFF

vanilla ice cream
1 half pint whipping cream
1 tablespoon sugar
2 ounces Triple Sec
2 ounces Cognac

2 ounces Grand Marnier
sliced fresh strawberries
   (save 1 whole berry for
   each serving)

Fill dessert glasses or champagne glasses with vanilla ice cream. Whip cream and add all remaining ingredients, except strawberries. Place sliced strawberries on top of ice cream. Pour cream mixture over all and top with a whole strawberry. Mint leaves can be placed under the strawberry garnish. Yield: 6 servings.

FRESH ORANGES AU GRAND MARNIER

SAUCE:

1 heaping tablespoon honey
   OR 1 tablespoon brown
   sugar
2 tablespoons orange
   marmalade

1 teaspoon Grand Marnier
1 teaspoon brandy
juice of ½ lemon
juice of 1 large orange

Combine all ingredients and mix well.

8 large navel oranges
¼ cup almonds, toasted

¼ cup shredded coconut

Peel the oranges, removing white pith. Cut into slices ⅛ inch thick. Arrange in layers in serving dish. Cover each layer with the sauce mixture. Chill overnight. Correct sweetness, if necessary. Serve very cold. Top this dessert with slivered, toasted almonds or shredded coconut. Yield: 6 to 8 servings.

"Serves beautifully in crystal or glass bowl."

AMBROSIA

6 large oranges
1 large coconut

¾ cup sugar

Remove orange sections from peel, being careful to remove all pith and skin. Remove brown skin from coconut and grate. Mix oranges, coconut and sugar. Chill for 1 hour or more before serving. For variety and color, add sliced strawberries and a small diced pineapple. A little dry sherry can be added to give this traditional Southern holiday dessert a different flavor. Yield: 6 to 8 servings.

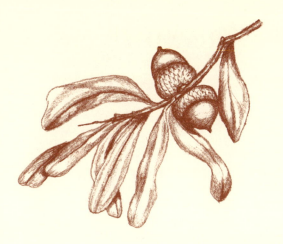

MERINGUE MOUNTAIN

6 egg whites
½ teaspoon cream of tartar
2 cups sugar
CHOCOLATE SAUCE

½ cup pecans, toasted
1 cup whipping cream,
   whipped

Beat egg whites and cream of tartar until frothy. Add sugar, 2 tablespoons at a time. Beat until very stiff and glossy. Draw circles on cookie sheet lined with brown paper about 2½ to 3 inches in diameter. Drop meringue into circles and carefully smooth tops. Bake at 250° F for 2 hours. Leave in oven overnight. To assemble, arrange 6 meringues in a circle; drizzle with a little CHOCOLATE SAUCE and sprinkle with a few pecans. Continue stacking until mountain is formed, topping each layer with a little CHOCOLATE SAUCE and some nuts. Serve with warm CHOCOLATE SAUCE and a bowl of whipped cream. Yield: 6 servings.

CHOCOLATE SAUCE:

2 (2 ounce) squares
   unsweetened chocolate
1 cup sugar
⅛ teaspoon cream of tartar

6 tablespoons evaporated
   milk
6 tablespoons dark rum
1 teaspoon vanilla extract
pinch of salt

Melt chocolate in a saucepan on very low heat. Stir until smooth and creamy. Blend in sugar and cream of tartar. Gradually stir in milk and rum, blending well. Heat for 1 minute. Add vanilla and salt, mixing until thick and smooth. Serve hot or cold.

VANILLA ICE CREAM WITH A LEMON TWIST

1 lemon rind, grated
1½ cups sugar
1 cup whipping cream

2 cups milk
juice of 4 lemons
1 teaspoon vanilla extract

Combine all ingredients and freeze in ice cream freezer.

MINT CHOCOLATE CHIP ICE CREAM

2 cups whipping cream
2 cups half and half
1 tablespoon peppermint
   extract

¾ cup sugar
⅛ teaspoon salt
8 drops green food coloring
¾ cup chocolate chip morsels

Combine all ingredients, except chocolate chip morsels. Freeze in ice cream freezer. After processing but before hardening, add chocolate chip morsels. Yield: 12 servings.

RICH NO-COOK ICE CREAM

2 pints whipping cream
2 cans condensed milk
2 teaspoons vanilla extract

2 eggs, beaten
1½ to 2 cups milk

Mix whipping cream, condensed milk, vanilla, eggs and milk. Freeze in ice cream churn. Yield: 12 servings.

VARIATION: add 1 quart crushed fruit or other flavorings.

GERMAN CHOCOLATE ICE CREAM

3 squares German sweet
   chocolate
1 cup milk
1 cup sugar

6 egg yolks, beaten
1 pint half and half
1 pint whipping cream

In double boiler melt chocolate in ½ cup of milk over low heat, stirring constantly. Remove from heat. Stir in rest of milk, sugar and egg yolks. Return to heat, stirring constantly, until sides bubble and mixture starts to thicken. Cool and add half and half and whipping cream. Freeze in ice cream churn. Yield: 2 quarts.

RASPBERRY SOUFFLÉ

1 (10 ounce) package frozen
   red raspberries
1 envelope unflavored gelatin
¼ cup cold water

4 eggs, separated
¾ cup sugar
½ teaspoon salt
1 cup whipping cream,
   whipped

Thaw raspberries, blend in blender. Sprinkle gelatin over cold water to soften. In top of double boiler beat 4 egg yolks until light. Gradually add ½ cup sugar and salt. Cook mixture over simmering water, stirring constantly until it is thickened. Remove from heat and add gelatin; stir until gelatin dissolves. Let mixture stand until it is cool, but not firmly set. Stir in raspberry purée. Beat egg whites with ¼ cup sugar until very stiff. Gently fold whites into cream. Fold all into raspberry purée. Pour mixture into a 1-quart soufflé dish that has been prepared by folding 6-inch wide piece of waxed paper in half and wrapping around soufflé dish to form a collar. Oil dish and collar. Chill 3 to 4 hours or until firm but spongy. Remove paper collar carefully before serving. Yield: 6 servings.

NOTE: Strawberries may be substituted for the raspberries.

COLD LEMON SOUFFLÉ

1 envelope unflavored gelatin
2 tablespoons cold water
½ cup lemon juice
grated rind of 4 lemons

1 cup sugar
1 cup whipping cream
1 cup egg whites (7-8)

In a small saucepan, sprinkle gelatin over 2 tablespoons cold water. Add lemon juice, lemon rind and sugar. Stir over low flame until gelatin and sugar are thoroughly dissolved. Chill until of syrup consistency. Beat whipping cream until stiff; beat in lemon-gelatin mixture. Beat egg whites until stiff; gently fold into lemon-cream mixture. Tie a double band of waxed paper around the top of a one-quart soufflé dish to form collar. Pour in the lemon soufflé and chill. Garnish with lemon slices and mint to serve. Yield: 6 to 8 servings.

APRICOT DELIGHT SOUFFLÉ

1 (8 ounce) package dried
    apricots
3 tablespoons sugar
1½ tablespoons lemon juice

⅛ teaspoon salt
⅓ cup sugar
6 egg whites

Cook apricots and sugar together in just enough water to cover. Blend in a blender to get 1½ cups of sweetened apricot pulp. Mix pulp, lemon juice and salt. Beat sugar into egg whites and fold in fruit mixture. Pile into lightly buttered 1 quart soufflé dish. Bake at 275° F for 30 to 45 minutes. Serve warm or cold. Yield: 6 servings.

DEMITASSE MOUSSE

¾ cup milk
½ teaspoon instant coffee
    powder
1 (6 ounce) package
    semi-sweet chocolate
    morsels

2 eggs
¼ cup brandy
½ cup whipping cream,
    whipped
1 teaspoon cocoa

Combine milk and coffee powder in a small saucepan; scald. Place chocolate morsels in electric blender; add scalded milk mixture and blend until smooth. Add eggs and brandy with blender running; then blend 2 additional minutes. Pour into 6 to 8 demitassee cups. Cover with buttered waxed paper; refrigerate several hours or overnight. Top with whipped cream and sift cocoa over top. Rum, creme de cacao or creme de menthe may be substituted for brandy. Yield: 6 to 8 servings.

ROSETTES

1 cup milk
2 teaspoons sugar
pinch of salt
4 eggs

1 teaspoon vanilla extract
1½ cups flour
confectioners' sugar

Mix all together, dip rosette irons into mix and fry in cooking oil 1½" deep.

ORANGE CHRISTMAS CHARLOTTE

2 tablespoons unflavored
    gelatin
1/3 cup cold water
1/2 cup orange juice
3/4 cup sugar
3 egg whites, stiffly beaten

1 pint whipping cream,
    whipped
ladyfingers
3/4 cup orange sections,
    drained
maraschino cherries

Soak gelatin in cold water. Then heat over boiling water. Add orange juice and sugar. Beat gelatin until foamy. Fold egg whites into gelatin mixture. Fold whipped cream into egg white-gelatin mixture. Turn into large glass bowl lined with ladyfingers. Chill for several hours or until firm. Unmold. Decorate with orange sections and cherries. Yield: 8 servings.

SOUTHERN CHARLOTTE

3 egg yolks
1 cup sugar
2 tablespoons unflavored
    gelatin
1 cup milk

4 egg whites, beaten
2 cups whipping cream,
    whipped
1/4 cup sherry

Beat egg yolks and sugar together in top of double boiler. Dissolve gelatin in milk for 5 minutes; heat and add to sugar and egg mixture. Cook in double boiler until it coats a spoon. Cool and pour over stiffly beaten whites. Fold in whipped cream and sherry. Pour into mold and refrigerate until firm. Yield: 6 to 8 servings.

CHOCOLATE CHARLOTTE

1 envelope unflavored gelatin
1/4 cup cold water
1/2 cup cream, scalded
1 1/2 squares (2 ounces)
    unsweetened chocolate

2/3 cup confectioners' sugar
3 cups whipping cream,
    whipped
1 teaspoon vanilla extract
ladyfingers

Soak gelatin in cold water. Melt chocolate over very low heat. Add 1/3 cup of sugar and cream. Add gelatin to mixture while hot; stir to dissolve. Chill. Stir as mixture begins to thicken, then fold in whipped cream and remaining sugar and vanilla. Line glass dessert bowl with ladyfingers. Pour in Chocolate Charlotte. Chill. Yield: 6 servings.

SHERRY ALMOND CREAM

2 tablespoons unflavored
   gelatin
1/4 cup cold water
1 cup boiling water
1 1/4 cups sugar

6 egg whites
1/2 teaspoon almond extract
1/3 cup sherry
1 cup blanched almonds

Soak gelatin in cold water in mixing bowl. Add boiling water and sugar; stir until dissolved. Chill until stiff; beat until frothy. Beat egg whites until stiff and add to mixture. Add almond extract and sherry; pour into 3-cup or larger mold, alternating layers of mixture with chopped almonds. Chill in refrigerator for 2 hours. Serve with SAUCE. Yield: 8 servings.

SAUCE:

1 pint sweet milk
6 egg yolks
1/4 cup sugar
1/8 teaspoon salt

1/2 pint whipping cream,
   whipped
3 tablespoons sherry
1/2 teaspoon vanilla extract

Scald milk in double boiler. Beat egg yolks with sugar and salt; stir into milk. Cook, stirring until mixture coats a spoon. Cool; add whipped cream, sherry and vanilla.

"Mold and sauce can each be made a day ahead of serving. Pretty in a tiered mold topped with sauce."

POT DE CRÈME

2 cups whipping cream
4 egg yolks
5 tablespoons sugar
1/8 teaspoon salt

2 tablespoons Grand Marnier
1 tablespoon grated orange
   rind

Place cream in a saucepan and bring it almost, but not quite, to a boil. Beat egg yolks, sugar and salt until light and lemon colored. Gradually add the cream to the yolks, stirring with a wire whisk. Place in double boiler and stir with a wooden spoon until custard thickens and coats the spoon. Immediately set into a bowl of ice water to stop cooking action. Stir to cool. Stir in Grand Marnier and grated orange rind. Pour into individual Pot de Cremes and chill thoroughly. When serving, garnish with a bit of finely grated orange peel or a candied violet. Can be made ahead. Yield: 6 servings.

FROZEN EGGNOG DESSERT

3 eggs, separated
½ cup plus 3 teaspoons
   sugar
3 tablespoons bourbon, plus
   1 extra for "the pot"
½ pint whipping cream,
   whipped

½ cup chopped pecans
½ cup maraschino cherries,
   chopped
2 cups vanilla wafers,
   crushed

Beat egg yolks until light and lemon colored. Add ½ cup sugar slowly and beat thoroughly. Add bourbon very slowly and continue to beat all the time. Beat egg whites until stiff and add 3 level teaspoons sugar as you would for meringue. Add egg yolk mixture to egg whites, folding gently. Add cream and fold into mixture. Fold in nuts and cherries. Line 2 old-fashioned ice trays with crushed vanilla wafers. Pour mixture on top of this and top with more crushed vanilla wafers. Place in freezer. Yield: 8 to 10 servings.

"This will keep for several weeks in the freezer."

Dessert Sauces

SOUR CREAM SAUCE FOR STRAWBERRIES

1 cup sour cream
1 teaspoon grated lemon peel

1 tablespoon lemon juice
½ cup confectioners' sugar

Beat sour cream, lemon peel, lemon juice and confectioners' sugar with electric mixer until light. Spoon over strawberries or serve in a separate container as a dip for strawberries and other fruit. Yield: 1 cup.

HARD SAUCE

½ cup butter, room
   temperature

1 cup confectioners' sugar
⅛ cup bourbon or brandy

Beat butter until creamy; add sugar gradually. Beat until well blended. Add bourbon to mixture when sauce is very smooth and not grainy. Place in pint jar with cover and chill until used. Use as an accompaniment to fruit cakes, mincemeat pies, cakes, plum pudding, etc. Best if prepared in advance. Will keep for two weeks in refrigerator. May be chilled in a mold for decorative look. Yield: 1 cup.

HOT CHOCOLATE SAUCE

2 cups sugar
½ cup cream
½ cup whole milk

3 squares unsweetened
   chocolate

Put all ingredients in top of double boiler and cook one-half to one hour, until thick. Beat well. Keep in the refrigerator. Reheat to serve. Yield: 1 to 1½ cups.

MELBA SAUCE

1 pint fresh strawberries
1 pint fresh raspberries

½ cup sugar or to taste
2 tablespoons lemon juice

Rub fresh strawberries and raspberries, both washed and trimmed, through a sieve. Pour the purée into the container of a blender; add sugar and lemon juice, and blend the mixture for 1 minute. Chill the sauce and serve it with poached fruit, cheesecake, ice cream, rice pudding or other puddings. Yield: 2 cups.

CHERRY WINE SAUCE

1 (16 ounce) can Bing
   cherries, pitted
1 tablespoon cornstarch

¼ cup sugar
¼ cup Burgundy wine

Drain cherries, saving the liquid. Combine cornstarch and sugar in saucepan. Slowly blend wine and juice with cornstarch and sugar. Boil for 2 minutes. Stir in cherries. Serve warm on Baked Alaska. Yield: 2 cups.

BLUEBERRY SAUCE

¼ cup sugar
1 tablespoon flour
pinch of salt
1 cup water
1 teaspoon fresh lemon
    juice

1 cup fresh blueberries,
    washed
3 tablespoons butter
¼ teaspoon ground
    cinnamon

In a saucepan combine sugar, flour and salt. Add water and lemon juice and cook the mixture until it is thickened. Add fresh blueberries and cook the mixture for 1 minute more. Remove the pan from the heat and add butter and ground cinnamon. Stir the sauce until the butter is melted and serve it hot with warm puddings, pound cake or pancakes. Yield: 2 cups.

CARAMEL SAUCE

1 cup brown sugar
½ cup white sugar
½ cup Karo syrup
½ cup cream

1 tablespoon butter
1 teaspoon vanilla extract
1 cup chopped pecans
    (optional)

Combine sugars and syrup. Cook until soft ball stage (234° F). Add cream, butter and vanilla. Pecans may be added. Serve over ice cream. Yield: 2 cups.

PINEAPPLE FRUIT DRESSING

½ cup sugar
4 teaspoons cornstarch
2 egg yolks, beaten
1 tablespoon vinegar

1 (12 ounce) can
    unsweetened pineapple
    juice
10 large marshmallows

Combine sugar and cornstarch in saucepan, blending well. Stir in egg yolks and vinegar. Slowly add pineapple juice. Cook over low heat until smooth and thickened, stirring constantly. Add marshmallows; stir until melted. Chill thoroughly. Keeps well in refrigerator. Remove from refrigerator 30 minutes before serving. Yield: 1 quart.

This is good on oranges and grapefruit in winter or melons and berries in summer.

Jams, Jellies, Pickles

Rich indeed is this section in its fruits for jams and jellies. Pickles, too, find a place on the pantry shelf. Mayhaw bushes with their bright fruit grow in moist places and blackberries can be found by roadsides and along fences. Wild plums are transformed into tart jelly or tasty sauce. Figs from backyard trees yield enough fruit for table and "putting up." Peaches can be transformed into pickles, chutney, and preserves.

Jams, Jellies, Pickles

The following eight recipes were taken to the Festival of American Folklife, held in 1980, at the Smithsonian Institute, Washington, D.C. by Mrs. Otiz Z. Miller (Peggy), Sylvester, Georgia by special request.

HOT PEPPER JELLY

1 cup bell peppers
½ cup hot pepper
3 banana peppers
1½ cups apple cider vinegar

6½ cups sugar
½ teaspoon salt
1 (6 ounce) bottle Certo
green or red food coloring

Take the seeds out of all the peppers and chop peppers. Mix vinegar, peppers, sugar and salt; bring to a boil. Boil for 20 minutes; add Certo and cook 1 minute. Add few drops food coloring, if desired. Pour into hot, sterilized pint jars and seal. Yield: 6 to 8 pints.

Note: Wear rubber gloves when handling hot peppers.

GRAPE JELLY

2 quarts grapes
2 quarts water

6 cups sugar

Wash grapes, add water, and bring to boiling point. Cook until grapes are soft. Take off stove and strain through cloth bag. Do not squeeze, if you like a clear jelly. Measure juices and bring to a boil. Add sugar gradually, stirring all the time. Cook rapidly until jelly begins to thicken. It will slide off spoon as one sheet. Put into hot, sterilized jars and seal. Yield: 8 half pints.

CORN COB JELLY

12 sweet corn cobs
4 cups water
1 box Sure-Jell fruit pectin

4 cups sugar
yellow food coloring

Boil cobs and water for 10 minutes. Remove from heat; strain juice into jelly kettle. Bring to a boil; add fruit pectin. Bring mixture to a rolling boil and add sugar. Boil 5 minutes. Skim and add yellow food coloring, if desired. Pour at once into hot, sterilized jars and seal. Yield: 6½ pints.

Never reduce the amount of sugar in the recipe when making jelly. The reduction of sugar will result in a syrup instead of a jelly.

MINT JELLY

2 cups water
1 cup vinegar
1 cup mint leaves and stems

6½ cups sugar
1 bottle Certo
green food coloring

Put water, vinegar, mint leaves and stems into pot; cook for 20 minutes. Remove mint leaves and stems. Add sugar and cook to boiling. Add Certo and cook 1 minute. Add green coloring, if desired. Pour into hot, sterilized jars and seal. Yield: 5 pints.

"A flavorful accompaniment for lamb."

CANTELOUPE-PEACH PRESERVES

4 cups canteloupe, peeled
2 cups peaches

5 cups sugar
2 tablespoons lemon juice

Wash and cut firm, ripe melon into 1-inch slices crosswise. Remove rind and seed. Cut slices into even pieces. Peel, pit and slice peaches. Mix fruit with sugar. Add lemon juice. Boil until fruit is clear. Simmer until thick, about 1 hour. Pour boiling hot mixture into hot, sterilized jars; seal at once. Yield: 6 half pints.

MAY HAW JELLY

4 cups prepared May haw   *5 cups sugar*
   juice
1 (1¾ ounce) box Sure-Jell
   fruit pectin

To extract juice from May haw berries, wash berries well, place in a 6 or 8 quart saucepan, and cover with water. Bring to a boil and cook over medium heat for 30 minutes. Cool.

Using a clean white pillow case and a large bowl, pour the cooled cooked berries into the pillow case-lined bowl. Mash the berries with a potato masher, then strain through the pillow case, squeezing the pulp as you strain the juice.

Measure 4 cups of juice and pour into 6 or 8 quart saucepan. Stir in Sure-Jell and bring to a full boil, stirring constantly. Stir in sugar and bring to a full rolling boil. Boil for 1 minute, stirring constantly. Remove from heat. Skim off foam. Pour hot jelly into hot, sterilized jars and seal with hot, sterilized lids. Yield: 6 half pints.

May haw is a tree sometimes twenty or thirty feet tall, an inhabitant of pine-barren ponds and the sandy margins of streams. Although extremely southern in distribution, it enjoys a wide range of popularity on account of the delicious preserves and jellies made from its bright red fruit. During May the markets of many southern towns dispose of large quantities of the fruit, which is eagerly gathered in all the region where it abounds. The May haw is the first of its kind to blossom and ripen its fruit, and besides, is readily known by the rusty tomentum on the under surface of the leaves.

WATERMELON JELLY

5 cups watermelon juice   *¼ cup lemon juice*
5 cups sugar

Bring the juice to a boil, add sugar a little at a time. Add all the lemon juice. Cook until the jelly will sheet off the spoon. Put into hot, sterilized jars and seal. Yield: 8 half pints.

Remember the fruit mixture will double or triple in size when it begins to boil, so use a large kettle.

GRAPE JAM

4 cups grapes
½ cup water

6 cups sugar

Place grapes and water in a large jelly kettle. Bring to a boil. Pour off juice. Put pulp through a sieve to remove the seeds and skins. Combine juice, pulp juice, and sugar. Cook for about 30 minutes. Put into hot, sterilized jars and seal. Yield: 8 half pints.

BLACKBERRY JELLY

3 cups blackberry juice
2 cups sugar

juice of lemon (optional)

To extract juice, put berries in boiler; add enough water to come just to top of berries. Bring to boil and cook until tender. Mash through colander. Strain juice through flour bag or several thicknesses of cheese cloth. Don't squeeze as this makes cloudy jelly. For every 3 cups of juice, use 2 cups of sugar. Cook until tiny bubbles are all over jelly, and it will sheet from a silver spoon. Let stand a few minutes; skim off sugar scum. Pour into hot, sterilized jars. NOTE: Be sure to have some half ripe berries. If not, squeeze a juicy lemon into juice before making jelly.

FIG PRESERVES

7 pounds figs
6 pounds sugar

8 cups water
1½ lemons, sliced thin

Wash figs and wipe dry. Mix together the sugar and water, heat to a hard boil. Put figs in one at a time and cook until they are clear and the syrup has thickened, about 2 hours. Add lemon slices during the last 30 minutes of cooking. Pack into hot, sterilized jars, trying to put a slice of lemon in each jar. Seal with hot, sterilized lids. Yield: 12 pints.

WATERMELON RIND PRESERVES

4 cups watermelon rind, cut
    in inch squares
2 tablespoons salt
2 quarts water to soak rind
1 (10 ounce) jar maraschino
    cherries
1 (8¼ ounce) can crushed
    pineapple

4 cups sugar
1 lemon, thinly sliced
2 tablespoons preserved
    ginger, thinly sliced
8 cups water.

Cut the green part of the rind off; soak the rind for 30 minutes in solution of salt and 2 quarts water. Drain, rinse with cold water. Place rind in large kettle. Add cherries, pineapple, sugar, lemon, ginger, and water. Bring to a boil. Cook until transparent, about 45 minutes to 1 hour. Pack into hot, sterilized jars and seal. Yield: 8 pints.

PUMPKIN CHIPS

1 firm dry pumpkin
1 dozen lemons

1 cup sugar to each cup
    chips

Peel pumpkin, cut in thin pieces about ½ inch square. Add sugar and juice of lemons—(save rinds). Let stand overnight. Boil until chips are transparent. Take chips out and boil syrup until it thickens a little. Cut up lemon rind and boil separately until soft. Add chips and rind to thickened syrup. Bring to boil. Place in hot, sterilized jars and seal. Yield: 6 to 8 pints.

House by the Side of the Road
Ashburn, Georgia

CUCUMBER CINNAMON RINGS

2 gallons large cucumber
   rings, peeled and seeded
2 cups lime
8½ quarts water
1 cup vinegar
1 tablespoon alum
1 bottle red food coloring

water enough to cover
2 cups vinegar
10 cups sugar
1 (3 ounce) package red hot
   cinnamon candies
2 cups water
8 cinnamon sticks

Let cucumbers stand in lime water for 24 hours. Drain then wash cucumbers in clear water. Soak 3 hours in cold water and drain. Simmer for 2 hours in vinegar, alum, food coloring and water. Drain. Make syrup of vinegar, sugar, candies, water and cinnamon sticks. Bring to a boil and pour over rings. Let stand overnight. First drain syrup off rings and reheat syrup and pour over rings again, let stand overnight. Drain syrup again; heat a second time and pour over rings that have been packed tightly into hot, sterilized jars and seal. Yield: 8 pints.

PEAR RELISH

15 pounds pears
5 onions
6 bell peppers (3 red and 3
   green)
2 pounds sugar

1 tablespoon salt
1 tablespoon mixed spices or
   allspice
1 tablespoon tumeric
5 cups vinegar

Peel and core pears. Peel onions, cut into quarters. Grind pears, onions, peppers in a food grinder. Combine mixture with sugar, salt, mixed spices, tumeric and vinegar. Bring to a boil and cook for 30 minutes. Put into hot, sterilized jars and seal. Yield: 12 pints.

APPLE CHUTNEY

10 pounds York apples
1 quart plus ⅔ pint white
  vinegar
3 pounds dark brown sugar
1¾ tablespoons ground
  garlic

1 (2¾ ounce) box mustard
  seed
1½ tablespoons red pepper
4¾ tablespoons salt
3 (16 ounce) boxes seedless
  raisins

Peel and core apples and slice thin. Put into large covered pot. Cover with 1 quart of vinegar to keep from sticking. Cook to mush, stirring often; cover. Make syrup of brown sugar and remaining vinegar. Boil about 5 minutes. Add to apples. Cover pot and simmer, stirring frequently. Put in garlic, mustard seed, red pepper, salt; stir. Add 1½ boxes of raisins, ground (a little bit at the time). Mix thoroughly. Let steam about 5 minutes covered. Add remaining raisins, not ground. Mash any pieces of apple. Cook about 45 minutes on low heat. Stir often as it will burn easily. Seal in hot, sterilized jars. Yield: 12 to 15 pints.

PEACH CHUTNEY

2 tablespoons salt
1 quart water
7 cups sliced fresh peaches
¼ cup cider vinegar
3 cups sugar
2 large cloves garlic
1 cup chopped onions

1 teaspoon ground ginger
¼ tablespoon crushed red
  pepper
¾ cup lime juice
1 cup raisins
½ cup chopped, candied or
  preserved ginger

Combine salt and water; pour over sliced fresh peaches. Let stand for 1 day. Drain. Combine the vinegar, sugar and garlic and bring to a boil. Add peaches and cook for about 45 minutes until liquid is clear. Remove peaches; reserve. Add onions, ground ginger, red pepper, lime juice and raisins and cook until thickened a bit—about 12 to 15 minutes. Add peaches and candied or preserved ginger. Bring to boil. Put into hot, sterilized jars and seal. Yield: 3 pints.

SPICED PLUMS

½ gallon plums
3 pounds sugar
1½ teaspoons ground cloves

1½ teaspoons cinnamon
1½ teaspoons allspice
1 pint vinegar

Put plums into large kettle. Cover plums with sugar, cloves, cinnamon, allspice and vinegar. Let stand overnight unrefrigerated. Boil until plums are tender and juice begins to thicken. Stir constantly after it begins to thicken. Put in hot, sterilized pint jars and seal. Yield: 6 pints.

MUSCADINE SAUCE

7 pounds grapes
4 pounds sugar
1 pint vinegar

2 teaspoons allspice
1 teaspoon cloves
2 teaspoons cinnamon

Separate pulp from hulls of grapes. Cook pulp in small amount of water until soft. (Does not take long.) Run through a colander to remove seed. Combine hulls and pulp, sugar, vinegar, allspice, cloves and cinnamon. Cook until thick like preserves. Put into hot, sterilized jars and seal. Yield: 12 pints.

MIMI'S RASPBERRY JAM

5 cups crushed raspberries
1 (1¾ ounce) box Sure-Jell
    fruit pectin

7 cups sugar

If berries are fresh you must wash, clean and pick out any bad berries before crushing. If berries were cleaned before frozen, then just thaw. Mix Sure-Jell with fruit. Bring fruit to a boil. Stir in all of the sugar and bring to a rolling boil this time, so that it can't be stirred down; keep it that way for 1 minute. Remove from heat and skim off the foam that has formed on top of mixture. Pour mixture while hot into hot, sterilized half pint size jars. If the fruit floats, invert the jar 30 minutes. Yield: 10 half pints.

STRAWBERRY PRESERVES

6 cups strawberries, washed   6 cups sugar
 and hulled

Place berries in a large, heavy saucepan. Pour sugar over them, but do not stir. Place the pan over medium heat. As soon as berries start to simmer, time the cooking for 25 minutes. Let cook without stirring. At the end of 25 minutes, pour into a bowl to cool. Cover and let stand overnight. Fill hot, sterilized jars and seal. Yield: 12 half pints.

WHOLE CRANBERRY SAUCE

4 cups cranberries   2 cups sugar
1 cup water

Wash and pick over cranberries. Put all ingredients into heavy saucepan and bring to a boil. Cook, stirring occasionally, until berry skins "pop" (You can hear them pop. This releases the soft, cooked center). Remove from heat and allow to cool. Pour into jars and store in refrigerator. Yield: 1 quart.

APPLE BUTTER

4 pounds apples   1½ teaspoons cloves
2 cups cider vinegar or water   ½ teaspoon allspice
sugar   grated rind and juice of 1
3 teaspoons cinnamon   lemon

Wash apples and remove stems; quarter. Do not remove core. Cook in vinegar until soft, about 1½ hours. Put the pulp through fine strainer. For 1 cup pulp add ½ cup sugar. Add spices, lemon juice and rind. Cook over low heat, stirring constantly, until sugar is dissolved. Cook, stirring frequently, until it sheets from a spoon, about 30 minutes. Put in hot sterilized jars and seal.

PEACH PICKLE

whole cloves
7 pounds peaches

1 pint vinegar
3 pounds sugar

Stick 2 cloves into each peeled peach. Bring vinegar and sugar to a boil. Pour over peaches. Let stand until next day, then cook until peaches are tender. Pack peaches in hot, sterilized jars. Cook juice until thick; pour hot juice over peaches, seal jars. Process in water-bath for 15 minutes. Yield: 4 quarts.

ZUCCHINI RELISH

10 cups ground zucchini
(small size)
2 to 3 cups onions (yellow or
white)
2 green bell peppers (more if
desired)
2 red peppers
1/3 cup canning salt

1 teaspoon tumeric
1 teaspoon nutmeg
1 teaspoon celery seed
1 teaspoon black pepper
1 tablespoon cornstarch
2 1/2 cups vinegar
4 cups sugar

Grind all the vegetables. Add canning salt; mix. Refrigerate overnight. The following day, drain ground mixture; rinse in cold water and drain again. Then mix the tumeric, nutmeg, celery seed, and black pepper. Add cornstarch, vinegar and sugar. Cook for 30 minutes; watch and stir often while cooking. Put into hot, sterilized jars and seal. Yield: 6 pints.

CLOSET PICKLES

cucumbers
distilled vinegar

5 pounds sugar
2 to 3 drops oil of cloves

Wash cucumbers and place, whole, in a wide mouth gallon jug. Cover with distilled vinegar. Place jug of cucumbers in paper bag, set in closet for 6 weeks.

Pour off vinegar, slice cucumbers and layer in gallon jug with sugar. Add oil of cloves. Place back in closet. About once a week, shake jar. When sugar is completely dissolved, put in pint jars. Does not have to be sealed or refrigerated.

PICKLED OKRA

4 pounds okra, washed,
   stemmed and trimmed
1 garlic clove per jar
1 hot pepper per jar
1 teaspoon dill seed per jar

1 teaspoon mustard seed per
   jar
2 cups cider vinegar
1 cup water
¼ cup salt

Pack sterile jars with okra, add to EACH JAR: garlic clove, hot pepper, dill seed and mustard seed. Bring vinegar, water, and salt to a boil. Boil for 5 minutes. Pour boiling mixture over okra and seal jars immediately. Let stand at least for 1 month before eating.

Wash all glasses, lids, jars and bands in warm, sudsy water. Rinse in hot water, and then boil them for 10 minutes. Leave the equipment in the hot water until they are used.

CHOPPED ARTICHOKE PICKLE

3 quarts chopped Jerusalem
   artichokes
1 quart chopped onions
6 green peppers

1 large cauliflower
1 gallon water
1 pint salt

Chop artichokes and onions. Cut peppers fine and break cauliflower into flowerets. Mix all together and cover with water and salt. Let stand 24 hours. Drain.

SAUCE:
1 cup flour
6 tablespoons dry mustard
1 tablespoon tumeric

4 cups sugar
2 quarts vinegar

Mix all dry ingredients for sauce and add enough vinegar to make a paste. Heat remaining vinegar and pour over mustard mixture. Boil until thick, stirring constantly; add vegetables and bring to a boil. While hot, pour into hot, sterilized jars and seal. Yield: 8 to 10 pints.

CRISP SWEET PICKLES

7 pounds cucumbers (small
  pickling variety is best)
2 cups pickling lime
2 gallons water
2 quarts cider vinegar
4½ pounds sugar

1 tablespoon salt
1 tablespoon celery seed
1 tablespoon whole cloves
1 tablespoon pickling spices
green food coloring (optional)

Slice cucumbers lengthwise and cut off seed centers. Slice each quartered length into halves or thirds. Mix lime in water. Soak sliced cucumbers in lime water for 24 hours, in glass or enamel containers (not aluminum). Drain cucumbers, rinse WELL and cover with ice water for 3 hours. Drain and cover with a mixture of the vinegar, sugar and seasonings. Boil for 30 minutes, then add some of the green food coloring, just for looks, if desired. Pack pickles into hot, sterilized jars (pints are best); pour hot juice over them, and seal. Yield: 10 pints.

ONION PICKLE

6 pounds onions
½ cup salt
crushed ice
5 cups sugar

5 cups white vinegar
2 teaspoons celery salt
1 teaspoon dry mustard
2 teaspoons tumeric

Slice onions. Layer onions, salt and ice in 3 layers. Let stand 2 hours. Squeeze hard to remove surplus ice, salt and water. Do not wash. Mix thoroughly sugar, vinegar, and spices. Bring to a hard boil, then add onions. Again bring to a hard boil for 3 minutes. Pour into hot, sterilized jars and seal. Yield: 6 pints.

R.D.

Ah! Men

Who were the James Beards and the Craig Claibornes of Albany's early days? Possibly they were the ones who cooked the meat for the July 4 barbecues and fish fries. Pork or kid cooked over open pits was the traditional fare at the barbecues and was served with Brunswick stew. Private ponds and streams abounded with fish. Men are taking more interest in the kitchen and often, now, in the home where both husband and wife hold outside jobs, they share in the preparation of meals. The backyard grill is their special sphere. Some of Albany's best men cooks share their recipes in this chapter.

Appetizers

PICKLED SHRIMP

1 small bottle olive oil
3 lemons, sliced thin
5 onions, sliced thin
1 box pickling spice

6 cups vinegar
4 pounds shrimp, cooked,
    peeled
3 tablespoons salt

Mix all ingredients thoroughly. Refrigerate. Stir occasionally.

MARINATED MUSHROOMS

1 pound mushrooms
½ cup salad oil
1 clove garlic, crushed
1¼ teaspoons salt
1 teaspoon mustard

1 tablespoon sugar
2 tablespoons water
¼ cup cider vinegar
⅓ cup olive oil

If mushrooms are small, wash and use whole. Large ones should be halved. Cook in ½ cup oil until they lose raw look. Mix other ingredients together, pour into pan. May be served hot or refrigerated and served cold. Yield: 1 pound.

"Very good in a tossed salad."

CRABMEAT DIP

3 (8 ounce) packages cream
    cheese
½ cup mayonnaise
garlic salt to taste
2 teaspoons prepared
    mustard

2 teaspoons Worcestershire
    sauce
1 teaspoon onion juice
¾ cup dry vermouth
dry mustard to taste
3 (6½ ounce) cans crabmeat

Mix all ingredients. Heat slowly over low heat, about 5 minutes. Use ⅓ of the above ingredients for a regular size batch which will serve 4 to 6 people when only one dip is being provided. Crabmeat dip may be frozen and reheated. Serve with crackers and keep dip hot enough until it just barely bubbles. Yield: 12 to 18 servings.

OYSTERS BU GAR´

1 pint oysters
Worcestershire sauce
Tabasco

salt and pepper
lemon juice
butter

Pour undrained oysters in a shallow baking pan. Sprinkle them generously with Worcestershire sauce. Sprinkle on Tabasco, salt, pepper and lemon juice. Put a small pat of butter on top of each oyster. Broil in oven until edges curl. Spear with toothpicks.

"This is a good and easy hors d'oeuvre."

BEER CHEESE

1 pound American cheese
1 pound sharp Cheddar
   cheese
1 tablespoon Worcestershire
   sauce
1 teaspoon salt

1 teaspoon dry mustard
2 teaspoons horseradish
dash red pepper
1 can beer at room
   temperature

Grate cheeses. Add all other ingredients and mix well. Serve with crackers.

Beverages

WHISKEY SOUR

1 (6 ounce) can pink
   lemonade
1 (6 ounce) can orange juice
6 ounces bourbon

4 ounces water
ice
maraschino cherry juice and
   cherries

Put first four ingredients in blender. If the blender will not turn, add a small amount of extra water. When blender is turning, add ice until this reaches the consistency of a frozen daiquiri. Add a little cherry juice. Pour in glasses and top with a cherry. Yield: 6 servings.

DONNEGAN

crushed ice   champagne
white rum

To each tall tumbler filled with crushed ice, pour in 1 ounce of white rum; fill with chilled champagne. These are better served for brunch when you can only have 2 and will eat a good meal immediately afterwards.

CURT'S FABULOUS SKINNY DIP

6 ounces light rum   2 tablespoons frozen orange
½ jigger grenadine   juice concentrate
½ banana   ½ lime
8 fresh strawberries   1 ounce package Sweet and
6 cubes fresh pineapple   Low

Fill blender ¾ full with ice; add light rum. (For those meaning serious business, add 7 or 8 ounces.) Add all other ingredients and mix until it reaches a smooth consistency. Serve in large wine glasses, 12 ounces per glass. Yield: 4 servings.

YELLOW BIRDS

1 banana   juice of 1 orange
8 ounces pineapple juice   1 tablespoon cherry juice
4 ounces rum   2 hands crushed ice
4 ounces vodka   orange slices
1 teaspoon confectioners'   cherries
   sugar

Blend banana; then add 4 ounces of pineapple juice in blender; mix well; pour up and reserve. In blender put rum, vodka, banana mixture and 4 ounces pineapple juice. Add confectioners' sugar, juice of 1 orange, cherry juice and at least 2 hands of crushed ice. Blend until ice is smoothly mixed. Pour up with a slice of orange and a cherry to garnish glass. Yield: 4 to 6 servings.

Soups

OYSTER STEW

½ cup butter
1 stalk celery, finely chopped
½ cup finely chopped onion
1 quart oysters

1 quart half and half
salt and pepper to taste
8 teaspoons sherry

In the top of a double boiler over medium heat, melt butter. Sauté celery and onion. Add oysters with liquor and heat thoroughly. Add half and half. Season with salt and pepper. Serve in bowls and float 1 teaspoon of sherry on top of each. Yield: 8 servings.

DAVID'S FISH CHOWDER

4 or 5 slices bacon, chopped
⅓ cup chopped onion
2 pounds haddock, chopped
2 cups diced potatoes
1½ teaspoons salt
⅛ teaspoon pepper
1½ cups water

1 cup White Sauce (see recipe)
3 tablespoons butter
2 tablespoons flour
1 teaspoon salt
1/16 teaspoon pepper
2 cups milk

Cook the bacon in a large saucepan until crisp; pour off all except 1 tablespoon of fat. Add onion; simmer 5 minutes until soft. Add haddock, potatoes, salt, pepper and water. Cook gently for 20 minutes. Add white sauce to fish mixture. In a small saucepan, melt butter; add flour, salt and pepper. Stir and blend thoroughly. Remove from heat; add to fish mixture. Gradually pour in milk. Cook on low until thick and smooth, stirring constantly. Yield: 4-6 servings.

SEAFOOD GUMBO

*1 six pack cold beer or bottle
of white wine "for the
cook"*
1 cup flour
½ cup olive oil
½ cup cooking oil
½ pound bacon, diced
1 pound okra, sliced
10 stalks celery, chopped
4 large onions, chopped
1 green pepper, chopped
2 cloves garlic, chopped
½ cup chopped parsley
1 quart chicken stock
4 cups Chablis
2 quarts water
½ cup Worcestershire sauce

Louisiana Hot Sauce, to taste
1 (6 ounce) can tomato paste
1 (6 ounce) can tomato sauce
2 tablespoons salt
2 bay leaves
¼ teaspoon thyme
¼ teaspoon rosemary
¼ teaspoon cayenne
*2 cups chopped cooked
chicken*
2 pounds cooked crabmeat
4 pounds raw shrimp
2 pints oysters
1 teaspoon molasses
1 tablespoon lemon juice
cooked rice

Preheat oven to 400° F. Make a roux by mixing flour, olive oil and cooking oil in oven-proof glass container. Bake for about 2 hours. Stir roux every 15 minutes. The roux should look like chocolate brownies when done. While this is cooking, have a cold beer or glass of wine. Dice bacon and fry in a heavy iron pot. Remove bacon, leave grease in pot, cook okra in bacon grease until slime is gone. Help yourself to beer or wine as necessary. This takes a long time.

When roux is done, add to bacon grease and okra. Add celery, onions, pepper, garlic and parsley. Cook 45 minutes at low heat, stirring constantly. A little more oil and chicken stock may be added if mixture is difficult to work. Add chicken stock, wine, water, Worcestershire, hot sauce, tomato paste, tomato sauce, salt, bay leaves, thyme, rosemary and cayenne. Simmer for 2½ hours. Enjoy beer or wine. The hard part is over! Peel shrimp at this time. Be careful—do not let gumbo stick.

(Recipe continued on next page.)

SEAFOOD GUMBO (continued)

Add chicken, crabmeat and shrimp about 30 minutes before serving. Add oysters and molasses during last 10 minutes. Add lemon juice and taste. It will be good if you did it right. Serve in soup bowl with about ¼ cooked rice and ¾ gumbo. Serve at once with French bread toasted with garlic butter. Gumbo is better after it is frozen or refrigerated. Make more than you need and enjoy it another day. Yield: 10 to 12 servings.

SHRIMP MULL

2 quarts water
2 (1 pound) cans tomatoes
1 can tomato soup
1 lemon, sliced
1 cup butter
1 cup diced salt pork
1 cup chopped onion
2 cloves garlic, sliced
1 cup sliced celery
1 teaspoon celery seed
15 drops Tabasco

1 (14 ounce) bottle tomato
    catsup
2 tablespoons Worcestershire
    sauce
¼ teaspoon curry powder
5 pounds raw shrimp, peeled
1 cup sherry
½ cup butter
cracker crumbs
rice

Into a heavy stewing kettle put water, tomatoes, soup and lemon. Brown in a frying pan salt pork, onion, garlic, and 1 cup butter. Transfer to stewing kettle. Add celery, celery seed, Tabasco, catsup, Worcestershire sauce and curry powder. Cook for 2 hours, low heat. Add shrimp. Cook gently for 1 hour. Add sherry and ½ cup butter. Thicken with cracker crumbs. Serve with rice. Yield: 12-15 servings.

JOHNNY REB CORN CAKES

1 cup stone ground cornmeal   1 teaspoon sugar
1 teaspoon salt   1½ cups boiling water

Mix cornmeal, salt and sugar. Add boiling water. Mix well. Batter will be thick. Drop by tablespoon on any well-greased frying pan or griddle. Use medium hot or 380° F for an electric frying pan. Do not touch or turn over for 6 minutes. At 6 minutes, turn over and cook for about 5 minutes. For thin, crispy Johnny Cakes, thin batter with milk or water (about ½ cup). Cook as above. Use only old fashioned pure cornmeal without enrichment or preservatives. Keep meal in refrigerator and it will last indefinitely. Yield: 8 to 10 cakes.

FISHERMAN'S HUSHPUPPIES

1½ cups cornmeal   1 cup minced onions
½ cup flour   1 (8 ounce) can of cut corn
1 teaspoon sugar   1 cup buttermilk
½ teaspoon salt   2 tablespoons oil (preferably
2 teaspoons baking powder   oil in which has been
1 teaspoon soda   fried)
1 egg, beaten   oil for frying

Sift dry ingredients. Stir in egg. Add minced onions and corn to mixture. Stir in milk to make a very heavy batter. Add oil. Heat a quantity of oil in a deep fryer. Spoon hushpuppy batter into desired size. Drop into hot oil. Brown well; drain. Serve hot with fried fish. Yield: 3 dozen.

Vegetables and Salads

"DOC'S" FRENCH FRIED ONIONS

2 large onions   ¾ cup water
1 cup flour   2 tablespoons oil
¼ teaspoon salt   1 egg white, stiffly beaten

Slice onions ⅛ inch thick. Soak in ice water for 1 hour. Drain on cloth. Mix the sifted dry ingredients. Add water and oil. Fold in egg white. Dip the onion slices in the batter. Fry in electric frying pan or deep fat fryer at 400° F. Brown one side and turn. Serve piping hot.

CAESAR SALAD

1 clove garlic
¾ cup salad oil
2 cups white bread cubes
2 eggs
3 tablespoons fresh lemon
 juice
2 teaspoons Worcestershire
 sauce
½ teaspoon salt

¼ teaspoon pepper
8 anchovy fillets, chopped
 (optional)
2 heads romaine lettuce,
 washed and chilled
¼ cup crumbled Bleu cheese
¼ cup grated Parmesan
 cheese

Crush garlic in small bowl; cover with ½ cup of oil. Refrigerate, covered, for 30 minutes. In ¼ cup salad oil in medium skillet, fry bread cubes until brown on all sides. Set aside. Cook eggs 1 minute in boiling water (may be used raw); set aside. In small bowl, combine the lemon juice, Worcestershire sauce, salt, pepper, and anchovies; mix well. Into large salad bowl, tear lettuce into bite size pieces. Drain remaining oil from garlic. Pour over lettuce; toss to coat evenly. Break eggs over salad; toss well. Pour on lemon mixture; toss well. Add bread cubes and cheeses; toss well. Serve at once. Yield: 8 to 10 servings.

GARLIC SALAD DRESSING

1 tablespoon Lawry's Season
 Salt
2 cloves garlic, pressed

⅓ cup salad oil
1 tablespoon vinegar

Place Lawry's Season Salt and garlic into a small wooden bowl. With a reversed spoon mix garlic and salt until salt is completely wet with juices of garlic. Add salad oil and continue to stir and mix. Add vinegar and mix well. Cover with foil and allow to set a couple of hours before using Pour over lettuce or spinach and toss, mixing thoroughly. Yield: ½ cup.

"The dressing adds a great taste to steaks when applied just before serving."

LOUISIANA CAJUN COLE SLAW

5 heaping tablespoons
  mayonnaise
2 heaping tablespoons
  Durkee's dressing
2 tablespoons olive oil
1 teaspoon Louisiana Hot
  Sauce
2 tablespoons catsup

1 teaspoon garlic salt
1 tablespoon wine vinegar
juice of 1 lemon
1 large head cabbage,
  shredded, well drained
2 medium onions, shredded
  into thin rings

Put mayonnaise and Durkee's dressing in a bowl large enough to hold complete mixture, but shaped so that ingredients can be beaten with a fork. Beat mayonnaise and dressing until combined; add olive oil slowly, beating all the while after adding olive oil. Add Louisiana Hot Sauce. Add catsup and keep beating. Add garlic salt. Add wine vinegar and beat thoroughly, adding lemon juice. Taste for salt and pepper; must be salty enough to salt slaw. Therefore, it can be a little saltier than if you were just doing the sauce alone. Place shredded cabbage and onion rings in large salad bowl. Pour sauce over and toss well. Chill 1 hour before serving. Yield: 8 servings.

BLEU CHEESE SLAW

1½ cups corn oil
⅔ cup vinegar
½ cup sugar
2 tablespoons grated onion
2 teaspoons salt
1 teaspoon celery seed

2 heads white cabbage,
  shredded
1 head red cabbage,
  shredded
3 (4 ounce) packages bleu
  cheese, crumbled

Mix oil, vinegar, sugar, onion, salt and celery seed. Pour over cabbage and chill several hours. Toss with bleu cheese at serving time. Yield: 16 servings.

Seafood and Fish

OYSTER LOAVES

2 cups corn flour or yellow
   corn meal
1½ teaspoons salt
½ teaspoon black pepper
½ teaspoon cayenne
4 dozen oysters, drained
1 quart peanut oil, heated to
   350° F.

2 loaves of French bread,
   each 20 inches long
½ cup butter, softened
2 cloves garlic, pressed
2 tablespoons minced parsley

Season corn meal or corn flour with salt, pepper, and cayenne; shake oysters in mixture. Fry quickly in hot oil until oysters float (about 1½ minutes). Allow oil to reheat before adding more oysters. Split French loaves horizontally and cut into thirds. Scoop out centers. Blend butter with garlic and parsley; spread onto bread. Broil 2 minutes. Pile oysters on and serve at once with the following:

sliced tomatoes
shredded lettuce
mayonnaise
tartar sauce

catsup
Tabasco
lemon wedges
horseradish

ORIENTAL KING MACKEREL STEAKS

2 pounds King Mackerel
   steaks or other fish steaks
¼ cup orange juice
¼ cup soy sauce
2 tablespoons catsup
2 tablespoons melted fat or
   oil

2 tablespoons chopped
   parsley
1 tablespoon lemon juice
½ teaspoon oregano
½ teaspoon pepper
1 clove garlic, finely chopped

Cut fish into serving size portions. Place in single layer in a shallow dish. Make sauce by combining remaining ingredients. Pour sauce over fish and let stand for 30 minutes, turning once. Remove fish, reserving sauce for basting. Place fish on well-greased broiler pan. Broil about 3 inches from source of heat for 4 to 5 minutes. Turn carefully and brush with remaining sauce. Broil 4 to 5 minutes longer or until fish flakes easily when tested with a fork. Yield: 6 servings.

SLICK'S CREOLE SHRIMP

2 onions, chopped
2 green peppers, chopped
3 celery stalks, chopped
1 clove garlic, minced
1 (17 ounce) can tomatoes
1 (6 ounce) can tomato
   paste
1 bay leaf

1 tablespoon brown sugar
1 tablespoon Worcestershire
   sauce
salt
pepper
2 pounds uncooked shrimp,
   peeled
rice

Sauté chopped onions, peppers, celery and minced garlic in oil. Add tomatoes, tomato paste, bay leaf, brown sugar, Worcestershire sauce, salt and pepper to taste. Cook slowly for at least 1 hour. Approximately 15 minutes before serving, add shrimp. Serve on a bed of rice. Yield: 6 servings.

SHRIMP AND EGGS BU GAR

½ pound shrimp
onions
green peppers
celery
½ stick unsalted butter

salt and pepper to taste
Tabasco
Worcestershire sauce
1 dozen eggs

Peel and devein shrimp. Sauté onions, green peppers and celery in butter about 5 minutes. Sprinkle with salt and pepper; add a few dashes Tabasco and Worcestershire sauce. Add the shrimp and cook until they are just pink. Beat eggs and add to shrimp mixture. Cook slowly until eggs are softly scrambled.

"Great for Sunday brunch."

SAUTÉED SHRIMP

1 pound fresh raw shrimp,
   shelled
¼ cup butter
juice of 2 lemons

cracked pepper
dash garlic salt
oregano (couple of dashes)

Prepare shrimp. Melt butter over medium heat. Add shrimp, lemon juice, pepper, garlic salt and dashes of oregano. Sauté slowly over low heat, tossing until shrimp turn pink—about 8 minutes. Yield: 2 servings.

SHRIMP BAKE

5 pounds medium shrimp
1 (16 ounce) bottle Wishbone
    salad dressing
1 pound margarine, melted

1 ounce black pepper
juice of 5 lemons (save rinds)

Preheat oven to 350° F. Put raw unshelled shrimp in roaster. Mix last four ingredients and pour over shrimp. Put a few lemon rinds in sauce. Cover tightly with aluminum foil. Bake for 45 minutes. Do not overcook. Serve with small bowls of the sauce for dipping after peeling the shrimp. Yield: 6 servings.

"Serve this with a salad and French bread."

Meats

BUDDY'S TENDERLOIN BÉARNAISE

4 filets (1¼ inch thick)
4 English muffins

Béarnaise sauce
bean sprouts

In a heavy skillet, sauté filets in butter for 5 to 6 minutes on each side. Place each filet on an English muffin that has been toasted with butter. Over the filets pour BÉARNAISE SAUCE. Top with bean sprouts that have been dropped in boiling water for 1 minute. Yield: 4 servings.

BÉARNAISE SAUCE:

2 tablespoons white wine
2 tablespoons tarragon
    vinegar
2 teaspoons tarragon
2 teaspoons minced green
    onions
3 egg yolks

2 tablespoons lemon juice
½ teaspoon salt
½ teaspoon freshly ground
    pepper
cayenne to taste
¼ pound butter, melted

Combine first 4 ingredients and heat in a saucepan until liquid is almost gone. In blender, mix egg yolks, lemon juice and seasonings. Pour in butter a little at a time, turning blender off and on between additions. Add the herbs and blend for 4 seconds. Yield: 2 cups.

CHILI

1 tablespoon bacon grease
3 medium onions, sliced
2 medium green peppers,
    diced
2 garlic cloves, minced
3 pounds lean ground beef
2 (15 ounce) cans red kidney
    beans

3 (16 ounce) cans tomatoes
2 (6 ounce) cans tomato paste
¼ cup chili powder
1 tablespoon salt
1 pound sharp cheese, grated
1 pound bacon, cooked and
    broken into bits
1 bunch spring onions, sliced

Using 4 to 5 quart pan, heat bacon grease and cook vegetables until tender. Add meat; brown, adding salt and pepper to taste. Combine all ingredients and simmer 1 to 1½ hours. Serve in bowls or over rice. Serve cheese, bacon and onions on the side as toppings. Yield: 8 to 10 servings.

SMOKED TURKEY

turkey
butter, melted

salt
garlic salt

Rinse turkey, salt inside and rub outside with butter, salt and garlic salt.

TO SMOKE ON THE GRILL: Start with lots of charcoal and keep adding during the day. Build fire on lower level right side of grill, and place the turkey on upper level left side, leaving left vents open and right ones closed, so that smoke will travel across the bird. Make a tent of aluminum foil; lay across top of turkey, breast side up. Put meat thermometer in the breast. Half way through cooking, turn bird so the other side is facing charcoal.

Place a pan under the bird to catch juices for gravy. The last couple of hours, take aluminum foil off so the turkey can brown. It usually takes the same time to cook as it would in the oven. Cook approximately 25 minutes per pound.

Green oak or hickory wood placed on top of coals, but not directly under meat being grilled, adds great flavor to grilled meats.

CHICKEN COUNTRY CAPTAIN

4 pounds chicken for frying
flour
salt
pepper
shortening
2 large onions, finely chopped
2 green peppers, finely
    chopped
1 garlic clove, finely chopped
1 teaspoon salt

2 teaspoons curry powder
½ teaspoon white pepper
2 cups tomatoes (canned)
½ teaspoon powdered thyme
½ teaspoon chopped parsley
3 tablespoons currants
2 cups hot cooked rice
½ pound almonds, roasted
parsley (to garnish)

Cut chicken in frying pieces and remove skin. Roll in flour, salt, and pepper. Fry in shortening. Remove from pan and place in lower half of roaster. Keep covered to keep warm—this is the secret of success. Into grease where chicken was fried put onions, green pepper and garlic. Cook very slowly, stirring constantly, until onions and peppers are tender. Season with salt, white pepper and curry powder. Add tomatoes, chopped parsley and thyme. Pour this mixture over chicken in roaster. If chicken is not covered, add a little water to skillet; pour over chicken. Cook about 45 minutes or until chicken is tender. Place hot rice in center of large platter. Remove chicken from roaster and place around rice on edge of platter. Now drop currants into sauce and pour over rice. Scatter roasted almonds over top of rice and sauce and garnish with parsley. *This makes a beautiful dish and is delicious. Serves 7 normal people, 8 ladies or 6 gluttons.*

BARBECUE PORK SPARERIBS

spareribs (allow ½ pound
    per person)
2 cups water

2 cups vinegar
2 tablespoons lemon juice
salt

Mix water, vinegar and lemon juice. Add salt until it will not melt into a solution. Add a bit more and heat to melt salt and keep solution warm. Place ribs over a slow fire and baste every 10 minutes with warm salty solution. The slow cooking makes for better tasting meat. Can use this same method for pork chops, pork loin or fresh ham.

AL'S PORK ROAST

whole loin
Chef Howell's Seasoning (or
   Lawry's Garlic Salt)

½ cup butter
3 lemons

Rub pork roast (whole loin) with Chef Howell's Seasoning or Lawry's Garlic Salt. Melt butter and add 2 or 3 lemons, squeezed. Place roast on rotisserie (with pan of tin foil in bottom of grill) over medium-low fire. After 1 hour pour lemon butter over roast and cook for 3 more hours, basting occasionally. Roast is done when it begins to pull away from bone. You can brown more by raising fire for 15 to 20 minutes. If not serving right away, wrap roast tightly in tin foil to keep it warm and retain juices.

MARINATED PORK CHOPS

½ cup lemon juice
½ cup soy sauce
½ teaspoon garlic powder

2 tablespoons chopped fresh
   ginger, or 2 teaspoons
   ground ginger
6 pork chops, 1 or 1½ inches
   thick

Combine above ingredients and pour over the pork chops in shallow dish. Refrigerate, covered, 6 hours or overnight, turning occasionally. Bake at 350° F for 45 minutes with half of the marinade; then broil until golden brown. This is an excellent idea for the outdoor grill. Yield: 6 servings.

CHICK-N-Q SAUCE

½ cup distilled vinegar
½ cup lemon juice
½ cup corn oil
1 tablespoon salt

1 teaspoon Accent
¼ teaspoon black pepper
1½ tablespoons dry mustard
sprinkle of cayenne pepper

Mix together in a small saucepan all ingredients. Bring to boil over medium heat, stirring frequently. Remove from heat. Brush chickens with sauce while on grill. Yield: sauce for 2 chickens.

CHARLES' BRUNSWICK STEW

8 pounds Boston butt
3 pounds chicken
3 cans cream style corn
1 can whole kernel corn
2 (32 ounce) bottles Hunt's
    catsup
½ bottle Worcestershire
    sauce

15 shakes hot sauce
3 tablespoons lemon
    juice
2 tablespoons vinegar
4 cans whole tomatoes,
    blended
1 can chicken broth

Cook Boston butt and chop fine. Cook chicken, debone and chop fine. Add all other ingredients and mix well. Cook on low heat about 1½ hours. Yield: 40 servings.

HARRY'S BAR-B-Q SAUCE

1 cup white vinegar
2 cups catsup
½ cup lemon juice
¼ cup margarine
1 tablespoon black pepper
1 cup water
1 tablespoon prepared
    mustard

1 tablespoon salt
1 tablespoon garlic salt
1 teaspoon Accent
3 ounces Louisiana Hot Sauce
1 teaspoon Worcestershire
    sauce
1 tablespoon brown sugar

Heat vinegar, catsup, lemon juice and butter to slow boil. Add all other ingredients and bring to slow boil. Let simmer over low heat with pan covered.

OPTIONAL: Add one pod of red pepper or one medium chopped onion to above. Cook pork, chicken or beef until done, then place meat in large pan, add sauce and simmer in oven for 15 minutes. Yield: 1 quart.

349

GRILLED QUAIL

6-8 quail, "picked, not   *1 stick margarine, melted*
skinned" and split down   *salt and pepper to taste*
back

Place birds in a flat grilling basket such as you might use for hamburgers. Baste birds with melted margarine. Season with salt and pepper. Have coals hot; place basket over coals, back side down. Cook 10 minutes. Turn breast side down, baste with melted margarine. Cook 10 minutes more. Yield: serve 2 quail per person.

Quail that are picked and not skinned have a different and far better flavor.

DOVE AND/OR QUAIL STROGANOFF

salt and coarse ground black   *½ cup white wine*
pepper   *½ teaspoon oregano*
12-18 doves OR 12 doves   *½ teaspoon rosemary*
and 6 quail   *1 (10½ ounce) can celery*
1 medium onion, chopped   *soup*
1 cup sliced fresh mushrooms   *1 tablespoon Kitchen*
OR 1 (4 ounce) can sliced   *Bouquet*
mushrooms   *1 cup sour cream*
⅔ tablespoon butter

Salt and pepper birds; place in heavy iron Dutch oven or casserole. Sauté onions (and mushrooms if fresh) in butter. Mix together with remaining ingredients (except half the wine and the sour cream) and pour over birds. Bake at 350° F for about 1½ hours. May be cooled and refrigerated overnight. This enhances the flavor. Add the sour cream and the remainder of the wine and bake uncovered 20 to 30 minutes. Serve over wild rice. Yield: 6 servings.

DOVE CASSEROLE

10 to 12 doves
flour, salt and pepper
cooking oil
1 onion, chopped

2 stalks celery, chopped
1 carrot, grated
2 cans beef consommé
2 tablespoons sherry

Dust birds in flour, salt and pepper. Brown evenly in hot cooking oil. Drain well. Place doves in casserole. Sprinkle with chopped vegetables. Pour consommé over all. Cover and cook in a 325° F oven for 1½ hours. Yield: 4 servings.

Sweets

MEXICAN WEDDING COOKIES

½ cup butter
½ cup confectioners' sugar
1 egg yolk

1½ cups flour
1 teaspoon vanilla extract
½ cup finely chopped pecans

Cream butter and sugar until smooth. Add yolk and flour, continue mixing and last add vanilla and nuts. Mixture should be very stiff. Roll into balls about the size of walnuts. Bake at 375° F for 12 to 15 minutes. Yield: 2 dozen.

POUND CAKE

1½ cups butter
1 (8 ounce) package cream
   cheese
3 cups sugar
6 eggs, extra large

3 cups cake flour, sifted twice
dash of salt
1½ teaspoons vanilla extract
yellow food coloring

Preheat oven to 325° F. Cream butter with cream cheese, then add sugar, little at a time, beat well after each addition. Beat in eggs, one at a time, until mixture is pale yellow or forms a ribbon. Then add flour, ¼ at a time, then salt, vanilla and dash of yellow coloring. Bake for 1½ hours.

"Someone (an ole-timer) said never to look at a pound cake until it has been in the oven 1 full hour."

SENATOR SAM NUNN'S FAVORITE
CHINESE ALMOND COOKIES

1 cup margarine	*1 teaspoon almond extract*
1 cup sugar	*2 cups flour*
2 egg yolks	*1 cup chopped almonds*

Cream margarine. Add sugar and beat until light and fluffy. Add egg yolks and almond extract; blend well. Add flour and almonds. Mix well. Form dough into one inch balls. Place on ungreased cookie sheet and flatten. Bake at 325° F for 15 minutes. When cooled, ice cookies with TEA ICING and top with whole almond. Yield: 3 dozen.

TEA ICING:

4 tablespoons instant tea	*½ cup margarine*
2 tablespoons milk	*2½ cups confectioners' sugar*

Dissolve tea in milk. Add margarine and beat well. Add sugar a little at a time beating until very fluffy.

CAMPERS CEREAL

1 small box oatmeal	*1 or 2 cups any chopped nuts*
1 small box Special K	*(pine nuts are especially*
1 jar wheat germ, plain or	*good)*
honeyed	*1 or 2 cups chopped dried*
1 small box Grapenuts	*fruit (apricots, prunes,*
1 box light raisins	*figs. etc.)*

Mix these together well with your hands and pour into some large plastic bags for easy carrying. This can be eaten dry or with fresh water in remote areas, with milk or cream in town. The best way to mix it is to pour it all into a large grocery bag and shake it up and down in the bag until it is mixed. This should be enough to last one person about a month. It is nutritious and will keep for months in a plastic bag.

Pickles

ARTICHOKE RELISH

2 quarts white vinegar
3 cups sugar
3 tablespoons whole mustard
   seeds
2½ pounds cabbage, chopped
1 quart chopped onions

6-8 bell peppers, chopped
1 (9 ounce) jar mustard
¾ cup flour
1 tablespoon black pepper
1 tablespoon tumeric
6 quarts chopped artichoke

Mix vinegar, sugar, mustard seeds and boil. Add cabbage, onions and green pepper. Mix mustard, flour, black pepper and tumeric in bowl. Add some of the hot vinegar mixture to mustard mixture and blend well. Then add mustard mixture to hot vinegar and vegetable mixture. Heat on low to medium heat for a few minutes. Be sure to stir all along as mixture will scorch. Add artichokes just before removing from heat. Seal in jars while hot. Process in hot water bath for 20 minutes. Yield: 8 quarts.

BREAD AND BUTTER PICKLE

2 quarts sliced, unpeeled
   cucumbers
salt
2 cups onion, cut finely
2 cups bell peppers, cut finely
2 teaspoons tumeric

2 teaspoons celery seed
3 sticks cinnamon
3 cups sugar
2 cups white vinegar
1 (4 ounce) jar cut pimento

Place cut cucumbers in large bowl. Sprinkle with salt (one handful) and let stand for 2 hours. Stir occasionally. Drain thoroughly. Place cucumbers and other ingredients, except pimentos, in large pot. Bring to boil, boil for 15 to 18 minutes. Add cut pimentos. Put into hot, sterilized jars and seal. Yield: 3 quarts.

Index

355

INDEX

INDEX

INDEX

INDEX

Mail to:

Quail Country
Smith House Publications
516 Flint Avenue
Albany, Georgia 31701

Please send me _____ copies at ...... 12.95 each $ _____

Plus postage and handling .... 1.55 each $ _____

Tax for Georgia residents .... .52 each $ _____

Enclosed is check or money-order .... TOTAL $ _____

Name _____

Address _____

City _____ State _____ Zip _____

Charge to: ☐ Visa   ☐ Mastercard

Acct. # _____ Expiration Date _____

Make check payable to Smith House Publications ☐ Please gift wrap.

☐ This is a gift. Enclosure card to read _____ .

- -

Mail to:

Quail Country
Smith House Publications
516 Flint Avenue
Albany, Georgia 31701

Please send me _____ copies at ...... 12.95 each $ _____

Plus postage and handling .... 1.55 each $ _____

Tax for Georgia residents .... .52 each $ _____

Enclosed is check or money-order .... TOTAL $ _____

Name _____

Address _____

City _____ State _____ Zip _____

Charge to: ☐ Visa   ☐ Mastercard

Acct. # _____ Expiration Date _____

Make check payable to Smith House Publications ☐ Please gift wrap.

☐ This is a gift. Enclosure card to read _____ .

- -

Mail to:

Quail Country
Smith House Publications
516 Flint Avenue
Albany, Georgia 31701

Please send me _____ copies at ...... 12.95 each $ _____

Plus postage and handling .... 1.55 each $ _____

Tax for Georgia residents .... .52 each $ _____

Enclosed is check or money-order .... TOTAL $ _____

Name _____

Address _____

City _____ State _____ Zip _____

Charge to: ☐ Visa   ☐ Mastercard

Acct. # _____ Expiration Date _____

Make check payable to Smith House Publications ☐ Please gift wrap.

☐ This is a gift. Enclosure card to read _____ .

I WOULD LIKE TO SEE THIS OUTSTANDING COOKBOOK IN THE FOLLOWING STORES:

Store Name _____

Address _____

City _____ State _____ Zip _____

Store Name _____

Address _____

City _____ State _____ Zip _____

I WOULD LIKE TO SEE THIS OUTSTANDING COOKBOOK IN THE FOLLOWING STORES:

Store Name _____

Address _____

City _____ State _____ Zip _____

Store Name _____

Address _____

City _____ State _____ Zip _____

I WOULD LIKE TO SEE THIS OUTSTANDING COOKBOOK IN THE FOLLOWING STORES:

Store Name _____

Address _____

City _____ State _____ Zip _____

Store Name _____

Address _____

City _____ State _____ Zip _____